On the Defensive

SHARON MARQUART

On the Defensive

Reading the Ethical in Nazi Camp Testimonies

UNIVERSITY OF TORONTO PRESS
Toronto Buffalo London

Toronto Buffalo London
www.utppublishing.com

ISBN 978-1-4426-5066-4 (cloth)

University of Toronto Romance Series

Library and Archives Canada Cataloguing in Publication

Marquart, Sharon, author
On the defensive : reading the ethical in Nazi camp testimonies / Sharon Marquart.

(University of Toronto romance series)
Includes bibliographical references and index.
ISBN 978-1-4426-5066-4 (bound)

1. Delbo, Charlotte – Criticism and interpretation. 2. Semprún, Jorge – Criticism and interpretation. 3. Auschwitz (Concentration camp) – In literature. 4. Buchenwald (Concentration camp) – In literature. 5. World War, 1939–1945 – Literature and the war. 6. Ethics in literature. 7. Witnesses in literature. I. Title. II. Series: University of Toronto romance series

PQ2664.E5117Z95 2015 809′.93358405317 C2015-900927-8

University of Toronto Press acknowledges the financial assistance to its publishing program of the Canada Council for the Arts and the Ontario Arts Council, an agency of the Government of Ontario.

Canada Council for the Arts Conseil des Arts du Canada

University of Toronto Press acknowledges the financial support of the Government of Canada through the Canada Book Fund for its publishing activities.

To Josh, for being there.

Contents

Acknowledgments

I benefited from the support of many people while writing this book. Special thanks go to David Caron, whose encouragement, guidance, and friendship helped to motivate me from the earliest stages of this project and to believe that it was worth pursuing. Juli Highfill has also been a tireless supporter who devoted extensive time to reading and offering detailed, illuminating commentary on drafts of the manuscript, even when my writing and thoughts were at their messiest. I am also indebted to Nathalie Freidel, Lisa Heldke, and Nicholas Theisen for their helpful responses to my work and suggestions for improvements. I would also like to acknowledge my intellectual debt to Ross Chambers, whose rigorous, lucid scholarship has long been an important influence. The flaws in this book are all mine.

For their friendship throughout this project, I am deeply indebted to Kara Barnette, Joel Carlin, Susan Carlin, Asem Ghabra, Jawad Ghabra, Hildegard Glass, Andrew Grace, John Harvey, Angela Jumbert, Julia Kleinheider, Julie-Françoise Kruidenier-Tolliver, Baraat Khudeir, Andreea Marinescu, Gabriela Maya, Ivan Mayerhofer, Marcel Muller, David Petterson, Tim Sundell, Colleen Theisen, Cedric Tolliver, and Stacey Triplette. You have all helped me manage in difficult times, and get joy out of the easy ones.

I am tremendously grateful to my editor at the University of Toronto Press, Richard Ratzlaff, whose dedication, advice, and support throughout the review and publishing process have been truly exemplary, and also to Miriam Skey and Barbara Porter at Toronto for their help preparing the manuscript. My thanks also go to the three anonymous readers of my manuscript for their detailed and engaged reports that made this book stronger, and to Noeline Bridge for constructing the index.

I owe many thanks as well to Wilfrid Laurier University, in particular to my colleagues in the Department of Languages and Literatures and the Centre for Memory and Testimony Studies, for their personal and intellectual support. I was fortunate to be the recipient of a research semester that allowed me to finish writing my book, and of grants from the Office of Research Services and the Office of the Dean of Arts at Laurier to help with its publication. Special thanks as well go to Gustavus Adolphus College for granting me library privileges that helped me track down many references in the book's final stages.

My final thanks go to my family for the support they have offered me, in particular to my brother Steve for his ability to always care for others no matter how daunting his own struggles may be. My cats, Alligator, Blixa, and Neville, forced me to take regular breaks from writing and to remain engaged in my surroundings. Finally, my husband, Josh Brown, has been my biggest supporter throughout, helping me through impasses, reading and editing every page of this book no matter how many times I asked, and continuing to believe in my abilities when my own belief was waning. Saying thank you is utterly inadequate, but for now it will have to do.

Abbreviations

ANR	*Aucun de nous ne reviendra*
CI	*Une connaissance inutile*
"Je me sers"	"Je me sers de la littérature comme d'une arme"
MNJ	*Mesure de nos jours*

On the Defensive

Introduction: On the Defensive: Reading the Ethical in Witness Literature

I do not know
if you can still
make something of me
If you have the courage to try ...

– Charlotte Delbo

[Je ne sais pas
si vous pouvez faire encore
quelque chose de moi
Si vous avez le courage d'essayer ...]

In a speech given in January 2005 to commemorate the sixtieth anniversary of the liberation of Auschwitz, French President Jacques Chirac concluded his solemn remarks on the memory of the Nazi camps by quoting extracts from a poem in Auschwitz survivor Charlotte Delbo's trilogy of memoirs *Auschwitz et après*. A member of the French Resistance who was part of the only convoy of female political prisoners sent to the camp from France, Delbo was being featured in the country's new national exhibition in Auschwitz as a survivor whose story had been deemed exemplary of the French experience of the Second World War by the national government. According to Chirac, Delbo's poem is representative of the terrifying, universal truths to which camp inmates bear witness, and the ethical duty of the French nation is to know these truths and never forget them. "O you who know" [Ô vous qui savez], Chirac began, quoting Delbo:

did you know that hunger makes the eyes sparkle that thirst dims them
O you who know

did you know that you can see your mother dead
and not shed a tear
O you who know
did you know that in the morning you wish for death
and in the evening you fear it [...][1]
Did you know that suffering is limitless
that horror cannot be circumscribed
Did you know this
You who know. (*Auschwitz and After* 11)[2]

[saviez-vous que la faim fait brilller les yeux que la soif les ternit
Ô vous qui savez
saviez-vous qu'on peut voir sa mère morte
et rester sans larmes
Ô vous qui savez
saviez-vous que le matin on veut mourir
que le soir on a peur [...]
Saviez-vous que la souffrance n'a pas de limite
l'horreur pas de frontière
Le saviez-vous
Vous qui savez.] (*ANR* 21–2)

Chirac ended his speech by offering Delbo a reassuring reply:

> Yes we know and we will never forget. We will never abandon our idea of mankind and his dignity. Conscious of all the irreparable things contained in these places, we will go forth this evening stronger, and with greater determination, in order to build a future of tolerance, of justice, and of peace.
>
> [Oui nous savons et nous n'oublierons jamais. Nous ne renoncerons jamais à notre idée de l'homme et de sa dignité. Conscients de tout ce que ces lieux récèlent d'irréparable, nous repartirons, ce soir, plus déterminés et plus forts, pour bâtir un avenir de tolérance, de justice et de paix.]

We now know the truth about what happened in Auschwitz, Chirac proclaimed, and we will use the knowledge that we have amassed, in part from survivor testimonies, to build a better and more ethical world for humankind.

An impressive moral gesture. But it completely ignores what Delbo has to say.

This is a book about our ethical responses to witness literature: about the social forces that seek to deny the disturbance of testimony by codifying our responses, and the well-intentioned people – from loved ones of disaster victims, to victims themselves – who unknowingly facilitate this denial. It is also a book about the defensive ways in which we react when people's experiences expose us to the limits of our understandings, and the contemporary theorizations of the ethical that promote our retreat from witnesses and their stories. It is, finally, a book about how survivors themselves strive to reconfigure these problematic modes of engagement through their narratives, resisting our desire to close ourselves off, withdraw, and turn a blind eye, working to include us in the communities they construct, and showing us ways to open ourselves up so we can be there for others without having recourse to rigid ethical behaviours that ignore the meanings victims give to their own experiences.[3]

Chirac's "yes we know" reply to Delbo's poem illustrates a key idea that I advance in this book – that the display of moral sentiments functions as a technology of repression by simultaneously recognizing the suffering of victims and turning a blind eye to their concerns. A pernicious way in which we deny the horrors of atrocity comes, that is, not from *silencing* witnesses, but from allowing their testimonies to circulate while controlling what counts as an ethical response to them. Scholars have observed that, since the 1990s in particular, the French state has routinely deployed moral sentiments in the public sphere as a way of evading its social problems rather than treating them. Didier Fassin, for example, suggests that this politics has a salutary power in society at large because, by demonstrating a concern for the misfortunes of others and acknowledging that the intolerable exists, we are able to preserve the idea we have forged of our own moral sense, our virtue, and our humanity (252).[4] However, as Fassin points out, this gesture only grants recognition to those aspects of victims' testimonies that reinforce our image of ourselves, and ignores experiences that fall outside of its bounds (254). Chirac's response to Delbo is an exemplary display of this repressive moral economy: he reads her poem as a testament to his understanding of the human, but pays no attention to the meanings that the work advances, independently, about the experience of atrocity.

Delbo's poem raises an additional point about the politics of the ethical that I propose in this book: that we reinforce these broader forms of denial at humbler levels of society by conceiving of knowledge as a stable category rather than as something that emerges from a perpetual process of reshaping and expanding. The indirect way in which the poem "O you who know" transmits this idea to its readers further indicates an approach witness narratives can use to resist exclusionary ethical responses and, I argue, to combat repressive displays of morality. Addressed to a knowledgeable "you," the poetic "I" alternates between using the verb "to know" [*savoir*] in the present and past – "O you who know/did you know" [Ô vous qui savez/saviez-vous que] – to emphasize that, before witnesses returned to tell their stories, "you" did not possess the knowledge that "you" now have. The poetic "I" presents the knowledge she acquired in the camps – knowledge of hunger, pain, fear, anguish, and death – through a series of rhetorical questions addressed to these supposedly knowledgeable readers that, while left unanswered, obviously lead us to see "no" as the only real response. "O you who know" calls on readers, in short, to recognize the pivotal role victims play in constructing knowledge about atrocity, and that this knowledge, in turn, is continuously subject to modifications whenever survivors bear witness.

However, Delbo's poem presents this series of questions as a statement in its own right – it ends with a period, not a question mark – which implies that the ultimate point is not just answering whether or not "you" knew what "you" now know thanks to witnesses, but the process of destabilization it takes "you" through. What "O you who know" seeks, in other words, is to alter the fixed relationship that readers maintain with knowledge, which it does not accomplish by directly stating its aim, but by drawing readers near and inviting them to share in the task of constructing meaning. Even for those who may disagree with the poem's critical commentary – or, in the end, feel attacked by it – this process creates a less alienating textual environment, because readers must involve themselves in the work and be engaged with it in order to understand the messages it conveys. The poem strives to include us all in the act of meaning-making, which keeps us from withdrawing into ourselves or becoming defensive because of our divergent views.

Witness texts represent collective disasters in these indirect manners, Ross Chambers tells us, in order "to cause some *disturbance* in well-established cultural regularities and routines" and, in so doing, to inculcate a shared sense of responsibility in readers that broader cultural forces otherwise seek to deny (xix–xx; emphasis in original).[5] But the form of denial that I document throughout this book results,

I argue, from the defensive ways in which well-intentioned people – that is, those who readily acknowledge their responsibility to others – respond when their knowledge of the ethical fails them. Dori Laub and Susan Brison have each observed that, when confronted with the kinds of existential questions that traumatic experiences raise, well-meaning individuals can react, unwittingly, in ways that harm or even retraumatize victims because of a need to maintain a sense of safety and control.[6] These defensive behaviours range from endowing survivors with a kind of sanctity, to being hyperemotional, or obsessing ourselves with fact-finding and "knowing it all" when we listen to or read testimonies, or even blaming and disparaging victims for what happened to them in order to leave our worldviews unscathed (Felman and Laub 72–3; Brison 9). Such reactions may help to reassure and protect us, but they also cause us to become mentally blocked off from survivors' stories and to deny them the intimacy and the space they need to bear witness to their ordeals and remaster their trauma.

I contend in this book that understandings of the ethical – understandings, that is, of our duties and responsibilities to others – perform a similar protective function in encounters that expose well-intentioned individuals to the limits of those same understandings. However, I argue that, unlike the behaviours discussed by Laub and by Brison, this defence mechanism is less a product of how people respond to the shattering effects of *trauma* than it is of how they cope with inhabiting positions of *epistemic instability*. In interactions with disaster victims, we desire to be there for them and to respond to their calls, but we also recognize that our knowledge of how to act in these encounters has not prepared us for the task. To cope with the shattering of our belief in our own capacities in these situations, we withdraw into the safety that our inadequate conceptualizations provide, and offer formulaic and inattentive responses that allow us to take action but that also ignore the singular calls of people in need. Our desire to act in the interest of others transforms into a desire to affirm our failed understandings of the ethical, which causes us to turn a blind eye to the needs of victims and, ultimately, to deny their concerns.

To invoke the idea of limits in a study of the Nazi camps and of witness literature is, of course, not new. From Theodor Adorno's early remarks on the barbarity of poetry after Auschwitz to the more recent works of scholars such as Berel Lang and Cathy Caruth – on the representation of limits and on trauma as an "unclaimed experience," respectively – much of the theoretical discourse produced about survivor testimony has emphasized the unrepresentable or unspeakable nature of the Holocaust and the fact that it challenges our conceptual frameworks to the point of breaking them. Yet, as Thomas Trezise has observed, because of its absolute and universalizing nature, "the routinely repeated claim that the traumatic experience of Holocaust survivors is unrepresentable or unspeakable" can actually have a "silencing effect on Holocaust survivor testimony or alternative responses" that readers or listeners may offer to it (*Witnessing* 211, 2).[7] I am persuaded by Trezise that, when bearing witness, survivors both need "to resort to conventional modes of communication in order to convey their traumatic experience to the world" and "to challenge convention so as to avoid either aestheticizing that experience or making too much sense of its senselessness" (3). An important role of listeners, readers, and viewers is, in turn, to help survivors reconstruct a sense of self and of community through their acts of witnessing – receiving their testimony being, in Trezise's understanding, "an ethical exigency that tests our ability to empathize" and requires us "to tolerate a tension between identification and estrangement" (223–4). Survivor testimonies are, in short, much more varied than theorizations of the unrepresentability or unspeakability of the Holocaust would suggest, and the concerns of both survivors and their audiences frequently diverge from and even challenge those same theorizations.

My concern in this book is to demonstrate how the ethical exigency of testimony causes well-intentioned respondents to become entrenched in the very conventions that they recognize as failures. I do not treat witnessing or the Nazi camp experience as a keystone for debates on representation or its closure in this study, nor do I seek to define the nature of the concentration camps, what it means to have survived them, or who is or is not a true or complete witness to them.[8] My aims and focus are much more modest: to try to understand how community norms of ethical conduct can cause the deep moral challenge posed by the experience of atrocity to be ignored or repressed both by victims and by the well-meaning people who listen to or read survivor testimonies.[9]

In order to avoid producing a universalizing account of this phenomenon that lumps the voices and concerns of all survivors into a mass and risks having the kind of silencing effect described by Trezise, I have limited myself here to an in-depth study of the testimonial writings of two widely read survivors that offer complex theoretical reflections on and demonstrations of this defence mechanism – Delbo and Buchenwald survivor Jorge Semprun, a Spanish political militant and French

Resistance fighter who was one of France and Spain's most famous and authoritative intellectual witness writers. I do not claim, moreover, that the works of these two survivors bear witness to this problematic ethical response in the exact same ways. I argue that Semprun's testimonial narratives document the forms of repression and exclusion that this reaction has caused within the survivor community – specifically, among the communist survivors of the Nazi camp at Buchenwald. These texts are also an example of writings that unwittingly enact this form of denial through the submissive role that their metacommentaries carve out for readers on subjects as diverse as fiction, authoritarianism, compassion, and fraternity. Delbo's works, in contrast, advance an extensive implicit critique of the ethics of well-intentioned respondents to atrocity – a group that includes people as diverse as men and women of the political deportee community, family members of victims, and ethically oriented readers of witness literature – and suggest ways in which their harmful reactions to victims can be resisted, modified, and ultimately dismantled. The extended dialogue I propose here between the writings of Delbo and Semprun points to a broader set of theoretical concerns pertaining to the ways in which community understandings of ethical behaviour can cause the singularity of victims' experiences to be repressed and ignored, and to the larger social and political impact that witness literature can have by changing the habits of ethically minded readers.

However, throughout this book, I also inscribe my analyses of Delbo and Semprun and the theoretical issues their works raise within the corpus of Nazi camp testimonies and their critical reception more generally. I turn here to a discussion of this broader context in order to suggest the importance of my theoretical concerns about the ethical for witness literature as a genre.

Robert Antelme's important witness narrative *L'espèce humaine* offers a complex example of how theoretical understandings can function as a repressive safety mechanism in the name of a community's ethics and will serve as my point of departure. A survivor of the Buchenwald work detail located in the German town of Gandersheim, Antelme was among the early wave of returnees to publish their testimonies in France after the Second World War, and he was recognized by prominent poststructuralist critics such as Maurice Blanchot and Jean-François Lyotard for the theoretical complexity of his reflections on the Nazi camps and the genre of testimony.[10] His work also offers one of the most influential articulations of internment in the system as an "unimaginable" experience by a witness. The most overt commentary on the phenomenon appears near the end of the work amid a description of Antelme's liberation from the Nazi camp system by Allied troops and is worth quoting at length:

> All the stories that the guys are telling are true. But it requires considerable artfulness to get even a smidget [*sic*] of truth accepted, and in the telling of these stories there wants that artfulness which must vanquish necessary disbelief. In all this, everything must be believed, but the truth can be more tedious to listen to than some fabulation. Just a piece of the truth would be enough, one example, one idea; but no one here has just one example to offer, and there're thousands of us. These soldiers are strolling about in a city where all the stories should be added end to end, and where nothing is negligeable [*sic*]. But no listener has that vice. Most consciences are satisfied quickly enough, and need only a few words in order to reach a definitive opinion of the unknowable. So in the end they come and go in our midst without strain, become accustomed to this spectacle of thousands of dead and dying. (Later on, when Dachau will be quarantined because of typhus, guys who want to get out of the camp at all costs will be put in prison.)
>
> *Unimaginable*: a word that doesn't divide, doesn't restrict. The most convenient word. When you walk around with this word as your shield, your step becomes better assured, more resolute, your conscience pulls itself together. (289–90; emphasis in original, translation modified)[11]

> [Les histoires que les types racontent sont toutes vraies. Mais il faut beaucoup d'artifice pour faire passer une parcelle de vérité, et, dans ces histoires, il n'y a pas cet artifice qui a raison de la nécessaire incrédulité. Ici, il faut tout croire, mais la vérité peut être plus lassante à entendre qu'une fabulation. Un bout de vérité suffirait un exemple, une notion. Mais chacun ici n'a pas qu'un exemple à proposer, et il y a des milliers d'hommes. Les soldats se baladent dans une ville où il faudrait ajouter bout à bout toutes les histoires, où rien n'est négligeable. Mais personne n'a ce vice. La plupart des consciences sont vite satisfaites et, avec quelques mots, se font de l'inconnaissable une opinion définitive. Alors, ils finissent par nous croiser à l'aise, se faire au spectacle de ces milliers de morts et de mourants. (Plus tard même, lorsque Dachau sera en quarantaine à cause du typhus, il arrivera que l'on mette en prison des détenus qui veulent à tout prix sortir du camp.)
>
> *Inimaginable*, c'est un mot qui ne divise pas, qui ne restreint pas. C'est le mot le plus commode. Se promener avec ce mot en bouclier, le mot du

vide, et le pas s'assure, se raffermit, la conscience se reprend.] (317–18; emphasis in original)

Antelme gives voice here to an oft-repeated concern of witnesses that echoes Delbo's "Ô vous qui savez": that most readers and listeners are too quick to come to definitive understandings about the unimaginable experience of atrocity, which results in the event, and the stories told by those who survived it, becoming commonplace and banal to non-deportees. A degree of artfulness is necessary to truly engage such an audience, to transmit some of the truth to them, and to maintain their interest, but most deportees do not employ it – or at least do not successfully employ it – when they bear witness. A hierarchy of witnessing is thus established, one in which the stories of the bulk of survivors risk being relegated to near oblivion by those who did not experience the camps because, while true, these narratives do not make use of the kinds of techniques needed to draw readers and listeners in and genuinely maintain their attention over time.

This preoccupation with responding to and engaging outsiders, however, also results in a survivor like Antelme, and the community of political deportees his work documents, embracing highly problematic theoretical understandings of group dynamics that his writing clearly, and even paradoxically, presents as lacking, if not failed. This tension is perhaps most noticeable in passages that focus on how some French internees conceptualized and practised solidarity in everyday camp life. In a discussion some starving deportees are having about the distribution and quality of food in their work detail while waiting for their daily soup ration, for example, the understanding of solidarity offered by a strong-spoken Resistance member called Jo serves to cut off all talk of their hunger:

> "Shut up. You're being a pain in the ass. We know we don't eat. We know we're hungry. You'll see how it is three months from now. Shut up, or you're going to go nuts. If you want to eat, it's easy. Go find a kapo[12] and kiss his ass. Wash his handkerchiefs and all that. Lick the *Meister*'s ass in the factory, point out to him which guy isn't working. That doesn't interest you? Then you won't eat. But don't talk about it all the time. You're political prisoners, for God's sake. The Resistance is still going on – do you understand that, or don't you? You're making everybody depressed, just listening to you."
>
> The guy talking this way is hungry too. He's very tall, very big. We call him Jo. The bones are showing on his face. Just a quarter-loaf and a little

water to fill up his huge frame. His body is starting to eat itself. (85–6; translation modifed)

["Fermez-là un peu. Vous nous emmerdez. On le sait qu'on ne bouffe pas. On le sait qu'on a faim. Vous verrez comment ça sera dans trois mois. Fermez-là, vous allez devenir fous. Si vous voulez bouffer, c'est facile: allez lécher le cul aux kapos ; lavez leurs mouchoirs et tout et tout. À l'usine, léchez le cul au meister, montrez-lui que le copain ne travaille pas. Ça ne vous intéresse pas ? Alors vous ne boufferez pas. Mais n'en parlez pas toujours. Vous êtes des politiques, nom de Dieu. Vous ne comprenez pas que ça continue la Résistance, non ? Vous foutez le cafard à tout le monde."

Celui qui parle comme ça a faim lui aussi. Il est très grand, très large. On l'appelle Jo. Les os apparaissent sur sa figure. Un quart de boule et de la flotte à mettre dans ce coffre immense. Son corps commence à se manger.] (95–6)

A logic such as this is frequently invoked by members of the deportee community depicted in Antelme's *L'espèce humaine* when discussing their group dynamics. The only way for deportees to improve the conditions of their internment would be to give in and collaborate with the enemy. Accepting their situation and their collective dehumanization should therefore be seen as an act that continues their struggle as combatants and displays their solidarity. The text's narrator offers a more intricate theorization of this politics a few pages later:

The more our condition as humans is contested by the SS, the more chances we have of being confirmed as such. The real risk we run is that of starting to hate another guy out of envy, of being betrayed by our longings, of abandoning others. From such risks no one can be relieved [...] You can recognize yourself and recall yourself rummaging like a dog among rotten leftovers. But, on the other hand, the memory of the moment when you didn't share with a friend what you should have shared with him will finally give rise to doubts even as concerns the former behavior. Conscience errs not when we "sink" to a "lower level," but when we lose sight of the fact that "downfall" must be of and for everyone. (96; translation modified)

[Plus on est contesté en tant qu'homme par le SS, plus on a de chances d'être confirmé comme tel. Le véritable risque que l'on court, c'est celui de se mettre à haïr le copain d'envie, d'être trahi par la concupiscence,

> d'abandonner les autres. Personne ne peut s'en faire relever [...] On peut se reconnaître et se revoir fouinant comme un chien dans les épluchures pourries. Le souvenir du moment où l'on n'a pas partagé avec un copain ce qui devait l'être, au contraire viendrait à faire douter du premier acte. L'erreur de conscience n'est pas de "déchoir," mais de perdre de vue que la déchéance doit être de tous et pour tous.] (107)

The slippage in Antelme's reasoning here is striking. While his commentary begins by rejecting the SS gaze that dehumanizes deportees, his insistence that deportees confirm their human status by resembling each other through degradation – that "downfall must be of and for everyone" – ends up reinforcing the very system it purports to resist. It is one thing to recognize that everyone has the *potential* for degradation and that no one is ultimately immune to or above it as Antelme's remarks in this passage first seem to suggest. It is quite another to embrace it as a unifying experience for all deportees that confirms their human status. This logic of solidarity-through-resemblance is frequently invoked by members of the deportee community described in Antelme's *L'espèce humaine*. Yet it is also an example of, to paraphrase Trezise, a way of identifying with others that leads to collective forms of estrangement within that very community because the image of the human through which these deportees resemble and identify with each other is the very one that the Nazis impose on them. The Nazi image is dehumanizing, not humanizing, and so, as *L'espèce humaine* clearly acknowledges, it results in the isolation of deportees from each other and their abandonment of responsibility to anyone but themselves. It is a theorization that ultimately serves to confirm the vision of the Nazis and to submit deportees to the dehumanizing order that their oppressors sought to create.

Antelme comments, himself, in the forward of *L'espèce humaine* on the complete dissolution of collective bonds among the deportees of Gandersheim and on the devastating effects this had on his community's struggle against the Nazis:

> Those who supervised us at Gandersheim were our enemies.
>
> The administrative system hence being the further sharpened instrument of SS oppression, any collective struggle was foredoomed to failure. That failure took the form of slow death at the hands of the SS and the kapos combined, and all attempts that were undertaken by some of us were in vain.

> In the face of this omnipotent coalition, ours became the humblest of objectives. It was only to survive. Our struggle, the best among us were only able to wage it in an individual manner. Solidarity itself became an individual affair. (5)
>
> [À Gandersheim, nos responsables étaient nos ennemis.
>
> L'appareil administratif étant donc l'instrument, encore aiguisé, de l'oppression SS, la lutte collective était vouée à l'échec. L'échec, c'était le lent assassinat par le SS et les kapos réunis. Toutes les tentatives que certains d'entre nous entreprirent furent vaines.
>
> En face de cette coalition toute-puissante, notre objectif devenait le plus humble. C'était seulement de survivre. Notre combat, les meilleurs d'entre nous n'ont pu le mener que de façon individuelle. La solidarité même était devenue affaire individuelle.] (10–11)

Unlike the deportee-run administration in the main camp in Buchenwald, which was infiltrated by communist Resistance members who worked clandestinely to defend deportees by covertly opposing SS orders, Gandersheim's was primarily composed of internees who sought the approval of their Nazi oppressors in exchange for privileges such as larger food rations, higher quality clothing, and less strenuous work. The fact that more ethically oriented and collectively minded individuals could not penetrate its ranks crippled any attempts at collective action among the deportee community, and turned the experience of solidarity in the work detail into a highly "individual affair." Throughout *L'espèce humaine,* Antelme, in turn, paints admiring portraits of those deportees who best exemplify this solitary struggle to resist and damning portraits of those who collaborated or gave in. His comments about Jo's massive body and emaciated face clearly draw our attention to the man's tremendous will to resist in his physically weakened state. Likewise, a young deportee named Jacques is compared to a saint for never once complaining about his situation or colluding with a kapo in spite of the severe malnutrition that resulted in his premature death. An internee known as Lucien, on the other hand, is condemned as being in the service of the Nazis for using his position as interpreter to receive privileges and special treatment rather than to protect his fellow inmates as does another French interpreter, Gilbert.

And yet Antelme's writing also registers and even valorizes relations that break from the dehumanized and solitary logic of solidarity promoted by members of the deportee community such as Jo and throughout the narrator's own commentary. Though the narrator offers comparatively little overt *theoretical* reflection on this behaviour, *L'espèce humaine* clearly draws our attention to deportees who recognize their responsibilities to others in spite of their dehumanization. One of the most memorable passages of the text praises an unnamed blind deportee for spontaneously sharing his ration of bread with Antelme and another "*copain*" named René when his only obligation in the eyes of their community was to worry about feeding himself. "The blind guy didn't say anything," Antelme matter-of-factly recounts (82). "He was powerful. A mother." Similarly, remarks made by a professor named Gaston Riby about the importance of collective activities such as singing and reciting poetry succeed in convincing even a hardened deportee like Jo to participate in them. "We've got to talk" [Il faut parler (211)], Gaston insists to the group before their gathering one Sunday near the end of the war (195):

> "Comrades, we thought we should take advantage of an afternoon like this to get together for a little while. We don't know each other very well, we yell at each other, we're hungry. We're locked into all that; we've got to get out of it. They wanted to turn us into animals by making us live in conditions that nobody – and I mean nobody – will ever be able to imagine. But they won't succeed. Because we know where we come from we know why we are here. France is free but the war is still continuing, it's continuing right here, too. If sometimes we don't even recognize our own selves, that's what this war is costing, and we have got to hang on. But in order to hang on, each one of us has got to get out of himself, he's got to feel responsible for everybody. They've been able to take everything away from us except what we are. We still exist. And it's coming, now. The end is in sight. But in order to make it till the end, and to resist them, and to resist the tiredness and giving up that threatens all of us – in order to do all that, I'm telling you again, we all have to hang on, and we all have to stick together."
>
> Gaston had brought all that out in one breath, in a loud voice that progressively rose. He was red and his eyes showed his tenseness. The guys were tense also, and they had applauded. (196)

> ["Camarades, on a pensé qu'il était nécessaire de profiter d'un après-midi comme celui-ci pour se trouver un peu ensemble. On se connaît mal, on s'engueule, on a faim. Il faut sortir de là. Ils ont voulu faire de nous des bêtes en nous faisant vivre dans des conditions que personne, je dis

personne, ne pourra jamais imaginer. Mais ils ne réussiront pas. Parce que nous savons d'où nous venons, nous savons pourquoi nous sommes ici. La France est libre mais la guerre continue, elle continue ici aussi. Si parfois il nous arrive de ne pas nous reconnaître nous-mêmes, c'est cela que coûte cette guerre et il faut tenir. Mais pour tenir, il faut que chacun de nous sorte de lui-même, il faut qu'il se sente responsable de tous. Ils ont pu nous déposséder de tout mais pas de ce que nous sommes. Nous existons encore. Et maintenant, ça vient, la fin arrive, mais pour tenir jusqu'au bout, pour leur résister et résister à ce relâchement qui nous menace, je vous le redis, il faut que nous tenions et que nous soyons tous ensemble."

Gaston avait crié cela d'un trait, d'une voix qui était devenue progressivement aiguë. Il était rouge et ses yeux étaient tendus. Les copains aussi étaient tendus et ils avaient applaudi.] (213)

Gaston's speech about solidarity contrasts starkly with the ideas on the subject advanced in the narrator's commentary and by a representative of the deportee community, such as Jo, who confines others to silence. While both Antelme and Jo (problematically) insist that it is by resembling others in their dehumanization and accepting it that deportees demonstrate their humanity, Gaston argues that this is actually done by resisting this dehumanization, by being together, by not retreating into themselves, and by not losing sight of their responsibilities to all deportees as a group. The narrator's description of the effects of this particular afternoon of singing and poetry recitals on his community lends support to Gaston's claims:

Light had returned to the block. For a moment, the stove had been forgotten; there weren't any peelings on top of it. The guys had gathered around the platform, and those who had at first remained on their pallets had decided to come down. If at any moment somebody had come into the block, he would have been witness to a strange sight. Everybody was smiling. (197)

[La lumière était venue dans le block. Le poêle avait été pour un moment abandonné. Il n'y avait pas d'épluchures dessus. Les copains s'étaient groupés autour du tréteau. Ceux qui d'abord étaient restés allongés sur leur paillasse s'étaient décidés à descendre. Si quelqu'un à ce moment-là était entré dans le block, il en aurait eu une vision étrange. Tous souriaient.] (215)

This is one of the rare instances in which *L'espèce humaine* depicts deportees opening up and engaging as a collective in an activity that helps them resist Gandersheim's dehumanizing conditions together, as a group. The disciplined Jo, we discover, has a strong nasal yet guttural singing voice that is well received by his comrades and inspires others to sing as well. The afternoon allows them to forget their hunger, to enjoy being with others, and to find relief from their miserable, dehumanized existence, if only for a very brief period of time.

My intention here is not to affirm or undermine any of these conceptualizations of solidarity, aesthetic experience, or the representation of the camp experience in *L'espèce humaine,* but rather to emphasize an ethical dilemma to which such obvious contradictions in a survivor narrative might point. Through these inconsistencies, it seems clear that Antelme's writing bears witness to the tremendous sense of responsibility witnesses feel to most of the members of their communities when representing them in their narratives. The narrator takes pains to justify, theorize, and defend the individualized model of solidarity practised by his fellow political deportees – they were clearly doing the best they could to make sense of and deal with their dehumanizing situation and were among the few with the courage to stand up to the Nazis at the time. Yet, as a text, *L'espèce humaine* also bears witness to the obvious failure of this theoretical understanding, in particular because it causes deportees to close themselves off and abandon their responsibilities to others in the camps. Antelme's writing quite obviously registers a longing for different kinds of relations between himself and others than those that dominate his community throughout their internment. In addition to the text's extensive, well-known reflections on the nature of singularity and of subjectivity, *L'espèce humaine* ends by recounting an exchange between Antelme and an anonymous Russian survivor just after liberation that is appreciative of the gentleness of the Russian's voice and demeanour, two qualities lacking from most deportee interactions recorded empathetically in the work.

But Antelme is also clearly compelled to pay tribute to his and his comrades' failed attempts at solidarity, presumably at least in part because, unlike those who collaborated, the actions of these deportees were clearly well-intentioned and made in an effort to resist. The easily satisfied audience of non-survivors reading his text might be too quick to make light of or to overlook such a crucial distinction, or even to condemn camp inmates for not doing more. In short, these contradictions in Antelme's writing illustrate just some of the ethical complexities to be negotiated in the act of witnessing. Survivors rightly feel a sense of duty to honour the memory of the dead and to defend the deportee community from the judgmental gaze of outsiders. Yet they also recognize the mistakes they and their comrades may have made throughout their experience, and the need to find more ethical ways of responding in the face of atrocity. In the case of Antelme's *L'espèce humaine,* the theoretical serves to protect the community described in the work and to justify its behaviour for a dismissive audience. Theorizing the importance of a term such as "unimaginable" to describe the camp experience can be seen as a way of defending witnesses and their community members because it emphasizes the extreme and destabilizing nature of the atrocious conditions deportees had to confront. To paraphrase Antelme, it further acts as a kind of shield for survivors, one that helps them pull themselves together and feel more assured in the aftermath of their experience. Such a theorization can also, however, unintentionally reinforce the dismissive behaviour of others because it lumps the experiences of deportees into an unimaginable mass. It masks the contradictions and inconsistencies that Antelme's testimony documents, and can thus easily morph into an absolute and universalizing truth that, to return once more to Trezise, limits the ways both survivors and their audiences may approach the act of witnessing.

Antelme's writing bears witness, in other words, to theory's status as a source of protection and strength for the deportee community that simultaneously draws attention from the failures of that community's theorizations of the ethical. The testimonial writings of Jorge Semprun clearly illustrate how this dynamic transforms into a full-fledged defence mechanism that represses the survivor community and reinforces broader forms of denial. His work thus occupies an important place in this book. Less well-known to North American audiences than survivors like Primo Levi, Elie Wiesel, or – because of his importance to French theory – Antelme, Semprun was one of the most important and politically influential witness writers in both France and Spain from the publication of his first Buchenwald memoir in 1963 until his death in 2011 at age 87. The son of a diplomat for Spain's Second Republic and grandson of five-time Spanish Prime Minister Antonio Maura, Semprun was one of approximately five hundred Spanish Republicans interned in Buchenwald for their activities in the French Resistance.[13] As a teenager, he had been exiled to France with the rest of his family at the outbreak of the Spanish Civil War, became a philosophy student in Paris before joining the Resistance, and was an important operative for the clandestine communist movement in Buchenwald thanks to his fluent German. After the war, Semprun devoted himself to politics, rising up the ranks of the Spanish Communist Party to become part of its Executive Committee that operated out of France, only to be banished in the early 1960s for his criticisms of the Party's abuses of power. He moved on to become one of the most recognized writers of the Deportation in France, an important voice during Spain's transition to democracy, Spain's Minister of Culture under the country's first socialist president (Felipe Gonzalez), and the scriptwriter for two of the most influential political films of the 1960s: Alain Resnais's *La guerre est finie* and Costa-Gavras's *Z*.[14]

Given Semprun's public status as a dedicated militant directly implicated in some of the most important cultural and political debates of his time, it is unsurprising and of course fitting that his witness texts have received extensive praise in France and Spain as well as in scholarship on the Nazi camps – in particular for their contributions to our understandings of totalitarianism and the creation of knowledge about atrocity. I propose here, however, that his works are also exemplary of the ways in which authoritative displays of knowledge – and, more specifically, of understandings of our humanity – function as tools of repression and exclusion within the deportee community. I show that Semprun's texts, in a manner similar to Antelme's, actually undo the theoretical understandings of the Nazi camps and of the "art" of witnessing for which his works have been so widely recognized, a fact that their narrators constantly work to cover up through their masterful displays. Theory actually functions as a safety zone in Semprun's concentration camp narratives, one that their narrators routinely retreat into when their experiences – including those that expose their ethical limits – make them anxious. What such texts ultimately point to, I argue, is the cathartic effect that these defensive theoretical displays have within the survivor community because of the paralysing fear that grips male political deportees in particular when exposed to the limits of their ethical knowledge. In an attempt to rid themselves of their own shortcomings as respondents to atrocity, these well-intentioned people seek to affirm and demonstrate a mastery of their preconceived theorizations of the ethical. But doing this causes them to deny the traumatic dimensions of their experiences – those aspects that can, in fact, never be fully controlled.

Denial, in this context, results from many members of the political deportee community idealizing rigid understandings of the ethical because of the difficulties they face when responding to atrocity both in the camps and when coping with their trauma in the aftermath.

Semprun's texts bear witness to a series of interactions in which political prisoners, including Semprun himself, even become hostile towards victims whose experiences do not fit into the forms they recognize. Community members who are too physically weak or not talented enough to speak masterfully, for example, are ignored because their experiences fall outside of the bounds of these fixed conceptualizations, or their narratives are perceived as flawed or deficient acts of witnessing that more articulate and knowledgeable speakers must discipline and correct. As in the work of Antelme, it is clear that these disciplinary actions are undertaken with a dismissive and too-easily satisfied audience of non-deportees in mind. But the ethical becomes repressive within the male deportee community because those aspects of victims' experiences that do not reinforce their group's agreed-upon understandings are either reshaped by others in order to resemble those understandings or are simply ignored. Displaying mastery of concepts replaces the desire to act in the interest of others within the community described in the narratives of a witness like Semprun, causing the suffering of real people to be repressed and the horrors of the camps to be denied.

Klaus Theweleit has noted that moments of display serve a similar repressive function among the militant men of *authoritarian* social formations. Organized public events in totalitarian regimes such as mass rituals, drills, and parades serve to constantly discipline these "soldier males." Over time, they come to conceive of these rigid displays as superior and liberating experiences that can ward off threats to their masculinity rather than as moments that repress, constrain, and cause anxiety in them. Participating in these public rituals helps to release and temporarily relieve their pent-up desires; however, these desires are liberated through predetermined paths that are ultimately controlled and manipulated by authorities, which only serves to dam them up until the next moment of display allows them to stream forth.[15] This continuous channelling of desire eventually causes these men to adopt a defensive and aggressive stance towards any of the real, living things in their surroundings that arouse them, to withdraw into intoxicating and hallucinatory mental states whenever they try to feel pleasure, and to seek to destroy anything that does not fit into the rigid forms they idealize.

Ethically oriented militants such as Semprun close themselves off and retreat from reality whenever real people in their surroundings activate their *ethical* desires. They further become incapable of remaining mentally present in encounters that destabilize their theoretical understandings of the ethical, and withdraw into themselves as a way of coping with their feelings of inferiority. In my analysis, in chapter 1, of Semprun's "compassionate" response in Buchenwald to the dying sociologist and theorist of collective memory Maurice Halbwachs, I demonstrate that this flight from reality occurs because authoritative members of the survivor community view their fixed ethical responses as a superior, "fraternal" way of being there for people in need that allows ethically minded people to show their courage and strength and to share in the experiences of their comrades. These displays help deportees to distance themselves from the destabilizing effects of the present, to master their frail and emaciated bodies, and to maintain their composure in the eyes of others. But they also unwittingly exert a kind of epistemic hegemony that ignores and, ultimately, denies the existence of any person or experience that challenges militants' ideas about the ethical.

Of course, not all survivors of atrocity engage in this exclusionary and repressive "ethical" behaviour when confronted with their limits. Auschwitz internee and Belgian Resistance member Jean Améry, for example, openly acknowledges the uselessness of his own ethics in the struggle to survive the Nazi camps as a "humanist intellectual." The son of an Austrian Jewish man raised Catholic by his non-Jewish mother after his father's death in the First World War, Améry entered the camps an atheist in spite of being deported to Auschwitz for his Jewish origins.[16] "I must confess that I felt great admiration for both my religiously and politically committed comrades," he reflects in *At the Mind's Limits* (12). "[W]e skeptical humanist intellectuals took recourse, in vain, to our literary, philosophical, and artistic household gods."

> I did not want to be one with my believing comrades, but I would have wished to be like them: unshakable, calm, strong. What I felt to comprehend [*sic*] at that time still appears to me as a certainty: whoever is, in the broadest sense, a believing person, whether his belief be metaphysical or bound to concrete reality, transcends himself. He is not the captive of his individuality; rather he is part of a spiritual continuity that is uninterrupted nowhere, not even in Auschwitz. He is both more estranged from reality and closer to it than his unbelieving comrade. Further from reality because in his Finalistic [*sic*] attitude he ignores the given contents of material phenomena and fixes his sight on a nearer or more distant future; but he is also closer to reality because for just this reason he does not allow himself to be overwhelmed by the conditions around him and thus he can

> strongly influence them. For the unbelieving person reality, under adverse circumstances, is a force to which he submits; under favorable ones it is material for analysis. For the believer reality is clay that he molds, a problem that he solves. (14)

Améry expresses admiration for his "believing" comrades here for qualities similar to the ones praised in the testimonies of political prisoners such as Semprun and Antelme. Committed internees remained calm and strong in the camps because their belief systems allowed them to transcend the miserable material conditions to which all were subjected, and to even influence and shape that reality thanks to their detachment from it. Unbelievers such as Améry were incapable of such transcendence precisely because of their attachment to the material world – they became overwhelmed when faced with the atrocious world of the camps, and captives of their individuality who were no longer capable of analysing reality or offering resistance to its forces. "[I]f the intellect was not centered around a religious or political belief it was of no help, or of little help," he tersely insists (15). "It abandoned us. It constantly vanished from sight whenever those questions were involved that were once called the 'ultimate' ones."

I argue that the testimonies of survivors like Antelme and Semprun reveal that many "believing" deportees were calm and strong in appearance only and grappled with the limits of their approaches just as much as an unbelieving humanist such as Améry did in the camps. As Antelme's *L'espèce humaine* suggests, community norms required political deportees to repress the acknowledgment of their limits, and to suffer in isolation as their belief systems failed. Critical responses to Semprun's work further indicate the problematic extent to which some influential readers of survivor testimonies – including prominent French intellectuals and scholars of witness literature – have also closed themselves off to the profound reflections on the humanist intellectual's relationship with the material world elaborated by Améry. I demonstrate in chapter 1 that this is due, in part, to an unwavering belief among these readers in the ability of *literary experience* to transcend the individual and the material world in the way that religious and political beliefs do according to Améry. At least for these particular readers, literature in fact has the status of the kinds of belief systems to which Améry opposes it: it is a source of tranquility and strength that allows readers to distance and defend themselves from the horrors of dehumanizing and destabilizing conditions. This desire to confirm a certain theoretical understanding of literature, however, makes readers blind to the inconsistencies that survivor narratives frequently expose about the literary in their own materiality as texts. Such readers dedicate themselves to mastering the new understandings that some survivors claim to elaborate. But these readers ignore and further reinforce the forms of exclusion and denial that such a belief in literature creates.[17]

The exclusionary and defensive behaviour I have identified here is not a response that militant men alone have when inhabiting unstable epistemic positions. A range of well-intentioned individuals – including female survivors, victims' loved ones, and readers of witness literature – withdraw into their failed understandings in this manner as a way of coping with their incapacities. However, through my analyses of the work of Charlotte Delbo in particular, I suggest that this reaction is most apparent in militant men because expectations of heroic male behaviour that are upheld as ideals of masculinity and ethical action within their communities exert tremendous pressure on them to appear as though they know how to act even when confronted with their limits. Traditional gender roles place greater demands on these men to act and take responsibility for others, yet, as Delbo succinctly puts it at the start of the second volume of *Auschwitz et après, Une connaissance inutile*, the women who engaged in the Resistance "had released them from all responsibility" from the very start [les femmes les avaient, dès le premier moment, déchargés de leur responsabilité (*CI* 10)] to defend and protect others on their own (*Auschwitz and After* 117). To borrow a phrasing from Marianne Hirsch and Leo Spitzer, gender emerges as significant in this book only to recede and make space for other concerns (198). The behaviour of the militant men of the Resistance makes visible ways in which the experiences of atrocity victims can become ignored or repressed by the moral sentiments of communities in general, and also indicates ways in which witness literature can offer a critical space of resistance to this pernicious form of denial.[18]

Delbo's testimonial writings offer a complex implicit critique of this defensive ethics that I seek to explicate here. Until fairly recently, her work has been less well-known to the French public than writings by survivors such as Antelme, Wiesel, or Semprun. However, she has been slowly gaining recognition in France and among scholars as an important writer of the Deportation, largely thanks to the richness and complexity of her Auschwitz trilogy, which was published in France in 1970 and 1971.[19] A member of the French Communist Party beginning in the 1930s and assistant to famed actor and director Louis Jouvet at the outbreak of the Second World War, Delbo was arrested on 2 March 1942, along with her husband Georges Dudach, for running a clandestine press that produced anti-Nazi literature. She spent a total of twenty-seven months in the Nazi camp system, including almost an entire year in Auschwitz, before being liberated from Ravensbrück, an all-women's concentration camp near Berlin, in April of 1945. After the war, Delbo returned to France, eventually disassociated herself from the Communist Party, and worked for the Centre National de la Recherche Scientifique, for the United Nations in Geneva, Israel, and Greece, and as an assistant to Marxist theorist Henri Lefebvre.[20] In France, Delbo was initially known more for her work as a playwright before a recent surge of interest in her concentration camp testimonies; however, in North America, she has been recognized for several decades for her survivor narratives and the theoretical reflections they advance about the experience of atrocity and the question of ethical responsibility.[21]

In my analyses of Delbo, I examine an aspect of her writing that has been ignored in previous scholarship – its use of various forms of irony – and argue that it be considered a key rhetorical device for combatting the retreat of well-intentioned individuals into the rigid ethical behaviours that cause their denial. As in the indirect approach used in the poem "O you who know," irony can create a more inclusive environment for those who are the targets of a text's criticisms because it invites all readers and listeners to share in the task of constructing meaning and to become intimately involved with a work. Wayne Booth, for example, has noted that, even if we ultimately reject a text's critical messages, we often have a feeling of camaraderie with authors who employ irony because of the "acrobatic skill" we must show in order to understand their conclusions (42). Booth remarks that often the predominant emotion when reading ironies

> is that of joining, of finding and communing with kindred spirits. The author I infer behind the false words is my kind of man, because he enjoys playing with irony, because he assumes *my* capacity for dealing with it, and – most important – because he grants me a kind of wisdom; he assumes that he does not have to spell out the shared and secret truths on which my reconstruction is to be built. (28; emphasis in original)[22]

Delbo, of course, is far from the only witness writer to employ irony in her testimonies. Ana Novac, for instance, makes extensive use of the device in her Auschwitz diary *Les beaux jours de ma jeunesse* as a distancing mechanism that keeps her from submitting herself to the dehumanization of the Nazi camp system throughout her internment. It performs a similar defensive function in the writings of Jorge Semprun, and is a tone that his narrators at times adopt to help maintain their composure and distance themselves from the world of the camps when confronted with their limits and incapacities.[23]

But the use of irony in Delbo's writing is less defensive in nature. In *Auschwitz et après*, a range of ironies – from verbal to dramatic to what Booth has dubbed "stable" – are deployed to reconfigure our problematic self-protective response to forms of human suffering that shatter our understandings. Irony does not have the status of a philosophical stance or mode of consciousness that Delbo's writing adopts in relation to the world of the Nazi camps, nor is it an informing principle of personality or way of life for survivors of atrocity more generally.[24] Rather, the examples of irony I analyse here are used as a rhetorical strategy at key points in Delbo's work in order to promote our attentiveness to victims and their concerns. In contrast to the "masterful" displays that appear in Semprun's narratives or the contradictions of Antelme's – both of which strive to cover up deportees' ethical shortcomings – the ironies in *Auschwitz et après* actually expose us to Delbo's limits as a respondent to atrocity in order to destabilize our relationship with knowledge. However – and again in contrast to some of her militant male counterparts – Delbo's writing does not attempt to transmit superior understandings of the ethical or new secret truths about atrocity and the human as do the ironies analysed by a scholar such as Booth. They also do not attempt to display that she, the author, is – to paraphrase Booth – our kind of woman or man. Delbo's ironies seek, rather, to emancipate us from the constraints of our ethical conventions in our encounters with people in need and to transform us from withdrawn meaning *confirmers* into members of a community of meaning *makers*. They do this by guiding us to recognize our own "acrobatic skill" even when we are at our weakest rather than Delbo's – or anyone's – exemplarity or mastery as a witness.

One way to appreciate the contrast between these various approaches to engaging readers of witness literature is to view them through the lens of Jacques Rancière's distinction between the methods that "ignorant masters" and "master explicators" use to instruct others and the dispositions that these methods cultivate in readers and listeners. Master explicators strive to transmit their knowledge, Rancière tells us, by explaining it in fragments and then revealing increasingly complex lessons once their pupils have mastered simpler ones. They thus gradually abolish the distance between their superior knowledge and the ignorance of others and guide others to their own level of expertise (*Ignorant* 3). While master explicators engage in this process in good faith, by proceeding in this fashion, they also cultivate dependency in their students, who feel that they must always have another master and his supplementary explications in order to understand and progress (21). Ignorant masters, on the other hand, seek to emancipate people from the "stultifying" order of explication by using their positions of authority, not to demonstrate their knowledge, but to verify that people are following their own intellectual routes: that people are conscious of their own intellectual power, attentive to their own intellectual acts, and vigilantly searching to move forward into new territories along their own distinct and unpredictable paths. What ignorant masters reject, in short, is a belief in superior and inferior intelligences and the binding of one mind to another, in place of which they assert the equality of the intellectual capacities of any human being and the ability of anyone and everyone to make new discoveries by themselves – that is, *without* following the lead of enlightened masters. Cultivating this disposition has a broader social impact, Rancière suggests, because it liberates people from the fiction of their own incapacities, which keeps them from submitting themselves to the domination of a society's elite or participating in their own social exclusion.

My central claim in this book is that theoretical ethical *knowledge* cannot prepare us to respond to the ethical *demands* of atrocity, and that confronting this fact puts us on the defensive. When conceiving of the ethical as a form of knowledge explicated and displayed by masters, survivor narratives perpetuate our dependence on understandings elaborated by others, thereby reinforcing the very "ethical" behaviour that causes us to freeze up and withdraw into rigid forms when confronted with victims and their concerns. They also reinforce the kind of dissolution of interpersonal bonds witnessed in the work of an Antelme, an undoing that the survivor himself attributes to an approach to collective resistance that depends on submission to and intervention from above. Such testimonies further reinforce broader forms of denial, I want to propose, because they cultivate our desire to preserve our image of our humanity rather than our awareness of the needs of others – the same disposition at work in France's state politics of the ethical as displayed by Chirac. The writings of a witness like Delbo seek to exert a radically different effect: they break the cycle of stultification and submission by presenting the ethical as a response that each of us must improvise in our encounters with any human being – a reaction that depends on our vigilance and attentiveness to the outside world, on using our own capacities when responding to people in need, on following intellectual routes that diverge from those of our masters, and on behaving in ways that will often differ from the responses previously sanctioned by our communities. To be there *for* others we must first "be there" *with* them and look at them through our own eyes – we must not transport ourselves into the safety of a concept and subject other people or ourselves to the domination of ethical knowledge or the repression caused by its display.[25]

But to advance such observations or theoretical insights directly would risk alienating the very people that witness narratives such as Delbo's work to include. Facing their shortcomings causes the well-intentioned individuals whose behaviour I analyse throughout this book to retreat from others and withdraw into themselves. Moreover, as Delbo herself acknowledges in regards to the ethically oriented *men* of the Resistance, overt statements would call attention to the weaknesses they feel they must hide from others and to their inability to live up to the ethical ideals they share as a community. While reflecting on how she and her fellow female political deportees attempted to communicate indirectly with these men during their imprisonment, Delbo comments, "they suffered [...] from not being able to protect us, to defend us, to take on destiny alone"[26] [ils souffraient [...] de ne pas être en mesure de nous protéger, de nous défendre, de ne plus assumer seuls le destin (*CI* 10)]. "We loved them. We told them with our eyes, never our lips. That would have seemed strange to them. It would have been like telling them that we knew how fragile their lives were"[27] [Nous les aimions. Nous le leur disions des yeux, jamais des lèvres. Cela leur aurait semblé étrange. Ç'aurait été leur dire que nous savions combien leur vie était fragile (9)]. Irony can help to disrupt our defensive ethical reactions and alleviate the kind of suffering we well-intentioned respondents experience by drawing attention to our courage and abilities rather than our failures. These emancipatory ironies can thus help to take the edge off these situations by offering others support and letting the fact that we know we are helping them remain unspoken.[28] Yet they also transform our approach to ethical commitment from the exemplary actions of a select, superior few to a process in which everyone must participate together, and that must always be improvised to discover the new. Confronting atrocity is a task that lies beyond both what knowledge can account for and what one person can manage alone.

We must build ethically minded people back up and draw them near to modify their ethics, keep them grounded, and keep them engaged. We must read their behaviour at once critically and compassionately, and show them the sympathy they are unable to have for themselves.

To approach testimonial narratives in this way, however, is to confront how the act of witnessing has been theorized in trauma studies and how the question of the ethical has been conceptualized in contemporary scholarship on the Nazi camps and on totalitarian oppression. Witnesses such as Semprun and Delbo call for bonds with their audiences that the patient-therapist model – the model on which scholars such as Shoshana Felman, Dori Laub, Dominick LaCapra, and Cathy Caruth base their understandings of the reader-text relationship elicited by survivor testimonies – cannot adequately account for.[29] It is clear that the works of survivors like Antelme, Améry, Semprun, and Delbo are addressed to a wide reading public that consists, not of therapists, but of people who do not have expertise in trauma recovery – an audience composed, in particular, of loved ones of camp victims and of survivors themselves, none of whom should respond as though they are knowledgeable authorities with definitive ideas to assert or should intervene in witness narratives as, to quote Laub, "one who knows" (63). The case of Semprun further presents us with a survivor recognized as an authoritative voice by society-at-large when testifying to the camp experience, one whose testimonies point to the dangers that such witnesses pose in the aftermath of disaster because of a collective need to be reassured. Survivors like Semprun announce that they have definitive understandings of the human to impart, and we obediently submit ourselves to their "masterful" displays.

Moreover, rethinkings of the ethical that have been advanced by Giorgio Agamben in his work on witnessing and by Jean-Luc Nancy in his conceptualization of community, I argue, promote at a theoretical level the very epistemic habits that I criticize here. Both authors claim to elaborate understandings of ethical commitment that we should embrace in light of the moral failures of the Nazi camps and, more broadly, of totalitarianism. Yet both also unwittingly defend the practice of ignoring victims when confronted with our own limits – Agamben by insisting that elaborating a new, more complete definition of the human is the ethical task we must take up to overcome the ethical shortcomings of camp deportees, and Nancy by promoting withdrawing from others and exposing our limits as responses that construct communities and resist totalitarian fusion. Such rigid formulations of the ethical ultimately lead, though, to the kinds of defensive reactions and displays that permeate both authoritarian societies and the ethically oriented communities that oppose them. They also, perhaps even more problematically, ignore what survivors actually do in their narratives in order to grapple with the ethical complexities of their experiences and engage and challenge their audiences. To combat the repression that passes for ethics, we must emancipate our responses from our theorizations and approach the ethical instead as demanding unending negotiations and improvisations – a process that requires us to turn towards others, step outside of our rigid selves, and remain attentive to the needs of others who may be struggling to articulate those needs themselves.

In each of the chapters in this book, I analyse in-depth how the defensive responses of well-intentioned people unwittingly contribute to a massive and pernicious way in which the horrors of atrocity are denied, and the experiences of victims are repressed and ignored. My first two chapters explore how the problematic dynamics of the male deportee community as documented in the work of Jorge Semprun have contributed to this denial. Chapter 1 focuses on how the authority to speak about atrocity can be established within this group by appropriating and filling in the gaps of well-established theoretical conceptualizations about literature and artistic experience and imposing them on survivors' experiences. This preoccupation with displaying mastery of the ideas of others, however, serves to repress victims and to blind readers to the limits of these ideas that the experience of atrocity continuously exposes. In chapter 2, I look at the ethical dilemmas that arise when "intellectual" witnesses attempt to speak for other members of the survivor community in their narratives. Since the immediate postwar period, French political returnees in particular have often stressed that an important role of the intellectuals among them is to produce narratives that account for *all* deportees' shared experience of trauma. I demonstrate, however, that these intellectual witnesses routinely ignore the concerns of others in order to speak in their name.

In chapters 3 and 4, I explicitly consider how some influential social and theoretical discourses have served to limit the acceptable range of ethical responses readers can offer to witness literature in a manner that echoes the processes at work within the male political deportee community. I discuss in the third chapter how Giorgio Agamben's highly influential observation that the concentration camp experience presents us with an ethical aporia actually serves to institutionalize the practice of turning a blind eye to others when our frameworks fail us. Agamben's argument that it is not decent for us to expect people to have been decent to each other given the miserable, dehumanizing conditions of their internment ignores a central concern of the works of survivors such as Charlotte Delbo: to teach us to react to others in more responsible ways and to resist and modify our problematic approaches to others. Chapter 4 again turns to the work of Delbo in order to explore how ideals of the couple contributed to the normalization and denial of concentration camp memory in the decades immediately following liberation. Scholars have noted that models of the happy middle-class couple played a crucial role in the exclusion of France's *colonial* past from its modern identity formations during this period by inspiring couples to close themselves off from the outside world rather than focus their attention on contemporary social and political struggles. I contend here that such ideals of coupledom further contributed to the exclusion of the horrors of the Second World War from French social space after the war's end by producing accounts of the Nazi camps that erased their uncontrollable and disruptive dimensions.

Blind moral displays of people like Jacques Chirac demonstrate the extent to which broader social forces still seek to codify our ethical responses to atrocity and ignore the concerns of individual victims. This book strives to understand our defensive ethics so we can break free of the repressive behaviours that unintentionally facilitate denial and submit us all to exclusion.

1 Literature, Theory, and Fraternity

I can't even manage to concentrate on this historic instant. I sense that I'm going to miss it, that it's going to pass me by, disappear, before I can become aware of it. Before I can digest its substantive and succulent juices. I must not be gifted for historic instants.

– Jorge Semprun, *L'écriture ou la vie*[1]

[Je n'arrive même pas à me concentrer sur cet instant historique. Je sens que je vais le rater, qu'il va passer, s'évanouir, avant que je n'en aie pris conscience. Que je n'en aie dégusté les sucs substantifiques et succulents. Je ne dois pas être doué pour les instants historiques.]

The opening scene of Jorge Semprun's 1994 witnessing narrative *L'écriture ou la vie* describes in detail the first instance in which the text's main character, "Jorge," is faced with telling people who did not experience Buchenwald about the horrors of camp life.[2] It is the day after the camp's liberation by Allied Forces, and the twenty-one year-old Spaniard and member of the French Resistance encounters three terrified officers in British uniforms while he is standing guard outside of one of the camp's former SS barracks. Two of the men are British, one of them French, and they all stare wide-eyed at the young survivor, waiting to hear what he has to say.

The passage's narrator carefully scrutinizes the French soldier before Jorge begins to speak. His demeanour is both joyful and fearful; a horrified look in the Frenchman's eyes contrasts starkly with the triumphant way in which he is wearing his French military badges.

"He must be about my age, maybe a few years older. I can sympathize," Semprun narrates [Il doit avoir mon âge, quelques années de plus. Je pourrais sympathiser (15)]. Jorge's first words are directly addressed to the Frenchman. "What is it?" Jorge drily and irritatedly asks. "Does the silence of the forest astonish you that much?" [Qu'y a-t-il? Le silence de la forêt qui vous étonne autant?] The soldier turns his head to look at the trees, and pricks his ears in response to the question. The British soldiers obediently follow his lead. "No, it isn't the silence" the narrator states. "They hadn't noticed anything, hadn't heard the silence. I'm clearly what's terrifying them, nothing else" [Non, ce n'est pas le silence. Ils n'avaient rien remarqué, pas entendu le silence. C'est moi qui les épouvante, rien d'autre, visiblement]. Though the officers probably perceived the survivor's Russian boots and German rifle as "reassuring" signs of authority at the time, the narrator surmises, it must be the look in Jorge's eyes that they find so terrifying. "No more birds," Jorge continues. "The smoke from the crematorium drove them away, they say. There are never any birds in this forest" [Plus d'oiseaux. La fumée du crématoire les a chassées, dit-on. Jamais d'oiseaux dans cette forêt]. The three wide-eyed officers listen attentively, and, the narrator guesses, try to understand Jorge's message. When Jorge further explains that it was the smell of burnt flesh that drove the birds away from the forest – "[l]'odeur de chair brûlée, c'est ça!" he exclaims (16) – the three already terrified men jump in horror. Though the three soldiers remain in Jorge's presence, they are unable to look at him for the rest of the time he bears witness to his experience of Buchenwald.

Witnessing narratives, whether oral or written, play crucial roles in transmitting the horrors of atrocity to those who are fortunate enough not to have experienced them. Much scholarship on survivor testimonies has focused on the challenging task with which readers and listeners are faced when they engage witnesses and their terrifying texts. In their landmark work on the genre, *Testimony*, Shoshana Felman and Dori Laub suggest that those who listen to or read narratives about "extreme human pain" and "massive psychic trauma" embark on "a journey fraught with dangers" because, through the act of listening to or reading the words of survivors, people can come to experience trauma themselves (57, 72). Felman and Laub define witnessing as a performative speech act that involves an "intimate bond" between a speaker and a listener, and propose that the role of the listener in this relation is to be a "blank screen on which a traumatic event comes to be inscribed" (57). But, because "[t]here is so much destruction recounted, so much death, so much loss, so much hopelessness" in survivor narratives (72), they suggest that readers and listeners frequently experience "a need, an urgency to pull back, to withdraw to a safer place," one in which they can protect themselves and "maintain a sense of safety in the face of trauma" (73).

The opening passage of *L'écriture ou la vie* points to a different kind of relation between witnesses and their listeners than Felman and Laub describe, one that I consider to be a *mise-en-abyme* of the relationship that certain kinds of readers have with survivor testimonies. Some readers pick up a text such as *L'écriture ou la vie* because they want to know more about the concentration camp experience, and they believe that a narrative written by a cultural authority such as Jorge Semprun, one of France and Spain's most famous witness writers since the 1960s, will give them the kind of information that will further their knowledge. In this chapter, I will examine in detail this "fraternal" relationship between listeners and "authoritative" witnesses, and between readers and witnessing narratives written by experienced authorities. I will focus on how such survivors establish their mastery as witnesses to atrocity by filling in the gaps of theoretical understandings of the "art" of witnessing elaborated by members of their communities. I will argue, however, that the writings of survivors like Semprun unwittingly expose their limits as authoritative witnesses to the experience of historical trauma and, in the process, the limits of both literature and theory as means of representing the horrors of camp life.

1 Mastery

Though he tried to write about his experience of the Nazi camps immediately after the Second World War, Jorge Semprun did not publish his first witnessing narrative, *Le grand voyage*, until eighteen years after his liberation from Buchenwald. The text won both the 1963 Prix Formentor and the Grand Prize of the French Resistance, and was immediately banned in Francoist Spain.[3] The publication of *Le grand voyage* marked a turning point in Semprun's life from Spanish political militant to one of France's most important Deportation writers. *L'écriture ou la vie* tells the story of Semprun's coming-to-writing, and describes how becoming a writer further signalled a change in the way he coped with his traumatic past. A political "life" that depended on Semprun distancing himself from and forgetting his traumatic memories gave way, the text shows, to an anguishing writerly existence in which he is constantly "driven back into the asphyxiation of [the] memory" [refoulé dans l'asphyxie de [la] mémoire] of the camps (146). The title *L'écriture ou la vie* refers to the dilemma with which Semprun had been faced since his liberation from Buchenwald: either "brutally" repress his traumatic memories in order to function in society and "live" (271), or distance himself from "life" by undertaking the "interminable task" of writing about what he calls "the experience of death" (319, 351). Though Semprun enjoyed a successful career as a writer in contemporary France and Spain, *L'écriture ou la vie* stresses that with it came "the full-fledged return of the old anxieties" [le retour en force des anciennes angoisses] that he had previously repressed in order not to be cut off from the world (293).[4]

Like all of Semprun's witness writings, *L'écriture ou la vie* is an autobiographical narrative in which the names of the text's first-person narrator and of the protagonist are both Jorge Semprun. The narrative is structured around the writer's experiences after his liberation from Buchenwald, and flashes forward and backward in time to comment on the steps he passed through to become a writer. The entire story is supplemented by an extended theoretical reflection on witnessing as a genre that comments on some of the narrative techniques that have been employed in Semprun's writings since *Le grand voyage*. As every critic who has written on the text has pointed out, *L'écriture ou la vie* presents within it a metacommentary on the genre of testimony which defends the use of the artificial techniques of fiction in order to transmit an "essential truth" about the experience of the Nazi camps to readers and listeners. In the process, the text reveals that Semprun has made use of these same techniques in all of his writings on Buchenwald; the text's narrator describes in detail how the author invents characters in his writing, gives fictitious names to real people, endows his "narrative I" with more knowledge than he could have possessed during his past experiences, and countless other "artificial" techniques that make his narratives fictional and factually inaccurate.[5] In spite of the fact that Jorge Semprun hid his use of fiction from his readers for over thirty years, scholars have primarily interpreted the use of artifice in his witnessing texts as an important contribution to understandings of the process of transmission and of the creation of knowledge about atrocity.[6] In his work on *L'écriture ou la vie,* David Carroll proposes that Semprun's use of fiction "defends the use of the imagination [...] for overcoming the shortcomings of first-person testimony and the restrictions of conventional historical representation" ("Limits" 69). This "shameless" reliance on fiction and artistic creation, Carroll suggests, is a way of stimulating "the imagination of listeners and readers" of Semprun's texts, which causes their audience "to experience the limits of empathy and the shock of non-identification," and, as such, "to imagine that the unimaginable occurred" (77). When performing this function, Carroll argues, fiction should not be seen as "a weapon to assassinate memory," but, rather, as "a means to enrich and complicate it," for it furnishes a type of narration that "could legitimately be considered one of the means of exceeding the limitations of historical representation and a way of phrasing what has not yet found its idiom in or as history" (78).

Susan Suleiman reflects more specifically on the way in which the first-person narrators in all of Semprun's writings make use of fiction in their commentary on the events that are evoked in the author's texts. Suleiman explains that, in all of his testimonial works, Semprun's narrator is, like Proust's in *À la recherche du temps perdu*, "perched at the top of a temporal edifice from which he can command the whole sweep of the past," an edifice in which he can "roam temporally at will" by leaping "forward and backward in time" ("Historical Trauma" 3, 6).[7] She interprets the narrator's use of fiction within this temporal edifice as the "literary performance" of the attempt to "work through" trauma in order to master and overcome it,[8] a process that involves the narrator of each of his texts "continuously revising" events from the author's past and making use of different forms of artifice in each rewriting (18, 6). As such, Suleiman proposes, fiction "is the poetic equivalent of revision" in Semprun's work, "or the process whereby the memory of a traumatic past event is not merely repeated but continually reinterpreted in light of the subject's evolving preoccupations and self-understandings" (6).[9] This "characteristic signature" of Semprun as a writer is most evident in *L'écriture ou la vie*, she argues, because the text's very structure is based on "revising" the writing subject's understanding of the events that took place on the day that he arrived in Buchenwald (6).

Both Carroll and Suleiman fail to note in their studies that the theoretical understandings of witnessing to which they refer are articulated by different characters who appear in *L'écriture ou la vie*. A close consideration of how the text's masterful narrator comments on and appropriates these in one scene in the text will serve as the starting point in this chapter for my analysis of the kind of reader-text relation whose limits are exposed in the course of the narrative. A passage that occurs near the work's halfway point is exemplary of how the narrator's theoretical reflections draw from those to which other characters give voice. In it, a group of French-speaking deportees, including the text's protagonist – Jorge – heatedly discuss the nature of their experience in Buchenwald while awaiting clearance to return to Paris in the German town of Eisenach. Jorge pursues an argument in the conversation with which readers are already familiar thanks to the narrator's previous interventions in the text – that "artifice" is needed for their testimonies to become "masterful" works of art which, in turn, will allow their stories to "evoke the imagination of the unimaginable" [susciter l'imagination de l'inimaginable] in the minds of listeners and readers – but it fails to convince any members of the collective until a university professor intervenes in support of it (165, 166). "I imagine there will be a considerable number of testimonies," the professor speculates:

> They will be worth what the acuteness and insight of a witness's look is worth ... And there will also be documents. Later, historians will collect, assemble, analyse both of these: they will make scholarly works out of them ... Everything will be said in them, mentioned ... Everything in them will be true ... except that the essential truth will be missing, a truth that no historical reconstruction will ever be able to attain, no matter how perfect or comprehensive it may be.
>
> [J'imagine qu'il y aura quantité de témoignages. Ils vaudront ce que vaudra le regard du témoin, son acuité, sa perspicacité ... Et puis il y aura des documents ... Plus tard, les historiens recueilleront, rassembleront, analyseront les uns et les autres: ils en feront des ouvrages savants ... Tout y sera dit, consigné ... Tout y sera vrai ... sauf qu'il manquera l'essentielle vérité, à laquelle aucune reconstruction historique ne pourra jamais atteindre, pour parfaite ou omnicompréhensive qu'elle soit.] (167)

The professor gives voice here to the idea cited in Carroll's study that history and experience offer different kinds of truths about events. "Historical truth," he explains, is an understanding that is constructed after an event that relies on "worthy" documents and witnesses, whereby worth is dependent upon the acuteness of a witness's sense of sight, and his or her ability to offer pertinent "insights" thanks to that sense of sight. "Essential truth," or the kind of understanding about the camps that survivors have to offer, he proposes further on in the passage, is only able to be transmitted by, as Jorge had previously argued, "literary writing" and "the artifice of a work of art" (167). "Everyone else looked at him, nodding their heads, apparently reassured to see that one of us is capable of phrasing our problems so clearly," the narrator explains [Les autres le regardent, hochant la tête, apparemment rassurés de voir que l'un d'entre nous arrive à formuler aussi clairement les problèmes (167)]. The professor turns to Jorge and smiles while concluding his remarks, undoubtedly a sign that he approves of the young survivor's ideas.

The professor's intervention serves both to authorize Jorge's understanding of the merits of "artistic" testimony within this collective by providing a more fleshed-out argument for its importance, and to change drastically the dynamic of the discussion. What begins as a "disorderly" [*confus*] conversation in which every survivor wants to make his voice heard – the narrator describes it as one in which "everyone has something of his own to say" [(t)out le monde a son mot à dire] – quickly transforms into a lecture in which the professor's ideas become a point of reference for those of the collective, and in which Jorge is his brightest pupil (165). The professor continues his reflections by suggesting that literary texts and works of cinematic fiction would best transmit the truth of experience because they "transcend" or "go beyond" what is contained in "simple testimonies," and Jorge rejoins, and ends, the conversation by literally filling in the gaps in the professor's way of speaking (169–70). "Maybe," the young survivor replies, interjecting his idea in the middle of one of the thoughtful ellipses that are characteristic of the professor's speech (170). "But what will be at stake will not be the description of horror. Not only, at any rate, nor even principally. What will be at stake will be the exploration of the human soul in the presence of the horror of Evil ... We need a Dostoyevsky!" [Peut-être. Mais l'enjeu ne sera pas la description de l'horreur. Pas seulement, en tout cas, ni même principalement. L'enjeu sera l'exploration de l'âme humaine dans l'horreur du Mal ... Il nous faudra un Dostoïevski!" (170)].[10] The narrator describes those listening to this conversation, or "the survivors who do not yet know what they have survived" [les survivants qui ne savent pas encore à quoi ils ont survécu], as left "utterly perplexed" by the character Jorge's words (170). The French expression that, literally translated, means "to be plunged into an abyss of reflection" [être plongé dans un abîme de réflexion], is employed to describe the overall effect that the conversation between Jorge and the professor has on its listeners (170).

The description of this conversation that takes place in Eisenach offers several important insights into how this collective conceives of the act of bearing witness, and how the narrator's theoretical understanding of "artistic" testimony is influenced by it. First, the passage suggests that the authority to speak about the experience of the camps is recognized and established in a certain way among French-speaking Buchenwald survivors. Those who, like the university professor, are more articulate and knowledgeable speakers – or what Jacques Rancière would call "master explicators" – "reassure" the collective with their ideas and are authorized to continue speaking.[11] The collective then listens in silence and "thinks about" this one speaker's ideas until someone, like Jorge, demonstrates that he is capable of understanding and revising them. This mode of listening entails allowing articulate speakers like the professor to finish their thoughts by not interrupting the ellipses in their reasoning, a process that, as the narrator's commentary describes, plunges less "knowledgeable" deportees into a figurative abyss, reflective as it may be. The description of this practice of collective witnessing maintains not only that the experience of atrocity establishes the authority to speak about it, but that master explicators who experience better understand experience because, like Jorge and the professor, they are better able to speak about it. This particular scene of collective witnessing suggests, in other words, that a deportee must be *authorized* to speak by a master in order for what he or she says about the experience of atrocity to matter for the collective as a whole.[12]

Second, this scene in Eisenach further suggests that the dynamics of this conversation are representative of the kind of relationship that the text's masterful narrator implicitly has with the way "knowledge" [*savoir*] is formed about experience. The narrator's comment at the end of the passage, that "those who do not *yet* know what they have survived" are left utterly perplexed by Jorge and the professor's exchange, indicates his belief in a "temporal" dimension to knowledge about experience. The use of the word "yet" [*pas encore*] implies that, once given enough time, the narrator believes that all of the survivors who are listening to Jorge and the professor will come to this knowledge that the two gifted speakers possess. By extrapolation, the narrator suggests that, because such witnesses can almost immediately incorporate the knowledge to be gleaned from their experiences into words, they need less time to obtain and articulate experiential knowledge. By sharing their knowledge about experience, that is, master explicators can serve as guides for others and save them time, a reason, perhaps, for the feelings of "reassurance" that Jorge and the professor appear to inspire in this particular collectivity.

A passage that occurs later in *L'écriture ou la vie* demonstrates that the ideas about fiction articulated by the professor in Eisenach profoundly influence the theoretical understanding of witnessing advanced by the text's masterful narrator throughout his commentary on the story of Jorge's coming-to-writing. The scene describes the first time after the war that Jorge sees newsreel footage of several concentration camps, including Buchenwald, after liberation. It is an unexpected encounter with his horrifying past: Jorge is sitting in a movie theatre a few months after his return waiting to see the cinematic adaptation of a Eugene O'Neil play, and footage filmed by the Allied forces when they arrived in the camps is randomly screened before it. The text's narrator describes the event as a moment of enlightenment for the character Jorge, one that allows the character to articulate some crucial elements of the theoretical understanding of witnessing that the narrator has been promoting since the beginning of *L'écriture ou la vie*. The narrator claims that, although the documentary images confirm for Jorge "the truth of lived experience" [la vérité de l'expérience vécue], they simultaneously accentuate "the difficulty experienced when trying to transmit it, to render it if not transparent, at least communicable" [la difficulté éprouvée à la transmettre, à la rendre sinon transparente du moins communicable (261)].

The narrator's understanding of Jorge's reaction seems to be a response that is conditioned by the professor's ideas about cinematic fiction that were made in Eisenach. The narrator further comments that, while the documentary images make the "naked horror" of the camps visible for their audience in an "historical" context, they depict it so as to become an "externalized reality of Evil" that fails to elicit an emotional response in him (260). "In fact, even though the images were depicting the naked horror, the physical degeneration, the effects of death, they were silent," he explains:

> Not only because, in accordance with filmmaking techniques of the era, they were filmed without simultaneously recording sound. They were silent mainly because they didn't say anything specific about the reality they showed, because they only offered fragmentary and disorderly messages. One would have had to *work on the body* of the film, on its very cinematic *material*: stopping the sequence of images occasionally to freeze a frame, offering close-ups of certain details, sometimes showing the action in slow motion, speeding it up at other moments. What was really needed was *commentary* on the images, to decipher them, to situate them not only in a historical context but *within a continuity of feelings and emotions*. And, in order to come as close as possible to the truth that was lived, this

> commentary should have been spoken by the survivors themselves, the Lazaruses of that long death. (my emphasis)
>
> [Les images, en effet, tout en montrant l'horreur nue, la déchéance physique, le travail de la mort, étaient muettes. Pas seulement parce que tournées, selon les moyens de l'époque, sans prise de son directe. Muettes surtout parce qu'elles ne disaient rien de précis sur la réalité montrée, parce qu'elles n'en laissaient entendre que des bribes, des messages confus. Il aurait fallu *travailler le film au corps*, dans sa *matière* filmique même, en arrêter parfois le défilement: fixer l'image pour en agrandir certains détails; reprendre la projection au ralenti, dans certains cas, en accélérer le rythme, à d'autres moments. Il aurait surtout fallu *commenter* les images, pour les déchiffrer, les inscrire non seulement dans un contexte historique mais *dans une continuité de sentiments et d'émotions*. Et ce commentaire, pour s'approcher le plus près possible de la vérité vécue, aurait dû être prononcé par les survivants eux-mêmes, les Lazares de cette longue mort.] (261–2; my emphasis)

In order for these images to transmit feelings and emotions about the experience of the camps, the narrator proposes, they need to be reworked in their "very cinematic material" so as to emphasize certain aspects of their "documentary reality," and commentary needs to be provided in order to situate the images within "a continuity of feelings and emotions." The narrator concludes his theoretical intervention by likening this way of "working the body" of these images to "treating documentary reality like a fictitious subject matter" (traiter la réalité documentaire comme une matière de fiction), as if this entire reflection is, once again, an attempt to "fill in the gaps" in the understandings about fiction that the university professor advances in Eisenach (262). In the narrator's use of the term, "fiction," in other words, refers to a way of representing reality that "works the bodies" of its material in order to make that material "cry out" to its audience and situate events within an "emotional" reality, a definition that seems to further demonstrate the way in which the survivor's body is "worked" by the professor's knowledgeable remarks while in Eisenach.

And yet ... The narrator's descriptions of the way the rest of the audience responds when confronted unexpectedly with images of the camps contradicts the theoretical understanding about fiction that he articulates throughout the passage. These same documentary images that don't "cry out" to him as a viewer because of their lack of commentary clearly evoke an emotional response in other audience members. "[I]n the silence of that movie theater," he narrates, "the whispers and murmurs died down [...] a horror and compassion-filled silence rigidly formed: a scandalized silence, too, most likely" [(D)ans le silence de cette salle de cinéma s'éteignaient les chuchotements et les murmures [...] se figeaient un silence d'horreur et de compassion: silence scandalisé, aussi, probablement (260)]. The ideas that the narrator articulates about the role that fiction plays in communicating emotional truths to outsiders are clearly ideas about how he needs reality to be "worked" for it to elicit any sort of emotional response in himself. They are an effect of the conversation described in Eisenach, and, in turn, a product of the narrator's implicit belief in the reassuring, guiding role that intellectuals play in the creation of knowledge about experience.

In light of this, the theoretical understanding of witnessing advanced by the "masterful" narrator of *L'écriture ou la vie* represents more than, as Suleiman contends in her study, the narrator's attempt to gain mastery over trauma by using artifice to revise his understandings of his experiences. It can also be read as an effect of the narrator's desire to perform the role of exemplary student who is capable of mastering the understandings about art to which knowledgeable figures such as the professor give voice. In the process, however, deploying "fictions" becomes a self-reflective practice for the text's narrator, one that, as the episode in the movie theatre demonstrates, allows him to communicate with himself while in the presence of others. The narrator imposes fictions on reality to make it speak to himself, fictions that others don't need for reality to have the same effect on them.

The narrator's initial theoretical intervention in *L'écriture ou la vie*, moreover, suggests that he conceives of his own masterful use of fiction as something that makes him an *exemplary* witness. It occurs in the first chapter of the text, while the character Jorge is still standing in front of the three horrified officers who refuse to look at him the day after Buchenwald's liberation. "I start to doubt the possibility of telling others about it," he declares:

> Not that what we lived through is indescribable. It was unbearable, which is something else entirely (that won't be hard to understand), something that doesn't concern the form of a possible account, but its substance. Not its articulation, but its density. The only ones who will manage to reach this substance, this transparent density, will be those able to shape their testimonies into *an artistic object*, a space of creation. Or of re-creation.

Only the artifice of a *masterly narrative* will prove capable of conveying some of the truth of such testimony. But there's nothing exceptional about this: it's the same with all great historical experiences. (my emphasis)

[(U)n doute me vient sur la possibilité de raconter. Non pas que l'expérience vécue soit indicible. Elle a été invivable, ce qui est tout autre chose, on le comprendra aisément. Autre chose qui ne concerne pas la forme d'un récit possible, mais sa substance. Non pas son articulation mais sa densité. Ne parviendront à cette substance, à cette densité transparente que ceux qui sauront faire de leur témoignage *un objet artistique*, un espace de création. Ou de recréation. Seul l'artifice d'*un récit maîtrisé* parviendra à transmettre partiellement la vérité du témoignage. Mais ceci n'a rien d'exceptionnel: il en arrive ainsi de toutes les grandes expériences historiques.] (25–6; my emphasis)

Masterly narratives that employ artifice, the narrator posits, will be able to "partially" transmit the truth that testimony has to offer about "unlivable" historical experiences such as that of the Nazi camps because they turn those experiences into "artistic objects." His reflections continue by suggesting that, because "language contains everything," everything about the experience of the camps can be put into words, and those who are unable to do so are lazy, bad thinkers, or lacking in courage:

In short, everything can always be said. The ineffable that people talk about so much is only an alibi. Or a sign of laziness. Everything can be said because language contains everything. You can talk about the craziest kind of love, the most terrible cruelty [...]

Everything can be said about this experience. It's a matter of thinking about it. And setting yourself to it. To have the time, no doubt, and the courage, of an unlimited narrative, probably an interminable one, illuminated – closed off, too, of course – by this possibility of pursuing oneself to the infinite. Even if it means repeating and rehashing things. Even if it means never emerging from it, to prolong death, if need be, in order to relive it over and over again in the threads of the narrative, in order to be nothing more than the language of this death, in order to live off of it, fatally.

[On peut toujours tout dire, en somme. L'ineffable dont on nous rebattra les oreilles n'est qu'alibi. Ou signe de paresse. On peut toujours tout dire, le langage contient tout. On peut dire l'amour le plus fou, la plus terrible cruauté [...]

On peut tout dire de cette expérience. Il suffit d'y penser. Et de s'y mettre. D'avoir le temps, sans doute, et le courage, d'un récit illimité, probablement interminable, illuminé – clôturé aussi, bien entendu – par cette possibilité de se poursuivre à l'infini. Quitte à tomber dans la répétition et le ressassement. Quitte à ne pas s'en sortir, à prolonger la mort, le cas échéant, à la faire revivre sans cesse dans les plis du récit, à n'être plus que le langage de cette mort, à vivre à ses dépens, mortellement.] (26)

The narrator's comments on witnessing here echo the understanding of the act of writing as a "transcription of the experience of death" mentioned above, an activity that cuts the survivor off from his surroundings such that he is constantly "asphyxiated" by his traumatic experience in his inhuman efforts to put his experience into words. It is undoubtedly an anguishing and haunting existence in which the survivor chooses to engage; but for whom does he endure the suffering he must go through to turn his experience into an artistic object? Upon whom, exactly, does this artistic mastery have an effect? Who is the audience that the narrator imagines for his masterly narratives? For whom does all of this mastery matter?

2 Fraternity

Renowned French sinologist Henri Maspero was one of the approximately 34,375 deportees who died in Buchenwald.[13] His son, François Maspero, reflects at length in his 2002 autobiography, *Les abeilles et la guêpe*, on the approach he has learned to adopt when listening to and reading survivor narratives in which his father's name appears. Maspero explains that, while he is wary of witnessing texts because of the factual errors they may contain, he appreciates the kinds of insights into camp life that "literary" testimonies like Semprun's can provide. "Jorge Semprun's intention – like Primo Levi's – was not to provide the kind of testimony that wants to have the precision of a factual account," Maspero explains:

Those kinds of testimonies, no matter how sincere they are, or how close they get to the minutest of facts, will never be able to communicate what is, in essence, incommunicable. What matters is not whether or not the witness has a perfect memory. What matters is that the reader, always outside, was not and will never be present in the camp. If, through writing – literary writing – something, even infinitesimal, can be transmitted about

> the camp and the smell of burnt flesh within it – an odour made more pungent every moment by the camp's crematorium – about the commingling of life and death in the camp, that makes up a thousand times for any factual imprecision.[14]

> [(L)e propos de Jorge Semprun – comme celui de Primo Levi – n'a pas été d'apporter un de ces témoignages qui veulent avoir la précision d'un procès-verbal. Ceux-là, si sincères soient-ils, et si minutieusement près des faits, jamais ne communiqueront ce qui, par essence, est incommunicable. La question n'est pas que le témoin ait, ou pas, une « mémoire de bronze ». La question est que le lecteur, toujours extérieur, n'a pas été et ne sera jamais présent au camp. Si, par l'écriture – l'écriture littéraire – quelque chose, même infime, peut passer de la vie du camp et de son odeur de mort – l'odeur à chaque instant prégnante du crématoire – de la vie et de la mort étroitement mêlées au camp, cela compense mille fois telle ou telle imprécision factuelle.] (44)

Maspero insists that, if messages about the "incommunicable" aspects of camp life can be transmitted through "literary" writing, then such testimonies more than make up for their historical flaws, a defence of fiction that is especially poignant considering the factual errors about his father that occur in Semprun's texts. As Maspero understands it, his father may be little more than a "shadow" that serves Semprun's needs as an author, but that author is also a concentration camp survivor whose "fallible" memory can be forgiven in light of the traumatizing events that he endured, and the horrifying images that have haunted him ever since. Such memory gaps – what Maspero, invoking a phrasing used in *L'écriture ou la vie*, calls "snow in the memory" [la neige dans la mémoire] – are a part of Buchenwald, and that is what a reader can find in "literary" testimonies like Semprun's. Maspero credits such an approach to reading *L'écriture ou la vie* for a new understanding of the idea of "fraternity," or of what dignified human beings could still find the "strength" and "courage" to share even in the most brutal of situations, that he finds in the text (20).

Indeed, in the final chapter of *L'écriture ou la vie*, the text's masterful narrator claims that an understanding of "the secrets of fraternity" is one of the important lessons to be learned from the events upon which he has been commenting for hundreds of pages, and a detailed examination of the phenomenon leads to some crucial insights about the reader-text relation whose limits are exposed in the course of the narrative (390). The importance of fraternity is established in the text's opening chapter in a passage that Maspero cites in his own reading of the text. After the narrator's initial theoretical intervention about "artistic" witnessing cited above, his commentary flashes back to describe Jorge's "fraternal" interactions in Buchenwald with his former sociology professor, Maurice Halbwachs, who died in the camp of dysentery less than a month before its liberation.[15] The narrator insists that the character Jorge learns the true meaning of the word "fraternity" from a look he reads in Halbwachs's eyes on the final Sunday of the man's life, and the details of how he arrives at this understanding are important. Over sixty years old when he entered Buchenwald in August of 1944, Halbwachs quickly succumbed to the difficulties of the Nazi order of things, and, along with Maspero's father, was placed in block 56 of the Little Camp with the staggering corpses known throughout the concentration camp system as the *Muselmänner*.[16] According to the descriptions contained in the first chapter of *L'écriture ou la vie*, Semprun visited Halbwachs during his free time every Sunday while the professor was still alive, and their conversations quickly became a one-way affair.[17] Within a few weeks, their discussions about literature, the professor's courses at the Sorbonne, and Allied victories taking place in France turned into Halbwachs listening in silence to the things his former student had to tell him because he no longer had the strength to speak.

The "death" of Maurice Halbwachs is described in several of Semprun's witnessing texts, yet another one of the author's experiences that, to paraphrase Susan Suleiman, is "continuously revised" in his work. In the opening chapter of *L'écriture ou la vie*, the narrator describes Halbwachs as having "reached the limits of human resistance" [parvenu à la limite des résistances humaines] when Jorge arrives in block 56 for his final "conversation" with the professor (37). His description of the visit reads:

> I *had taken* the hand of Halbwachs. He *hadn't had* the strength to open his eyes. I *had felt* a response only from his fingers, a light squeeze: an almost imperceptible sign.
>
> The professor Maurice Halbwachs *had reached* the limits of human resistance. He *was slowly being emptied* of his substance, having reached the final stage in which dysentery *was overtaking him* with its stench.
>
> A bit later, while I *was talking* to him about anything that came into my head so that he could hear a friendly voice, he suddenly *opened* his eyes. Distress and shame at his decaying body *were* readable in them. But also a flame of dignity, of conquered but intact humanity. The immortal glimmer of a

> look that *sees* death's approach, that *knows* exactly where it stands, that *has considered* it from all angles, that *takes* account of, on one hand, the risks, on the other, what is to be gained, freely: with sovereign power. (my emphasis)

> [J'*avais pris* la main de Halbwachs qui *n'avait pas eu* la force d'ouvrir les yeux. J'*avais senti* seulement une réponse de ses doigts, une pression légère: message presque imperceptible.
>
> Le professeur Maurice Halbwachs *était parvenu* à la limite des résistances humaines. Il *se vidait* lentement de sa substance, arrivé au stade ultime de la dysenterie qui l'*emportait* dans la puanteur.
>
> Un peu plus tard, alors que je lui *racontais* n'importe quoi, simplement pour qu'il entende le son d'une voix amie, il *a soudain ouvert* les yeux. La détresse immonde, la honte de son corps en déliquescence y *étaient* lisibles. Mais aussi une flamme de dignité, d'humanité vaincue mais inentamée. La lueur immortelle d'un regard qui *constate* l'approche de la mort, qui *sait* à quoi s'en tenir, qui en *a fait* le tour, qui en *mesure* face à face les risques et les enjeux, librement: souverainement.] (36–7; my emphasis)

The gradual shift from past to present tenses in the narrator's description of Halbwachs's look is striking. Though distress, shame, dignity, and humanity were all readable in the man's eyes, only their "dignified," or "immortal," aspects persist into the present. The narrator's commentary remains in the present tense, and becomes more fragmentary, until the end of the passage:

> So, in a sudden panic, not knowing if I *can* invoke some God to accompany Maurice Halbwachs, conscious that a prayer is needed, however, choked by emotion, I *say* out loud, trying to master my voice, to make it sound like it should, a few lines of Baudelaire. It's the only thing that *comes* into my head.
>
> O death, old captain, it is time, let's weigh anchor …
>
> Maurice Halbwachs' look *becomes* less fuzzy, *seems* to be amazed.
> I *continue* to recite. When I *come* to
>
> … our hearts that you know are filled with beaming rays,
>
> a faint smile *appears* on Maurice Halbwachs' lips.
> He *smiles*, dying, his fraternal look on me. (37–8; my emphasis)

[Alors, dans une panique soudaine, ignorant si je *puis* invoquer quelque Dieu pour accompagner Maurice Halbwachs, conscient de la nécessité d'une prière, pourtant, la gorge serrée, je *dis* à haute voix, essayant de maîtriser celle-ci, de la timbrer comme il faut, quelques vers de Baudelaire. C'est la seule chose qui *me vienne* à l'esprit.

Ô mort, vieux capitaine, il est temps, levons l'ancre ...

Le regard de Halbwachs *devient* moins flou, *semble* s'étonner.
Je *continue* de réciter. Quand j'en *arrive* à

... nos coeurs que tu connais sont remplis de rayons,

un mince frémissement *s'esquisse* sur les lèvres de Maurice Halbwachs.
Il *sourit*, mourant, son regard sur moi, fraternel.] (37–8; my emphasis)

The use of the present tense here draws the reader's attention to the fact that this entire episode with Halbwachs is a memory from the narrator's past, one that he relives, and maybe even revises, when it resurfaces in his mind. The narrator presents his complete understanding of what the look of Maurice Halbwachs teaches him about the experience of "fraternity" in the camps at the end of the chapter:

[T]he look of my people, when it was still there, as fraternal as it was – because it was – sent me to death. This was the substance of our fraternity, key to our destiny, sign of belonging to the community of the living. We were living together this experience of death, this compassion. Our being was defined by this: to be with the other in the death that was approaching. Rather that was nurtured within us, that spread over us like some luminous evil, like some sharply focused light that devoured us. All of us who were going to die had chosen the fraternity of this death out of a taste for freedom.

That is what I learned from the gaze of Maurice Halbwachs, as he lay dying.

[(L)e regard des miens, quand il leur en restait, pour fraternel qu'il fût – parce qu'il l'était, plutôt – me renvoyait à la mort. Celle-ci était substance de notre fraternité, clé de notre destin, signe d'appartenance à la communauté des vivants. Nous vivions ensemble cette expérience de la mort, cette compassion. Notre être était défini par cela: être avec l'autre dans la mort qui s'avançait. Plutôt qui mûrissait en nous, qui nous gagnait comme un mal lumineux, comme une lumière aiguë qui nous dévorerait. Nous tous qui allions mourir avions choisi la fraternité de cette mort par goût de la liberté.

Voilà ce que m'apprenait le regard de Maurice Halbwachs, agonisant.] (39)

"Being with the other while death approaches" and "living the experience of death together" define "fraternal" relations for the narrator of *L'écriture ou la vie*. Members of this "community" of men must deploy signs like those readable in the look of Maurice Halbwachs in order to demonstrate that they share in this understanding about death, and belong among the living. "We were nothing else, nothing more – nothing less either – than that approaching death," the narrator states (31). "The only difference between us being the time that separated us from it, the distance still left to travel" [Nous n'étions rien d'autre, rien de plus – rien de moins, non plus – que cette mort qui s'avançait. Seule différence entre nous, le temps qui nous en séparait, la distance à parcourir encore]. The experience of death is the essence of the experience of fraternity in Buchenwald, the narrator explains, and the kind of compassionate relations in which this community of deportees had the strength to engage are defined by their knowledge of its approach.

Given Jorge Semprun's admitted use of fiction that occurs in later passages of *L'écriture ou la vie*, and, as my analysis in part 1 demonstrated, the narrator's preoccupation throughout the text with "mastering" the material his professors provide him, this account of Jorge mastering his voice in order to recite Baudelaire's "Le voyage" to Maurice Halbwachs should be greeted with scepticism by any reader. As Maspero himself remarks, doesn't the whole scene seem "too beautiful to be true" (25)? Did Jorge Semprun really have the presence of mind while interned in Buchenwald to offer up Baudelaire for his dying professor? Does the narrator of *L'écriture ou la vie* only think to recite the poem after the fact, from his future position, as a way of making up for something Semprun failed to do in the past and is haunted by in the present? And what did Halbwachs really smile at, if he smiled at all? Isn't the lesson that the narrator "learns" from Halbwachs's look just another example of his self-reflective and fictionalizing behaviour? Isn't it just another instance in which he receives a smile of approval from a professor, as he did in Eisenach, one that authorizes his theoretical ideas? And, perhaps most importantly, isn't the way the two men "master" and "work" their bodies – through the gaze, the smile, the voice – absurd given the abject context? Why, in other words, does a compassionate response require so much corporeal discipline?

Though sceptical of its historical accuracy, Maspero reads this passage with Halbwachs, and the lessons about fraternity that the narrator extracts from it, as a testament to "what can never be taken away from man," one that affirms that the experience of the literary is something "in which all human beings can share" [en quoi tout être humain peut communier], given that they have enough "courage" and "strength" (22, 23). "In Jorge Semprun's use of the term, fraternity [...] comes from sharing the only two things that could still be generously shared, provided that (and what a stipulation!) someone had the courage, the will, the strength," Maspero proposes:

> One of them is this immaterial good, conserved, affirmed, constituted by ideas, interrogations, research, creation, the aspiration to *something else*, things that used to be and still are, I still believe in spite of anything people may say, what gives sense to the human condition. Writing or life, Baudelaire or a bowl of soup? The bowl of soup will never abolish Baudelaire.
>
> The other is the anguish of imminent death – which is something that supposedly cannot be shared. (emphasis in original)
>
> [La fraternité dont parle Jorge Semprun [...] relève du partage des deux seuls biens qui pouvaient être encore partagés sans parcimonie, à condition (et quelle condition !) d'en avoir eu le courage, la volonté, la force.
>
> L'un est ce bien immatériel, conservé, affirmé, constitué par les idées, les interrogations, les recherches, la création, l'aspiration à *autre chose*, qui étaient et qui sont, je l'espère encore envers et contre tout, ce qui donne sens à la condition humaine. L'écriture ou la vie, Baudelaire ou un bol de soupe ? Le bol de soupe, jamais, n'abolira Baudelaire.
>
> L'autre est l'angoisse de la mort imminente – ce qui, justement, est réputé ne pouvoir être partagé.] (20; emphasis in original)

For Maspero as a reader, the way that literature is deployed as a symbol of "fraternity" in the scene with Maurice Halbwachs offers confirmation of his previously held beliefs in what gives sense to the "human condition." But his reading fails to recognize that when the death of Maurice Halbwachs is revisited in later passages of *L'écriture ou la vie*, the narrator reveals new, and sometimes contradictory, information about the event. And each of these revisions undoes the understanding of the relationship between literature and fraternity that is articulated at the end of the text's first chapter.

An analysis of the first instance in which this occurs in the narrative will bring us back to our discussion of the reader-text relation whose limits are exposed in the work. This initial revision of the death of Maurice Halbwachs takes place in the second chapter, titled "Le Kaddish," when Jorge finds himself in a situation similar to the one he has previously experienced with his professor. He and a comrade discover a dying Jewish man still alive among a pile of corpses after Buchenwald's liberation, and Jorge takes the agonized man in his arms and speaks to him softly while his comrade goes for help. The man is reciting to himself the Kaddish, the Jewish prayer for the dead, and the narrator immediately flashes back to the opening scene with Halbwachs as he compares the physical state of the two men.

> He no longer had the strength to speak, Halbwachs. He had crossed further into death than this unfamiliar Jewish man I was now hunched over. The latter still had the strength, unimaginable really, to recite to himself the prayer for the dead, to accompany his own death with words meant to celebrate death. To make it immortal, in any case. Halbwachs no longer had the strength. Or the weakness, who knows? It was no longer a possibility for him, in any case. Or a desire, including the desire to die. It's only from life, from the knowledge of life, that one can desire to die. This deadly desire is a reflex of life.
>
> But, quite visibly, Maurice Halbwachs could no longer desire anything, not even death. He was beyond, no doubt, in the pestilential eternity of his decomposing body.
>
> [Il n'avait plus la force de parler, Halbwachs. Il s'était avancé dans la mort encore plus loin que ce Juif inconnu sur lequel je me penchais maintenant. Celui-ci avait encore la force, inimaginable par ailleurs, de se réciter la prière des agonisants, d'accompagner sa propre mort avec des mots pour célébrer la mort. Pour la rendre immortelle, du moins. Halbwachs n'en avait plus la force. Ou la faiblesse, qui sait? Il n'en avait plus la possibilité, en tout cas. Ou le désir, y compris celui de mourir. Ce n'est qu'à partir de la vie, du savoir de la vie, que l'on peut avoir le désir de mourir. C'est encore un réflexe de vie que ce désir mortifère.
>
> Mais Maurice Halbwachs n'avait visiblement plus aucun désir, même pas celui de mourir. Il était au-delà, sans doute, dans l'éternité pestilentielle de son corps en décomposition.] (60–1)

Though the narrator had previously insisted that the look in Halbwachs's eyes demonstrated that he was conscious of his fate, a "sign" that he belonged to the community of the living, in this episode with the dying Jew, he revises his previous statement, and stresses that it was no longer "possible" for Halbwachs to "desire death" because he was so close to it. It is only from the knowledge of life, the narrator implies, that one can desire death, and Halbwachs no longer had the strength to desire anything. His narration continues by mentioning Jorge's reaction to the smell of Halbwachs's decomposing body.

> I took him in my arms, brought my face near his; I was overwhelmed by the fetid fecal odour of death that was growing in him like a carnivorous plant, a venomous flower, dazzling filth. I told myself, with deliberate derision, to help myself traverse this unlivable moment, to at least live through it without giving in to it, in line with a rigorous kind of compassion that isn't pathetic; I told myself that I had at least learned that in Buchenwald: how to identify death's many smells. The smell of smoke from the crematorium, the smells from the block where the invalids were housed and from the barracks of the *Revier*. The smell of leather and cologne on the *Sturmführer* S.S. I told myself that this was significant knowledge, but was it practical knowledge? How can one say anything to the contrary? (emphasis in original)

> [Je l'ai pris dans mes bras, j'ai approché mon visage du sien, j'ai été submergé par l'odeur fétide, fécale, de la mort qui poussait en lui comme une plante carnivore, fleur vénéneuse, éblouissante pourriture. Je me suis dit, dans un moment de dérision délibérée, pour m'aider à traverser cet instant invivable, à le vivre sans complaisance du moins, dans la rigueur d'une compassion non pathétique, je me suis dit que j'aurais au moins appris cela, à Buchenwald, à identifier les odeurs multiples de la mort. L'odeur de la fumée du crématoire, les odeurs du block des invalides et des baraques du *Revier*. L'odeur de cuir et d'eau de Cologne des *Sturmführer* S.S. Je me suis dit que c'était un savoir pertinent, mais était-ce un savoir pratique? Comment jurer du contraire?] (61; emphasis in original)

Jorge retreats into irony in order to get himself through this "unlivable" moment with the fetid Halbwachs while still showing the professor a kind of "rigorous" compassion. Here, it is a recitation in his head of the things he "knows" about the overwhelming smells of Buchenwald that takes place, and the beauty of Baudelaire is nowhere to be found. In this passage, recitation is clearly an act that allows Jorge to distance himself from the events of his present so he can remain in another person's presence in appearance only, and not an act that allows him to share in another's experience of imminent death. Recitation, that is, is a practice that allows the man both to distance himself from the horrifying events of his present, and to "be with the other" as a "compassionate" physical presence once those around him are in a physical state to which he does not know how to respond. The narrator then reveals that Maurice Halbwachs did not die in Jorge Semprun's arms, but, in fact, two full days later: "That Sunday, the final Sunday, I was forced to leave him," he reveals, "to abandon him to the solitude of his death [...] He had held out two days longer, forty-eight more eternal hours" [Ce dimanche-là, le dernier dimanche, j'avais été contraint de le quitter, de l'abandonner à la solitude de sa mort [...] Il avait donc tenu deux jours encore, quarante-huit heures d'éternité de plus (62)]. Did Halbwachs open his eyes again before he died? Was he "conscious" of his fate until the end? What kind of suffering was his during those last eternal days?

In spite of this admission, however, the narrator of *L'écriture ou la vie* still insists at the end of his flashback that he "had lived the death of Maurice Halbwachs" on the final Sunday of the man's life, and his justification for this statement offers important insights into the reasons why his commentary continuously aims to cover up the limits of his understandings that are exposed in the narrative (63). The narrator's explanation for this idea about "living the death of the other" occurs much later in the text when reflecting on Wittgenstein's famous proposition "Mein Tod ist kein Ereignis meines Lebens. Meinen Tod erlebe ich nicht," and the mistakes that he made at different points in his life when translating it from German to French (226).[18] The narrator comments on two different translations Jorge has given of the second part of the statement – "one cannot live death" [on ne peut vivre la mort], and "death is not a lived experience" [la mort n'est pas une expérience vécue] – before offering his current, and correct, understanding of Wittgenstein in French (225).

> Of course [...] death cannot be a lived experience – *vivencia* in Spanish – we have known this since Epicurus. Nor can it be an experience of pure consciousness, of the *cogito*. It will always be a mediated experience, conceptual; the experience of a social fact or practice. But this is a patently obvious insight that belies extreme spiritual poverty. In fact, to be rigorous, Wittgenstein's statement should be read as such [...] *my* death is not an event of *my* life. I will not live *my* death. (emphasis in original)
>
> [Sans doute [...] la mort ne peut-elle être une expérience vécue – *vivencia*, en espagnol – on le sait au moins depuis Épicure. Ni non plus une expérience de la conscience pure, du *cogito*. Elle sera toujours expérience médiatisée, conceptuelle; expérience d'un fait social, pratique. Mais c'est là une

> évidence d'une extrême pauvreté spirituelle. En fait, pour être rigoureux, l'énoncé de Wittgenstein devrait s'écrire ainsi [...] *ma* mort n'est pas un événement de *ma* vie. Je ne vivrai pas *ma* mort.] (225–6; emphasis in original)

The narrator distinguishes here between the experience of death as a social construct, and the experience that any one person has of his or her own death, and he appropriates his ideas from a philosophical authority in order to advance them. "Death" will always be an experience that is mediated by social facts and practices, he explains, whereas, as his corrected translation of Wittgenstein demonstrates, one's own death ("ma mort") cannot be a "lived event." The suggestion is that to "live" an event is to experience it through mediation, and once one is no longer capable of this, one is socially "dead."

For the narrator to say, then, that he "lived" the death of Maurice Halbwachs, is to say that he experienced the moment at which his socially based knowledge about death could still make sense of, or "share in" what Halbwachs was going through. However, after this moment, the human body becomes nothing but decomposing organic matter for Jorge's knowledgeable gaze. The social dies when Jorge's knowledge of human experience fails, and Halbwachs lives on in a state that others ignore. In light of this revelation, Jorge may, as Maspero proposes in his reading, share in Halbwachs's experience of "the anguish of imminent death" as a social fact in the description provided in the opening chapter of *L'écriture ou la vie*. But the young Resistance fighter further recognizes the limits of this shared understanding, and experiences both the anguish of knowing that Halbwachs is living on in a state that nothing has prepared either of them for, and the anguish of knowing that he himself no longer knows how to respond to his professor's agony. Jorge responds to this dilemma by withdrawing into himself and turning away from his dying professor. Baudelaire marks this moment after which he no longer knows how to respond to Halbwachs's suffering; in *L'écriture ou la vie*, literature is located at the cusp of the recognizable and the unknown, the point at which it abandons everyone to the agony of solitude.

In addition to the contradictory vision of the death of Maurice Halbwachs that it offers, this episode with the dying Jewish man also points to a particular way that the narrator of *L'écriture ou la vie* and the character Jorge make use of fiction when they traverse anguishing experiences. After his revelatory flashback to the "death" of Maurice Halbwachs, the narrator returns to his experience with the dying Jew and responds to the situation by telling the suffering man about a fictionalized version of a past event in his life. "I don't want to live the death of this anonymous, perhaps Hungarian, Jew," the narrator explains:

> I take him into my arms, I speak softly into his ear. I tell him the story of the young German soldier who was singing *La Paloma*, and who Julien and I gunned down. But I don't speak to him about Julien, I speak to him about Hans. On the spot I begin to invent Hans Freiberg, my imaginary Jewish friend, my combatant Jew, to keep this anguished man company, this anonymous Jew that I want to see survive his own death. I tell him the story of Hans, a story that I have just invented, in short, to help him live.[19] (emphasis in original)

> [(J)e ne veux pas vivre la mort de ce Juif anonyme, peut-être hongrois. Je le tiens dans mes bras, je lui parle doucement à l'oreille. Je lui raconte l'histoire du jeune soldat allemand qui chantait *La Paloma* et que nous avons abattu, Julien et moi. Mais je ne lui parle pas de Julien, je lui parle de Hans. Je commence à inventer à l'instant même Hans Freiberg, mon copain juif imaginaire, mon Juif combattant, pour tenir compagnie à cet agonisant, à ce Juif anonyme que je voudrais voir survivre à sa propre mort. Je lui raconte l'histoire de Hans, que je viens d'inventer, pour l'aider à vivre, en somme.] (66; emphasis in original)

Again, the use of the present tense alerts readers to this passage's status as a resurfacing memory for the text's narrator. Questions of historical accuracy aside, the way that fiction is deployed here clearly reveals its self-reflective nature for both the narrator and the character Jorge. In this instance, it is used as a weapon to combat the anguish of not knowing (or having known?) how to act when faced with the death of an anonymous man, and its absurdity as a practice that can "help" another person "live" cannot be overlooked. In this instance, fiction clearly serves to distance the survivor from the experience of death, not to share in it, and its recitation is a matter of his own survival, something that helps him remain in the physical presence of others whose distance from death is far less than his own. His compassion depends on distance, and not on being there.

This particular practice of recitation carries over into the accounts of Jorge's post-camp life contained in *L'écriture ou la vie*, as well. The narrator's descriptions of Jorge's reactions during the ceremony at which he is awarded the Prix Formentor for *Le grand voyage* are particularly striking in this regard. The "historic moment" that changes the course of the survivor's life turns into another instance in which he must distance himself from the experience of his surroundings in order to get through it while maintaining an air of dignity. Heads of the most prominent publishing houses in the world have come to meet Jorge, and to present him with translations of his first text that will be in world-wide circulation, but he is completely incapable of focusing on the event taking place before him. The narrator's commentary reads:

> I should be moved, it's an historic moment. I should say: for me, in my personal history, it's a privileged moment. But I'm distracted, I'm thinking of a whole list of other things, many faces resurface in my memory, things clang around a bit, I can't manage to concentrate on this historic moment […]
>
> I can't even manage to concentrate on this historic moment. I sense that I'm going to miss it, that it's going to pass me by, disappear, before I can become aware of it. Before I can digest its substantive and succulent juices. I must not be gifted for historic instants.
>
> So that my head wouldn't spin, and to keep myself from being carried away by the flattering words, the applause, the radiant smiles of my friends who were in the room, I quietly recite to myself the editorial comments that Jean Paulhan drew up for the manuscript of my novel.[20]
>
> [Je devrais être ému, c'est un instant historique. Je veux dire: pour moi, dans mon histoire à moi, c'est un instant privilégié. Mais je suis distrait, je pense à des tas d'autres choses, de multiples visages surgissent dans ma mémoire, ça se bouscule un peu, je n'arrive pas à me concentrer sur ce moment historique […]
>
> Je n'arrive quand même pas à me concentrer sur cet instant historique. Je sens que je vais le rater, qu'il va passer, s'évanouir, avant que je n'en aie pris conscience. Que je n'en aie dégusté les sucs substantifiques et succulents. Je ne dois pas être doué pour les instants historiques.
>
> À tout hasard, pour que la tête ne me tourne pas, pour ne pas me laisser griser par les paroles flatteuses, les applaudissements, les sourires radieux des amis qui se trouvent dans la salle, je me récite à voix basse le texte de la note de lecture que Jean Paulhan a rédigée pour le manuscrit de mon roman.] (334–5)

Recitation in this instance is an activity that distances Jorge from the destabilizing effects of his resurfacing memories, and from the anxiety of the events of his "historic" present, the result being that he is incapable of registering any of the important aspects of or of being moved by this important moment of his writerly life. The narrator's description of his failure to take in these events as his inability to "déguster les sucs substantifiques et succulents" echoes the organic imagery evoked in his description of the death of Maurice Halbwachs in the text's second chapter. A cloistered "revenant" who is unable to "digest the substantive and succulent juices" of the present, Jorge repeats here the behaviour that had previously helped him survive the horrifying experience of Buchenwald. This recitation, in other words, exposes the survivor as a man incapable of paying attention to the things happening before his eyes in moments of historical importance, an exposition that appears to call into question what his narratives have to offer about the experience of any event of historical importance, including that of the Nazi camps.

L'écriture ou la vie clearly paints the portrait of a distanced and distracted survivor-witness, one who uses recitation, literary or otherwise, as a way of maintaining his composure so he can continue to be with others in appearance only. Of course, given the utter horror of the events that he experienced, one can hardly blame the man for engaging in practices that distance him from the present so as to ensure his survival, and to appear compassionate to those in his presence. But, to return to Maspero's evaluation of Semprun's "literary" witnessing texts, this also suggests that the inaccuracies that occur in *L'écriture ou la vie* are representative of something other than the "fallibility" of a narrator-witness whose traumatic experiences are responsible for the "snowiness" of his memories. This fuzziness, and the resultant "gaps" in the text that the narrator tries to theoretically comment away or cover up with literature, are, one might say, a testament to the anxiety that overcomes him when faced with experiences for which all of his knowledge leaves him unprepared. Literary recitation marks this anguishing limit at which the survivor must look away and distance himself from his present as a matter of survival, and in order to be compassionate without being, in his words, "pathetic." If, then, there is, as Maspero argues, a message pertaining to the "incommunicable" aspects of camp life to be retained from "literary" testimonies such as Semprun's, it is a message about what happens to deportees when the knowledge they possess can no longer account for what goes on in front of their eyes. Far from a "bien immatériel" that gives sense to the human condition, literature, in this particular context, is a safety zone into which survivors can retreat when they are confronted with historical events that make them feel, understandably, overwhelmed. In *L'écriture ou la vie*, the beauty of Baudelaire, and of literature, is nothing but a cover for the unknown matter that those who recite it can no longer stand to perceive.

So what does this mean for readers of witnessing texts like *L'écriture ou la vie*? What, that is, can readers hope to learn from "literary" testimonies such as those written by Jorge Semprun? My analysis until this point suggests that it is a message about how literature and theory serve as covers for the blind-spots of knowledge more than anything else. But it is also, and perhaps more important, a message about how a reader's desire for "literary" knowledge can make him or her blind to what a testimonial narrative does in its textual material. Such is the case of François Maspero, whose wariness of the historical reliability of the genre does nothing to combat his desire to learn the exact lessons that a literary witness claims to be transmitting through his masterful works of art. The narrator authoritatively announces that the "secrets of fraternity" are to be found in the text, and obedient student-readers of literature set out to try to master his ideas about them, perhaps in the hopes of filling in their gaps with revisions of their own.

In another digression that occurs during the awards ceremony for the Prix Formentor, the narrator himself imagines a similar pedagogical function for his metacommentary vis-à-vis his implied reader. He takes his understandings to serve, like those of the professor in Eisenach, as a lecture for a reader who hangs on his every reassuring word. In it, the narrator explains his reasons for not sharing more information with his reader about a train ride he made with Dolores Ibárruri in 1956, and about the Kafka text that accompanied him on his voyage.[21]

> If I weren't in Salzburg, on the first of May 1964, at the end of the celebratory dinner for the Prix Formentor; if I wasn't seeing in this moment, after Ledig Rowohlt and Claude Gallimard, Giulio Einaudi coming towards me in order to give me a copy of the Italian edition of *The Long Voyage*, I would undoubtedly take advantage of the chance offered to me for a digression on the trip from Prague to Bucarest. But I will not offer this digression, brilliant through it would have been, just like I didn't offer one on Kafka just a little bit ago.
>
> You sometimes have to know how to hold yourself back, to keep your reader craving more.

> [Si je n'étais pas à Salzbourg, le 1er mai 1964, à la fin du dîner de gala du prix Formentor; si je ne voyais pas en ce moment, après Ledig Rowohlt

> et Claude Gallimard, Giulio Einaudi venir vers moi pour me remettre un exemplaire de l'édition italienne du *Grand voyage*, sans doute profiterais-je de l'occasion qui m'est offerte d'une digression à propos du voyage de Prague à Bucarest. Mais je ne ferai pas cette digression, pour brillante qu'elle eût pu être, pas plus que je n'ai fait un excursus à propos de Kafka, il n'y a guère.
>
> Il faut savoir se retenir, parfois, laisser le lecteur sur sa faim.] (338)

A once-brilliant student whose experience of trauma and mastery of artistic knowledge have turned him into an exemplary witness, the narrator conceives of himself as a purveyor of the informative understandings that his obedient audience craves. Withholding this information becomes a way of stringing these eager readers along in his narratives, and of subjecting such followers to the blindness of his literary ways.

What kinds of readers exhibit this insatiable desire for the information that witnesses such as the masterful narrator of *L'écriture ou la vie* have to offer? One need, in fact, look no further than the text's opening scene. The three officers in British uniforms who listen intently, and unguardedly, in order to hear whatever messages Jorge may be trying to transmit to them, are the textual representation *par excellence* of the kinds of readers who allow authoritative narrators to guide them through their reading of a text. Such readers and listeners become incapable of contemplating horror through their own eyes, and entangled in the self-reflective blindness of their exemplary heroes. Testimonies from any disaster do not need to be masterfully "worked" by survivors to make us feel something when they speak of the horrors that haunt their lives. A testimony like *L'écriture ou la vie* points us towards the dangers that any reader faces when approaching a literary testimony for information about unfamiliar events that have traumatic effects. We must be wary when engaging the works of masterful authorities like Jorge Semprun, no matter how much we want to be reassured.

2 Speaking for Others

> It is no doubt at times necessary to speak in the name of the drowned. Speak in their name, in their silence, to give their words back to them.
>
> – Jorge Semprun

> [Sans doute faut-il parfois parler au nom des naufragés. Parler en leur nom, dans leur silence, pour leur rendre la parole.]

Speaking for others is both a necessary and a problematic practice in witness literature. Auschwitz survivor Primo Levi suggests that this paradoxical aspect of the genre arises from the position of privilege that all survivors occupy in relation to the experiences they describe. People who live through historically traumatic events are the only ones who can speak to the experience of them, but because they are among the few who survived, they are "exceptions" who can only speak "by proxy" for the many who died (*Drowned* 83). "We who were favored by fate tried, with more or less wisdom, to recount not only our fate but also that of others," Levi explains in his collection of essays *The Drowned and the Saved*. "[B]ut this was a discourse 'on behalf of third parties,' the story of things seen at close hand, not experienced personally." When speaking for those who cannot speak for themselves, survivors can only tell stories from their perspectives as privileged outsiders who lack lived knowledge of the experiences they saw take place. These narratives cannot bear witness to the experience of death in the camps, but without them, the circumstances surrounding those deaths would never be known to the outside world.

The practice of speaking for others has taken on ethically and historically problematic dimensions in some of the most influential testimonies produced by France's political deportee community. Buchenwald survivor and Trotskyist militant David Rousset's reflections on the nature of the Nazi camps are a particularly striking example. The first concentration camp survivor to describe in detail the logic of the Nazi order of things and its mechanisms of repression for French audiences after liberation, Rousset problematically states in his seminal work *L'univers concentrationnaire* (1946) that the differences between the *extermination* camps in which Jews were massacred during the Second World War – what he calls "camps of destruction"– and the *concentration* camps in which political deportees were imprisoned – or "normal camps" – should be seen only as differences in "degree" and not in "nature." "Between these camps of destruction and the 'normal' camps, there is not a difference in nature, but only of degree," Rousset explains:

> Buchenwald had its hell: Dora, the underground V2 factory; weeks without returning to the surface, sleeping eleven people on two straw mattresses, eating and sleeping underground next to the latrines; every evening, hangings, and the obligation to be present at each slow and precise hanging; very often, roll call on Sundays; and the "Muslims," the weak, separated from the others, sent on transports to be killed in the camps in the East. In Neuengamme, people were hanged in the courtyard and the detainees gathered there were forced to sing as one throughout the entire ceremony. In Helmstedt, people were hanged in the dormitories.[1]

> [Entre ces camps de destruction et les camps "normaux," il n'y a pas de différence de nature, mais seulement de degré. Buchenwald avait son enfer: Dora, la fabrique souterraine des V2; des semaines sans remonter à la surface, coucher onze sur deux paillasses, manger et dormir dans le souterrain à côté des latrines; tous les soirs, des pendus, et l'obligation d'assister à la pendaison lente et raffinée; très souvent, le dimanche, l'appel; et les "musulmans," les faibles, mis à part, envoyés en transport de destruction pour les camps de l'Est. À Neuengamme, on pendait dans la cour et, tout un temps, les détenus rassemblés devaient chanter pendant toute la cérémonie. À Helmstedt, on pendait dans notre dortoir.] (57)

All deportees, no matter the camp, experienced a torturous kind of hell, Rousset states, and he implies that all deportees resemble each other and share the same essential experiences as a collective.[2] While deportees in both concentration camps and extermination camps all experienced horrifying forms of suffering, such elisions of the differences between camps as well as between the experiences of Jews and political deportees led to an all-encompassing line of thinking about the Second World War in France in the immediate postwar era in part because of the nation's universalizing Republican tradition.[3] As Annette Wieviorka has observed, this tradition was incapable of recognizing a distinctly Jewish history within its borders – in the French Republican tradition, all individual citizens, including Jews, are divested of their particularistic affiliations such as ethnicity or religion, and aspire instead to a universal and abstract idea of the human to which everyone can supposedly belong.[4] This universalizing logic resulted, however, in a broader cultural tendency throughout the postwar era to speak of the genocide of European Jews as but one aspect among others of the French concentration camp experience, and to deny the different kinds of ordeals that Jews and political deportees endured in the Nazi system.[5]

In this chapter, I want to consider a less-examined consequence that such universalizing logics have had for World War Two memory. I examine here the harmful effects that these all-encompassing conceptualizations of the camp experience have exerted within the political deportee community itself. For this, I turn to an analysis of the kind of "speaking for" that occurs in the works of Jorge Semprun. In a manner similar to Rousset, Semprun claims throughout his works that one of his roles as an "intellectual" witness is to speak for other survivors by producing narratives that bear witness to *all* survivors' shared experience of the Nazi camps. Yet all of his Buchenwald memoirs, I argue, portray Semprun as a witness who routinely silences his fellow survivors in order to speak for them as a collective. I will examine here this problematic relationship between intellectual survivors and the community of political deportees for whom they claim to speak, and the ethical dilemmas that such a dynamic lays bare. The testimonial narratives produced by such intellectuals *can* speak for others, I propose, but only because they point readers towards those experiences that are necessarily denied by the approach such survivors take to witness writing.

1 The Intellectual

Jorge Semprun was expelled from the Spanish Communist Party in 1964 for his criticism of the abuses of power committed by the international communist movement during and after its Stalinist era.[6] His writings routinely denounce the kinds of authoritarian practices that took place while he was a member of the Party's leadership. In his most inflammatory work on the subject, *Autobiografía de Federico Sánchez*, Semprun explains that his disillusionment with the Party stemmed from the way it refused to remember its suppression of critical thinking, and its elimination of dissenting members from its ranks through banishment and/ or murder. Semprun contends in the text that

> Communist memory in reality is a way of not remembering: it does not consist of recalling the past but of censoring it. The memory of Communist leaders functions pragmatically, in accordance with the political interests and objectives of the moment. It is not a historical memory, a memory that bears witness, but an ideological memory. (*Autobiography* 182)

> [La memoria comunista es, en realidad, una desmemoria, no consiste en recordar el pasado, sino en censurarlo. La memoria de los dirigentes comunistas funciona pragmáticamente, de acuerdo con los intereses y los objetivos políticos del momento. No es una memoria histórica, testimonial, es una memoria ideológica.] (241)

Written and published during Spain's transition to democracy, *Autobiografía de Federico Sánchez* tells the story of Semprun's expulsion from the Party in order to revive the oppressive past that it was trying to hide from the Spanish public after Franco's death. As the narrator proclaims in the text: "I am not going to do like the rest, like almost all of the rest of the leaders formed in the era of Stalin. I am not going to shut away my memory under lock and key" [No voy a hacer lo mismo que los demás, que casi todos los demás dirigentes formados en la época de Stalin. No voy a cerrar a cal y canto mi memoria (129)].[7]

Nearly every critic who has written on Semprun has noted that his "characteristic signature" as a writer is the endless revisitation and reinterpretation of the past that occurs in his texts. In her work on Semprun's *Autobiografía de Federico Sánchez*, Ofelia Ferrán has argued that the narrative techniques it employs are meant to reinforce the author's critique of the Communist Party's repression of memory ("Memory" 198).[8] Semprun's criticism of the suffering for which he was responsible as an "intelectual estalinizado," she suggests, represents the kind of self-critical confrontation with the past in which the Party refused to engage while he was a member of its leadership and during Spain's transition to democracy (205).[9] Most important, Ferrán proposes that the structure of the narrative – which, in Semprun's typical fashion, jumps forward and backward in time to evoke memories of the past while commenting on them from the present of writing – differs drastically from the kind of authoritarian discourse denounced in the author's textual commentary. "Throughout this kaleidoscopic recuperation of memory," Ferrán explains,

> the work is overtly self-reflexive, highlighting at every turn the process of its own writing. This de-naturalizing, relativizing self-reflexivity will ultimately stand in sharp contrast with the discourse of the Communist Party that Semprun had critiqued in 1964 and continues to critique in 1977, an intransigent, mythifying discourse completely closed to any form of questioning, much less dissent. (199)

Ferrán argues that, unlike the leaders of the communist movement, Semprun questions "any and all reconstructions of the past" in *Autobiografía de Federico Sánchez* by reviving his memories and drawing attention to how he constructs his own text. In the process, she proposes, Semprun exposes all reconstructions of the past as "based on textual interpretations, therefore never fully complete and always open to reinterpretation and dissent" (217).

Published three years after *Autobiografía de Federico Sánchez*, Semprun's 1980 Buchenwald memoir *Quel beau dimanche!* advances an understanding of the intellectual that also arises from a critique of authoritarian practices. Yet several important passages in the text portray Semprun as an intellectual witness whose criticisms of authoritarianism blind him to the harmful effects of his own self-reflexive ways. I suggested in the previous chapter that Semprun's well-known use of fiction throughout his works be considered, in fact, a self-reflective practice, one in which the first-person narrators and protagonists of his testimonies engage to distance themselves from the horrors of the camps, to model their own identity as "exemplary" witnesses, and to shape the events that unfold in the camps so they can find themselves in them. His conceptualization of the intellectual witness is also self-reflective in nature, and leads, in practice, to such witnesses seeking to shape the narratives of other survivors in order to better resemble their own. Semprun certainly recuperates and reinterprets the past in his metacommentaries throughout *Quel beau dimanche!* But, in his interactions with other survivors, he refuses to give them the space they need to engage in a process similar to his own. Semprun's writing is *self-reflective* and not *self-reflexive* in these moments, I ultimately propose, because it seeks to impose and naturalize the witness's own ideas about the Nazi camp experience rather than denaturalize his theoretical conceptualizations, engage in a self-critical confrontation with them, or create space for forms of testimony that diverge from his own. A close examination of the phenomenon will serve as the starting point for this analysis of how intellectual witnesses speak for other survivors through the writer's Buchenwald narratives.

Quel beau dimanche! is the most overtly political of all of Semprun's works about the Nazi camps, and contains the author's most elaborate reflections on the intellectual witness. The first-person narrative is structured around one Sunday afternoon in Buchenwald, and flashes forward and backward in time to comment on Semprun's tenure as a clandestine operative in Franco's Spain, the internal power struggles of the international communist movement, and the author's banishment from the Party in the sixties. The criticisms of authoritarianism that Semprun voices in *Quel beau dimanche!* stem largely from the treatment he received from Party members because of his privileged social background. The son of a Second Republic diplomat and grandson of five-time Spanish Prime Minister Antonio Maura, Semprun was exiled to France with the rest of his family at the outbreak of the Civil War. He was a philosophy student in Paris before joining the French Resistance, and spoke fluent Spanish, French, and German when he arrived in Buchenwald. It was his knowledge of German that caused him to come under the protection of Buchenwald's clandestine communist movement soon after his arrival in the camp. He was placed in the camp's deportee-run administration – the *Arbeitsstastik* – in which the Party's German-speaking operatives manipulated Gestapo documents to protect certain internees from hard physical labour or deportation to camps with harsher living conditions.[10]

While Semprun's elite education rendered him useful to Buchenwald's communist organization, his background also drew the suspicion of many people in the movement. Several passages in *Quel beau dimanche!* indicate that Party members symbolically exclude Semprun from their ranks both in Buchenwald and after because of his social background. Semprun's first interaction in the text with the German internee in charge of the *Arbeitsstatistik*, Willy Seifert, is exemplary in this regard. The passage describes the day of Semprun's arrival in the *Arbeitsstatistik*, and Seifert remarks upon meeting him that it is the first time that the movement has sent a philosophy student to work in the bureau. "Usually," Seifert explains, "the pals sent to me are proles" (45)

[D'habitude, les copains qu'on m'envoie sont des prolos (47)].[11] Semprun interprets Seifert's use of the words *copain* (German *Kumpel*) and *prolo* (German *Prolet*) – words that he had always used interchangeably before his deportation to Buchenwald – as an attempt to deny him access to the "communist universe." His lengthy commentary reads:

> But that day, Seifert had quietly thrown me back into my singularity – that is, into the suspect universality of my class background. I might at most be a pal, *ein Kumpel*, but I would never be a prole, *ein Prolet*. Never, that much was certain. Thus those passwords that had seemed to me to open up the doors of a fraternal world, in which each individual would be judged by what he did and treated according to his needs suddenly turned against me. I was sent back by those words into the sulfurous hell of ontology. Here, I was no longer to be judged by my actions, but classified according to my being, and, what was more, that part of my being that was most external to me, that most inert, adhesive part of me for which I could never assume responsibility: my social being. (47)

> [Seifert, ce jour-là, d'une voix calme, me rejetait dans ma singularité, c'est-à-dire dans la suspecte universalité de mes origines de classe. À la rigueur, je pouvais être un copain, ein *Kumpel*, mais je ne serais jamais un prolo, ein *Prolet*. Jamais, c'est certain. Ainsi, ces mots de passe qui m'avaient semblé ouvrir les portes d'un univers fraternel, où chacun serait jugé d'après sa pratique, et traité selon ses besoins, ces mots se retournaient tout à coup contre moi. J'étais renvoyé par ces mots dans l'enfer sulfureux de l'ontologie. Voici que je n'étais plus jugé selon mes actes, mais bien classé en fonction de mon être, et encore, mon être le plus extérieur à moi-même, la part de moi la plus inerte et visqueuse, dont je ne pourrais jamais assumer la responsabilité: mon être social.] (48)

Semprun explains here that Seifert's comments "classify" him according to the "suspicious universality" of his privileged "social being," and, as such, judge him for an aspect of his life that he cannot personally control. This conflicts with Semprun's "fraternal" understanding of communist doctrine, which entails judging others only for the actions that they perform, and never for their class origins.

For different reasons, Semprun maintains in *Quel beau dimanche!* that his background also causes his exclusion from the community of Republicans with whom he works as a clandestine operative in Francoist Spain in the fifties and sixties. Only twelve years old at the outbreak of the

Civil War, Semprun was too young to have been a Republican soldier, and he proposes that this causes veterans of the conflict to approach interactions with the leader they know as "Federico Sánchez" with caution. "They had fought during the civil war, they had sustained the party organization with their ebbing strength during the terrible years, they had been in prison. They were shrouded in glory, secrets, and doubts," Semprun reflects (34–5) [Ils avaient fait la guerre civile, ils avaient tenu l'organisation du parti à bout de bras, dans les années terribles, ils avaient été en prison. Ils étaient couverts de gloire, de secrets et de doutes (38)].

They would look at me. They knew that I was "Sanchez"[12] of the Central Committee and the Politburo. They listened to me. But when they first met me, I could see by the look in their eyes that they were wondering who I was, where I'd sprung from. "Sanchez"? What was this "Sanchez"? I was not a leader out of history. Nor was I old enough to have taken part in their civil war. I didn't share the same experiences, the same obscure, tragic complicities, the same glorious and wretched memories. Nor did we have the same things to forget – I mean the same wish to forget certain episodes in a long, bloody history.

"Sanchez"? The veterans would shake their heads. That didn't bother me. I liked to listen to their stories, to build up with their help a collective memory. But even better I liked to be "Sanchez," with no links to their past, linked, rather, to the future of our struggle. (35)

[Ils me regardaient. Ils savaient que j'étais "Sanchez," du Comité central, du Bureau politique, ils m'écoutaient. Mais je voyais bien à leur regard, les premières fois, qu'ils se demandaient qui j'étais, d'où je sortais. "Sanchez"? C'était quoi, "Sanchez"? Je n'étais pas un dirigeant historique. Je n'avais pas non plus l'âge d'avoir fait leur guerre. Nous n'avions pas les mêmes références, les mêmes obscures et tragiques complicités, la même mémoire glorieuse ou misérable. Nous n'avions pas non plus les mêmes oublis. Je veux dire: la même volonté d'oublier certains épisodes d'une longue histoire sanglante.

"Sanchez"? Ils hochaient la tête, les anciens combattants. Ça ne me gênait pas. J'aimais bien écouter leurs récits, recréer avec eux une mémoire collective. Mais j'aimais plutôt être "Sanchez," délié de ce passé, lié plutôt à l'avenir de notre lutte.] (38)

Semprun believes that members of the Republican community are suspicious of him because he does not share their memories of the Civil

War, and his descriptions here echo the critique of the leaders of the communist movement cited above. Like the Party's authoritarian leaders of the fifties and sixties, Semprun proposes that Republican veterans remember the past in a way that censors it in order to forget any wrongdoings for which they may have been responsible. His insistence at the end of these remarks that he "likes" being marginalized by collectives that adopt these dogmatic approaches to their memory posits his own role in these groups as a disruptor of their dominant practices. As Semprun explains later in the text, behaving in this contrarian fashion distinguishes him from the Party's authoritarian thinkers who act only as "timorous, devious functionaries, attentive to the slightest wind that blew through the corridors, antechambers, and seraglios of the apparatus" (205) [fonctionnaires timorés et retors, attentifs au vent qui souffle dans les couloirs, les antichambres et les sérails de l'Appareil (186)].

Moreover, a passage that occurs near the halfway point of *Quel beau dimanche!* indicates that Semprun conceives of this "suspicion" that he arouses in other Party members as something that makes him a representative communist intellectual. His lengthy commentary on the subject follows a description of the astonishment that one of his comrades in the French Resistance feels upon learning of his privileged background. "I must say, I'm getting rather sick of my social background" [Je dois dire, mes origines sociales commencent à m'emmerder (185)], Semprun grumbles (203). "Or, rather, the way it is used against me, the way it is thrown in my face" [Ou plutôt, la façon dont on les utilise contre moi, la façon qu'on a de me les jeter à la figure].

> I shall always be suspect, then, whichever side I'm on, for inversely identical reasons. One day I shall have to explain to them, all of them, what a Communist intellectual is. Before this book comes to an end, I must explain to them in greater detail that it is precisely my suspect side that is of most value, that is my raison d'être. If I were not suspect, I would not be a Communist intellectual *from* the bourgeoisie, but an intellectual *of* the bourgeoisie. [...] If I am suspect, it is because I have betrayed my class. [...] I am a traitor to my class because I have had the vocation, the will, the capacity – the luck, too – to betray, with my own class, all classes, class society as a whole, because my role (and I'm speaking here in the first person only metaphorically, out of convenience, of course: I am speaking not about myself but about the Communist intellectual, generically) is precisely that of negating classes as such, class society in whatever form it presents itself ... (206; translation modified, emphasis in original)

> [Je serai donc toujours suspect, d'un côté comme de l'autre, pour des raisons inversement identiques. Un jour, il faudra bien que je leur explique, aux uns et aux autres, ce que c'est qu'un intellectuel communiste. Avant même la fin de ce livre, il me faudra leur expliquer plus en détail que c'est mon côté suspect, précisément, qui fait mon intérêt, qui est ma raison d'être. Si je n'étais pas suspect, je ne serais pas un intellectuel *issu* de la bourgeoisie, mais un intellectuel *de* la bourgeoisie [...] Si je suis suspect, c'est parce que j'ai trahi ma classe [...] Je suis un traître à ma classe parce que j'ai eu la vocation, la volonté, la capacité – la chance aussi – de trahir avec la mienne toutes les classes, la société de classes dans son ensemble, parce que mon rôle (et je ne parle ici à la première personne que par métaphore ou facilité de langage, bien entendu: il ne s'agit pas de moi, mais de l'intellectuel communiste en général, génériquement) mon rôle en tant qu'intellectuel communiste est précisément celui de nier les classes en soi, la société de classes sous quelque forme qu'elle se présente ...] (187; emphasis in original)

What makes Semprun a true communist intellectual, he argues here, is his betrayal of his privileged class origins, an act that participates in what he believes to be the primary objective of the movement: the creation of a classless society. The implication is that, in order for Semprun to perform his function as an intellectual, he must constantly strive to arouse suspicion, which entails continuously challenging the categories into which he is placed, and remaining the Party's perpetual outsider. Semprun turns his marginalized status within this collective into an integral part of his identity as a communist intellectual, and claims it as the ideal position from which to wage the battle against class-based forms of oppression.[13]

However, Semprun's understanding of the role played by intellectuals in bearing witness to atrocity in *Quel beau dimanche!* adheres, precisely, to a class-based division of labour. His reflections on the phenomenon occur in the context of a conversation that he has years after liberation with a fellow Buchenwald survivor named Fernand Barizon. Barizon tells Semprun disjointed and confusing stories about their shared experiences in Buchenwald, and Semprun speculates that it is because members of the working classes like Barizon are not gifted storytellers that "dominant minorities" (such as intellectuals) are always the ones who must put history into words:

> At Nantua, as I listened to Fernand Barizon's rigmarole, I wondered why it is always the same people who tell stories, who write history [...] I ended up by putting the question in parentheses, thanks to a temporary,

compromise formula: The masses may make history, but they certainly don't write it. It is the dominant minorities – which on the left are called "vanguards" and on the right, and even in the center, "natural elites" – that write history. And rewrite it, if need be, if the need is felt, and, from their dominant point of view, the need is often felt. (62–3)

[À Nantua, en écoutant le brouillamini de Fernand Barizon, je me demandais pourquoi ce sont toujours les mêmes qui racontent les histoires, qui font l'histoire [...] j'avais fini par mettre la question entre parenthèses, grâce à une formule provisoire de compromis: les masses font peut-être l'histoire, mais elles ne la racontent sûrement pas. Ce sont les minorités dominantes – qu'on appelle à gauche "avant-gardes" et à droite, voire au centre, "élites naturelles" – qui racontent l'histoire. Et qui la récrivent, au besoin, si le besoin s'en fait sentir, et le besoin s'en fait, de leur point de vue dominant, souvent sentir.] (62)

Readers recognize here Semprun's criticisms of communist authoritarianism examined above: "dominant minorities" are responsible for constructing historical narratives; but, in the process, they rewrite the past in accordance with their needs in the present. Semprun further ventures to suggest that, even though people like Barizon are unable to tell compelling stories about their personal experiences, doing so is the only way for people to truly "live" them:

Perhaps that isn't the problem for them, recounting convincingly the life of the camps. Perhaps the problem for them is quite simply that they have been there and survived.

Yet it isn't so simple. Has one really experienced something that one is unable to describe, something whose minimum truth one is unable to reconstruct in a meaningful way – and so make communicable? Doesn't living, in the full sense of the term, mean transforming one's personal experience into consciousness – that is to say, into memorized experience that is capable at the same time of integration into the future? But can one assume any experience without more or less mastering its language? The history – the stories, the narratives, the memories, the eyewitness accounts in which it survives – lives on. The text, the very texture, the tissue of life. (61–2)

[Peut-être n'est-ce pas leur problème, de raconter de façon convaincante la vie des camps. Leur problème, peut-être est-il tout simplement d'y avoir été et d'y avoir survécu.

> Pourtant, ce n'est pas aussi simple. A-t-on vraiment vécu quelque chose dont on n'arrive pas à faire le récit, à reconstruire significativement la vérité minime – en la rendant ainsi communicable? Vivre vraiment, n'est-ce pas transformer en conscience – c'est-à-dire en vécu mémorisé, en même temps susceptible de devenir projet – une expérience personnelle? Mais peut-on prendre en charge quelque expérience que ce soit sans en maîtriser plus ou moins le langage? C'est-à-dire l'histoire, les histoires, les récits, les mémoires, les témoignages: la vie? Le texte, la texture même, le tissu de la vie?] (61)

While Semprun acknowledges that some camp survivors are not talented enough to speak convincingly for themselves, he stresses that experiences must be put into words and made "communicable" in order to be "mastered," and that those who cannot are not really alive. A possible implication would be that, because, in Semprun's understanding, intellectual witnesses are skilled at composing narratives about their experiences, their task is to tell stories about their collective's experience, which people like Fernand Barizon can then reference in order to "live" those experiences as well. The problems inherent in such a view are patently obvious: intellectuals furnish the survivor community with orderly narratives about their shared experiences, but their stories necessarily reflect their own interests, and their own visions of the past. The self-reflexivity of Semprun's writing may, as Ferrán argues, question any and all reconstructions of the past, but, in *Quel beau dimanche!* it also forces less talented witnesses to make sense of their past experiences through its endless reconstructions. Intellectual witnesses like Jorge Semprun may claim to speak for the "mass" of survivors, but their narratives always shape the experience of atrocity according to their own needs, and the privileged, self-reflective position from which they speak in the present of writing.

2 Writing

While Jorge Semprun may be Spain's best-known communist survivor of the Nazi concentration camp system, the primary site of the Republican experience of the camps is not Buchenwald, but Mauthausen.[14] Classified by the Nazis as one of their severest camps, Mauthausen primarily housed prisoners that Germany categorized as incapable of rehabilitation, and those condemned to it were meant to experience prolonged suffering before they died from exhaustion.[15] Approximately seven thousand Spaniards who sought refuge in France after Spain's Civil War were imprisoned in the camp because, as David Wingeate Pike has noted, the Nazis viewed them as "inveterate enemies" of the fascist cause who deserved the worst punishments Germany could devise for them (*Spaniards* 11).[16] The circuitous route that most Republicans took to Mauthausen began with internment in refugee camps in the south of France and incorporation into special work details of the French army. After Pétain's armistice with the Nazis in 1940, Spain's Republicans were arrested, transferred to prisoner-of-war camps in Germany, denied POW status, and, from there, deported to Mauthausen. Nearly five thousand Spaniards perished in the camp, and only one hundred of its survivors returned to live in Franco's Spain after the end of the Second World War.[17]

As Semprun explains throughout his works, though he tried to write about his experiences in Buchenwald immediately after liberation, he did not publish his first text about the camps, *Le grand voyage*, until eighteen years after his return. Semprun's 1994 text *L'écriture ou la vie* tells the anguishing story of his coming-to-writing, and specifically links his ability to write about his time in Buchenwald to a series of conversations in 1961 with a Mauthausen survivor named Manuel Azaustre. Like *Quel beau dimanche!*, *L'écriture ou la vie* is an autobiographical narrative in which the names of the text's first-person narrator and protagonist are also both Jorge Semprun. The narrative is structured around the writer's experiences immediately after his liberation from Buchenwald, and flashes forward and backward in time to comment on the steps he passed through to become a writer.

A detailed analysis of Semprun's interactions with Manuel Azaustre in *L'écriture ou la vie* offers important insights into how intellectual witnesses speak for other survivors through the writer's work. These exchanges with Manuel take place while Semprun is working in Madrid as the Spanish Communist Party's head of clandestine operations. Semprun is forced to listen in silence to Manuel's testimonies about the camps because, as a clandestine Party leader, he is not allowed to reveal anything about his true identity to any of his operatives. Had he not been constrained by his position, Semprun insists that he would have intervened in Manuel's "disorderly" narratives as a fellow survivor in order to correct their flaws. His commentary reads:

> It was disorganized, confused, too wordy, mired in details: there wasn't any overall vision, everything was seen in the same light. In sum, a firsthand

account that was rough, unpolished. A jumble of images, an avalanche of facts, impressions, pointless commentary.

I champed at the bit, unable to intervene with questions, to make him bring order and meaning to the chaotic nonsense of his torrent of words. His undeniable sincerity had been reduced to rhetoric, his truthfulness no longer even seemed convincing. But I couldn't say anything to him, I couldn't help him give shape to his memories, since he was not supposed to know that I, too, had been deported. Since I could not possibly share this secret with him. (240)[18]

[C'était désordonné, confus, trop prolixe, ça s'embourbait dans les détails, il n'y avait aucune vision d'ensemble, tout était placé sous le même éclairage. C'était un témoignage à l'état brut, en somme: des images en vrac. Un déballage de faits, d'impressions, de commentaires oiseux.

Je rongeais mon frein, ne pouvant intervenir pour lui poser des questions, l'obliger à mettre de l'ordre et du sens dans le non-sens désordonné de son flot de paroles. Sa sincérité indiscutable n'était plus que de la rhétorique, sa véracité n'était même plus vraisemblable. Mais je ne pouvais rien lui dire, je ne pouvais pas l'aider à mettre en forme ses souvenirs, puisqu'il n'était pas censé savoir que j'avais moi aussi été déporté. Puisqu'il n'était pas question que je lui fasse partager ce secret.] (310)

Semprun outlines here two distinct listening protocols for those who engage survivor testimonies, one for people who experienced the Nazi camps, and one for people who did not. His harsh criticisms of Manuel's shortcomings as a storyteller, and his insistence that, if not confined by his position, he would have intervened in the conversation to help give the man's narratives a more "orderly" and "meaningful" form, indicates that survivors should listen critically to each others' testimonies, and correct other returnees when they speak about their experiences. Semprun's desire to act in this way clearly conforms to the problematic understanding of the intellectual witness's role elaborated throughout *Quel beau dimanche!* He believes he can shape the Mauthausen survivor's stories because of his guiding role as an intellectual witness, but he is blind to the self-reflective nature of the narratives he constructs. Because of the constraints imposed on him by the Party, though, he behaves in the way in which he implies outsiders should act in conversations with survivors: he keeps his identity a secret, and patiently listens while Manuel tells him about Mauthausen.

This inability to intervene in Manuel's testimony further exposes some of the hidden assumptions upon which Semprun bases his understanding of the intellectual witness. Semprun justifies his desire to speak for a survivor from a different camp in this passage by insisting that all concentration camp survivors share the same experience, and should be able to "find themselves" in each other's narratives:

> Obviously, there were differences between Buchenwald and Mauthausen: the deportees experienced very specific circumstances in each of the Nazi camps. In its essence, however, the system remained the same. The regimentation of daily life, the tempo of work, the hunger, the lack of sleep, the constant persecution, the sadism of the SS, the madness of the veteran detainees, the knife fights over control of personal fiefdoms of power: essentially the same. Yet I couldn't make sense of what Manuel A. had to say. (240)

> [Certes, entre Buchenwald et Mauthausen il y avait eu des différences: dans chacun des camps nazis l'existence des déportés a été soumise à des circonstances spécifiques. L'essentiel du système, pourtant, était identique. L'organisation des journées, le rythme de travail, la faim, le manque de sommeil, les brimades perpétuelles, le sadisme des S.S., la folie des vieux détenus, les batailles au couteau pour contrôler des parcelles du pouvoir interne: l'essentiel était identique. Je ne m'y retrouvais pourtant pas, dans les récits de Manuel A.] (309)

Of course, Semprun recognizes, there were differences between the existences that deportees led in Buchenwald and Mauthausen, but, because the Nazis organized the space of each concentration camp in roughly the same way, he claims, like David Rousset, that the "essential" nature of the experience is the same for all survivors. This definition of collective experience, in other words, is both a product of a totalizing understanding of the dominant order that punishes, and an effect of the shared experience of trauma. Semprun's problematic desire to shape Manuel's testimonies into something in which he can "recognize" himself, then, is also a desire to recognize the repressive mark of the Nazi system in the speech of fellow survivors.

To connect these ideas to the understanding of the intellectual witness articulated in *Quel beau dimanche!*, this interaction with Manuel indicates that Semprun's witness writings conceive of speaking for others not only as a self-reflective act that shapes the past according to a witness's needs in the narrating present. It is also an attempt to wash out the differences between the experiences of the various camps of the Nazi system, and of the individual deportees who were interned in them. In the process, this practice seeks to replace singular accounts of the camps with a masterly narrative about them, one that allows survivors to connect with each other's experiences only through the punishments to which the Nazis subjected them all. The absence of Manuel's testimony from *L'écriture ou la vie* testifies to one of the harmful effects that this kind of "speaking for" exerts on other survivors: their singular voices are subsumed and silenced by a narrative that claims to speak in the collective's name.

Other passages in *L'écriture ou la vie* further demonstrate that this totalizing view of survivors' experience as a collective profoundly influences Semprun's understanding of how intellectual witnesses write about the experience of atrocity. In his commentary on a conversation that he has with two female aide workers in the days after Buchenwald's liberation, Semprun describes himself as nothing more than a "conscious residue" of the experience that survivors share. The reflection is occasioned by a question that one of the aide workers asks while Jorge gives them a guided tour of Buchenwald. Pointing at the crematorium, the woman asks, "[i]s that the kitchen?" (119) [(c)'est la cuisine, ça? (160)]. Commenting on this question, Semprun reflects:

> For a fraction of a second, I wished I were dead. If I had been dead, I wouldn't have been able to hear that question. I was suddenly horrified at myself for being able to listen to that question. For being alive, in short. An understandable reaction, even if it was absurd. Excessive, at least. Since this question about the kitchen infuriated me precisely because I wasn't really alive. If I hadn't been a small fragment of the collective memory of our death, this question wouldn't have left me so angry. Fundamentally, I was nothing other than a conscious residue of all that death. An individual patch in the impalpable material of that shroud. A dust mote in the ashy cloud of that agony. A still-flickering light from the extinguished star of our dead years. (119–20)

> [J'ai souhaité d'être mort, pendant une fraction de seconde. Si j'avais été mort, je n'aurais pas pu entendre cette question. J'avais horreur de moi-même, soudain, d'être capable d'entendre cette question. D'être vivant, en somme. C'était une réaction compréhensible, même si elle était absurde. Excessive en tout cas. Car c'est précisément parce que je n'étais pas vraiment vivant que cette question à propos de la cuisine me mettait

hors de moi. Si je n'avais pas été une parcelle de la mémoire collective de notre mort, cette question ne m'aurait pas mis hors de moi. Je n'étais rien d'autre, pour l'essentiel, qu'un résidu conscient de toute cette mort. Un brin individuel du tissu impalpable de ce linceul. Une poussière dans le nuage de cendre de cette agonie. Une lumière encore clignotante de l'astre éteint de nos années mortes.] (160)

Semprun explains here that his horrified reaction to the woman's question is an effect of his "essential" identity as a camp survivor. Semprun is "nothing more" than the aggregate of survivors' shared experience of death, and he proposes that his responses are entirely conditioned by the Nazi's order of things. Recognizing this "essential identity," in turn, is an important part of Semprun's understanding of writing. In the final chapter of *L'écriture ou la vie,* he defines writing as an ascetic activity that allows him to "recognize" the traumatic marking that all survivors share:

> [W]riting, if it claims to be more than a game, or a gamble, is but a long, endless labor of ascesis, a way of casting off one's self by keeping a firm hold on oneself. Becoming oneself through recognizing and bringing into the world that *other* one always is. (295; emphasis in original)

> [(L')écriture, si elle prétend être davantage qu'un jeu, ou un enjeu, n'est qu'un long, interminable travail d'ascèse, une façon de se déprendre de soi en prenant sur soi: en devenant soi-même parce qu'on aura reconnu, mis au monde l'autre qu'on est toujours.] (377)

Semprun understands writing here as a practice that helps survivors take leave of the "other" that is always found within the self by recognizing that otherness as a part of themselves. To write, in other words, is to choose to engage in the endless process of bringing out the other that grafts itself onto one's selfhood, an other that will always be integral to one's self no matter how much one writes about it.

But, as Susan Brison has pointed out, traumatic experiences leave marks of "otherness" that exert horrifying and disruptive effects on survivors, an idea that an earlier passage of *L'écriture ou la vie* indicates Semprun knows only too well.[19] In it, Semprun is listening to his friend, the French literary critic Claude-Edmonde Magny, read a letter that she wrote to him about some poems he composed before being arrested by the Gestapo in 1943.[20] It is the fall of 1945, and Magny digresses from her reading to comment on the silence that has enshrouded Semprun's experience of the camps ever since his return to Paris several months prior. "I know others in the Resistance who have come back from deportation" [Je connais d'autres résistants revenus de déportation (213)], she tells Semprun (162). "They're all possessed by a true frenzy of communication ... of attempts at communication, anyway ... You, you maintain the most perfect silence" (162) [Ils sont tous saisis par un véritable vertige de communication ... De tentative de communication, en tout cas ... Un délire verbal du témoignage ... Vous, c'est le silence le plus lisse (213–14)]. She pauses to pour a few drops of coffee into her cup when Semprun suddenly interjects for the first time since his return:

> "Those beautiful Sundays!" I exclaim. "In the afternoon, after roll call, when we'd devoured our Sunday noodle soup, I'd go off to the Little Camp ... Those too sick to work were in Hut 56 ... We'd gather there around the bunk assigned to Halbwachs and Maspero ... The loudspeakers were playing songs sung by Zarah Leander ... That's were Schelling came up, a *Bibelforscher* – a Jehovah's Witness – talked to me about him."
>
> She listens with such keen attention that deep lines appear in her face. But I'm worn out, and pause to rest. (163; emphasis in original)

> [– Les beaux dimanches! ai-je dit alors. L'après-midi, une fois l'appel terminé, la soupe aux nouilles dominicale dévorée, je descendais dans le Petit Camp ... La baraque 56 était celle des invalides inaptes au travail ... Nous nous réunissons autour du châlit de Halbwachs et de Maspero ... Les haut-parleurs diffusaient des chansons de Zarah Leander ... C'est là que Schelling m'est apparu, un *Bibelforscher* m'en a parlé ...
>
> Elle m'écoute avec une attention tellement aiguë que les traits de son visage se creusent. Mais je suis épuisé, je marque un temps d'arrêt.] (215; emphasis in original)

The fragmentary nature of Semprun's testimony here calls to mind the criticisms of Manuel Azaustre's Mauthausen narratives. Semprun's disorderly remarks do not present a cohesive vision of his experience, but, rather, an avalanche of images and facts about his time in Buchenwald. Magny continues to listen intently as Jorge struggles to describe the obstacles he faces when trying to write about his anguishing experience:

> "My stumbling block – but it's not a technical problem, it's a moral one – is that I can't manage, through writing, to get into the present ... So all

my drafts begin before, or after, or around, but never *in* the camp … And when I finally get inside, I'm blocked and cannot write. Overwhelmed with anguish, I fall back into nothingness: I give up … only to begin again elsewhere, some other way … And the same thing repeats itself."

"That's understandable," she says softly.

"It's understandable, but it's killing me!"

She stirs a useless spoon around in her empty coffee cup.

"It must be the path you'll have to take as a writer," she murmurs. "An ascetic path: to put an end to all that death through writing."

She's probably right.

"Unless it puts an end to me!"

That's not just a play on words, and she knows it. (166; emphasis in original)

[Mon problème à moi, mais il n'est pas technique, il est moral, c'est que je ne parviens pas, par l'écriture, à pénétrer dans le présent du camp, à le raconter au present … Comme s'il y avait un interdit de la figuration du présent … Ainsi, dans tous les brouillons, ça commence avant, ou après, ou autour, ça ne commence jamais dans le camp … Et quand je parviens enfin à l'intérieur, quand j'y suis, l'écriture se bloque … Je suis pris d'angoisse, je retombe dans le néant, j'abandonne … Pour recommencer autrement, ailleurs, de façon différente … Et le même processus se reproduit …

– Ça se comprend, dit-elle d'une voix douce.

– Ça se comprend, mais ça me tue!

Elle tourne vainement une cuiller dans sa tasse de café vide.

– C'est sans doute votre chemin d'écrivain, murmure-t-elle. Votre ascèse: écrire jusqu'au bout de toute cette mort …

Elle a raison, probablement.

– À moins qu'elle ne vienne à bout de moi!

Ce n'est pas une phrase, elle l'a compris.] (218–19)

Semprun is overwhelmed by anxiety whenever he attempts to write about his time in Buchenwald in the immediate postwar period – the marks left on him from the experience are too painful for anyone to confront directly. His descriptions of this excruciating ordeal suggest that the disorderly manner in which he tells his story is caused by this inability to write about his traumatic experiences. Writing may help give order to experience, but trauma is a state of disorder that can never be completely organized and mastered. To return to Semprun's criticisms of Manuel's testimonies, the interaction with Claude-Edmonde Magny also implies that Semprun's critique of the Mauthausen survivor's stories is really a critique of himself, and of the flaws that appear in his own acts of witnessing. Semprun's desire to perform the role of corrective guide for his fellow camp survivor is really a desire to rid himself of his own shortcomings as a witness to atrocity, and to master the traumatic aftereffects of his experience in Buchenwald.

Yet *L'écriture ou la vie* indicates that not being able to speak for Manuel's experience of Mauthausen is what finally allows Jorge Semprun to write about Buchenwald. Semprun explains that after a week of listening patiently as an outsider to Manuel's narratives, the traumatic memories of Buchenwald that he had been brutally repressing for years in order to function in society return to him in his sleep, and he suddenly knows he can write the book about the camps that he abandoned shortly after his conversations with Claude-Edmonde Magny in 1945. Semprun notes:

> For fifteen years, snow had never fallen on my sleep. I'd forgotten it, repressed it, censored it. I mastered my dreams, cleansing them of the snow and smoke over the Ettersberg. Sometimes, it's true, I felt a pang in my heart. An instant of anguish tinged with nostalgia [...]
>
> But the snow had disappeared from my sleep.
>
> I awoke with a start, after a week of Manuel A.'s stories about Mauthausen. It was in Madrid, on the Calle Concepción-Bahamonde, in 1961. But now that I think about it, "with a start" is not the right choice of words. Because I did wake up all at once, and felt immediately lucid, alert. But it wasn't anxiety or stress that awakened me. I was strangely calm, serene. Everything now seemed clear to me. I knew how to write the book that I'd had to abandon fifteen years before. Rather, I knew that I could write it, now. Because I'd always known how to write it: what I'd lacked was courage. The courage to confront death through writing. But I no longer needed this courage. (241–2)

> [Depuis quinze ans, jamais la neige n'était plus tombée sur mon sommeil. Je l'avais oubliée, refoulée, censurée. Je maîtrisais mes rêves, j'en avais chassé la neige de la fumée sur l'Ettersberg. Parfois, certes, une douleur aiguë, brève, m'avait traversé le cœur. Un instant de souffrance mêlée de nostalgie [...]
>
> Mais la neige avait disparu de mon sommeil.
>
> Je me suis réveillé en sursaut, après une semaine de récits sur Mauthausen de Manuel A. C'était à Madrid, rue Concepción-Bahamonde, en

> 1961. Mais le mot "sursaut" ne convient pas, réflexion faite. Car je m'étais réveillé d'un seul coup, certes, j'avais aussitôt été en éveil, lucide, dispos. Mais ce n'était pas l'angoisse qui me réveillait, l'inquiétude. J'étais étrangement calme, serein. Tout me semblait clair, désormais. Je savais comment écrire le livre que j'avais dû abandonner quinze ans auparavant. Plutôt: je savais que je pouvais l'écrire, désormais. Car j'avais toujours su comment l'écrire: c'est le courage qui m'avait manqué. Le courage d'affronter la mort à travers l'écriture. Mais je n'avais plus besoin de ce courage.] (311–12)

Recognizing the shortcomings of Manuel's narratives, and not intervening to correct them, gives Semprun the "courage" he needs to confront his anguishing experiences through writing, the result of which is the text *Le grand voyage*. In order to write about his experience of atrocity, Semprun must act like an outsider in his conversations with other camp survivors, and not try to shape their testimonies into something in which he can recognize his own traumatic markings. A possible implication is that Semprun behaves in his corrective way as an "intellectual witness" because he lacks belief in his own abilities, a behaviour in which he engages because, understandably, he is unable to face his overwhelming experiences on his own.

If Jorge Semprun's Buchenwald writings are able to speak for the experience of other concentration camp survivors, it is not because, as Semprun claims, they serve as "masterly" guides for the entire survivor community to reference in order to make sense of their individual experiences. Rather, it is because they direct us towards the unknown experiences of people like the Mauthausen-survivor Manuel, and towards the disorderly parts of a survivor's self, that are necessarily denied by any act of witness writing. This leaves us with another paradox about witnessing as a genre: masterful witness narratives speak for others only because they point readers towards the denials upon which such writing depends.

3 Seeing Responsibility

I couldn't have made it
if no one had seen me
if you hadn't been there.

– Charlotte Delbo

[Moi je n'aurais pas tenu
si personne ne m'avait vu
Si vous n'avez pas été là.]

In the influential text *Remnants of Auschwitz: The Witness and the Archive,* one argument pursued by Giorgio Agamben is that a new understanding of the relationship between the human and the non-human emerges from the Nazi camps, and that this understanding has important ramifications for how we conceive of the ethical obligations we have to others. Agamben primarily bases this argument on the way relatively healthy internees responded in the camps to deportees who were thought to be beyond help because they appeared to have lost their will to live and their ability to speak, and staggered about their daily tasks more like walking corpses than human beings. Known throughout the camp system as *Muselmänner,* these deportees were an unbearable sight for many prisoners, Agamben tells us, because they were humans who seemed to have lost their "human" qualities; the degrading conditions of the camps seemed to strip them of their senses of dignity, self-respect, and decency, and this led many deportees to categorize them as non-humans and turn a blind eye to their plight.[1] Agamben argues that this response points to the inadequacy of many of our definitions of the human, and that we must rethink these definitions in order to include forms of humanity like the *Muselmänner* within them. If there is a zone of the human in which concepts like dignity, self-respect, and decency no longer make sense, Agamben explains, "then they are not genuine ethical concepts, for no ethics can claim to exclude a part of humanity, no matter how unpleasant or difficult that humanity is to see" (63–4).[2]

At the same time, however, Agamben contends that survivors should not be judged or held responsible for their failure to see and help internees who no longer appeared to be human beings while they were in the camps. Drawing primarily on the work of Primo Levi, who is one of the few camp survivors to attempt to bear witness to the plight of the *Muselmänner*, Agamben further advances the idea that the Nazi camps represent a zone of non-responsibility, one that "allowed for neither summary judgments nor distinctions" in regards to the behaviour of deportees (47). In order to survive the degrading conditions in which they were imprisoned, Agamben reasons, *Muselmänner* and other deportees alike had to abandon their humanity and their responsibilities to others upon entering the camps (59–60).[3] He argues that what a site like Auschwitz presents us with, then, is an ethical aporia: "it is the site in which it is not decent to remain decent, in which those who believed themselves to preserve their dignity and self-respect experience shame with respect to those who did not" (60). One of the tasks of survivors, in this context, is to testify to this shame they experience in the face of the non-human – in their narratives, survivors become "witness to [their] own disorder, [their] own oblivion as subject" when speaking of the plight of the *Muselmänner* and the form of humanity that they embody (106).[4] Thus, Agamben stresses, the genre of testimony is not for those few deportees who retained their dignity in the camps. Such deportees may be able to bear witness to their own faith or strength, but "they would not be able to bear witness to the camp[s]," and to the reconfigured understanding of the human that emerges from them (60).

This particular line of thought that Agamben elaborates in *Remnants of Auschwitz* accounts poorly for the way a survivor narrative like Charlotte Delbo's *Auschwitz et après* frames the question of responsibility in the Nazi camps.[5] However, as in *Remnants of Auschwitz*, the relation between deportees and their comrades who appear to have lost their "human" qualities occupies a central place in Delbo's witness writing. A member of the only convoy of female political prisoners sent to Auschwitz from France,[6] Delbo spent a total of twenty-seven months interned in various camps in the Nazi system, and, throughout her trilogy, she presents her own survival as the result of her group's collective struggle to make it out of the camps alive. A staggering number of the women who were deported with Delbo died in the first six months of their internment in Auschwitz – one hundred and seventy-three out of a total of two hundred and thirty. Nonetheless, the group also had one of the highest survival rates in the history of the camp,[7] and it lost none of its members to the Nazi system once they were transferred out of Auschwitz to various other camps for the remainder of their internment.[8] *Auschwitz et après* presents us with a community of women who do not abandon their responsibilities to others upon entering the camps and, in contrast to Agamben's analysis, offers many examples of deportees being able to see and, in certain situations, even help and come to understand prisoners who appear to have been stripped of their "human" qualities.[9]

While Delbo does not call on readers to judge or blame those deportees who fail to see and help others during their internment, I will argue here that one of the primary concerns of a testimony like *Auschwitz et après* is to teach us to react to others in more responsible ways when we find ourselves in situations that shatter our understandings of the human. Delbo's writing in this testimony recuperates "non-human" figures such as the *Muselmänner* as figures of human resistance that *can* be understood, and it stages ethical encounters with this form of humanity that make readers see their responsibilities towards it in spite of an initial lapse in understanding. My contention here is that witness writing such as Delbo's rejects Agamben's idea that elaborating a new, more complete definition of the human is the ethical task we should take up in light of the Nazi camps. Instead, it presents the ethical as a kind of positioning in which we look, in spite of our fear and repulsion, at forms of humanity that are difficult to see because of their incomprehensibility, and in which we open ourselves up to others when we are confronted with the limits of our understandings.

1 Looking

Published as a trilogy in 1970 and 1971, *Auschwitz et après* is composed of an assemblage of narratives and poems that reflect on the experience of deportation, internment, and return.[10] It offers what Thomas Trezise has called a "fragmentary articulation of trauma and survival" ("The Question of Community" 860): the poems and short prose pieces interspersed throughout it disrupt any "rigorous narrative continuity" that readers may seek (859), and, within its longer prose pieces, the text's narrator frequently jumps forward and backward in time to relate her experiences before and after the time she spent in the Nazi system. Each volume of the trilogy is structured around a different stage of the experience that Delbo and her fellow deportees endured at the hands of the Nazis and their collaborators. Volume 1, titled *Aucun de nous ne reviendra,* focuses almost exclusively on the first gruelling weeks of the group's internment among the general population in Auschwitz's women's camp.[11] Volume 2, *Une connaissance inutile,* recounts events from the French prisons in which members of the convoy were incarcerated before their deportation and from the later stages of their internment in Auschwitz and in Ravensbrück, an all women's camp outside of Berlin that most of the surviving convoy members were transferred to after the year they spent in Auschwitz.[12] The final volume, *Mesure de nos jours,* is set in postwar France, and contains the testimonies of different survivors who recount their experiences both in Auschwitz and afterwards as they struggle to reintegrate themselves into French society.

As Neil Levi and Michael Rothberg in particular have observed, in addition to describing the atrocities that Delbo witnessed, the trilogy also looks beyond her personal story to offer "categories for theoretical reflection" on the Nazi camp experience and its aftermath (25). Scholars have largely centred their analyses on the trilogy's theoretical understanding of the act of reading, and, more specifically, on the different ways in which Delbo's writing attempts to disrupt, for ethical reasons, how readers categorize and identify with the experiences and events it recounts. Trezise, for example, proposes that *Auschwitz et après* leads readers to question the "interpretive frameworks" with which they initially approach witness texts by using a type of phenomenological description called "eidectic reduction" to make readers bear responsibility in the act of witnessing ("The Question of Community" 866, 876).[13] Delbo's writing does this, he argues, in order to expose readers to "the discrepancy between ignorance and knowledge" that deportees struggled with when they arrived in the Nazi camps and to force readers to look inside of themselves to fill in the narrative's gaps (877, 860). Patricia Yaeger further suggests that the trilogy tries to "ward off the empathy" that readers "want to inhabit," which it does to strip us of the "comforting illusions" we have about what it means to feel compassion for the experiences of others (402, 410). *Auschwitz et après* evokes readers' empathy only to "burn it away," Yaeger notes, and this causes readers to step back from the intimate relationship they seek out with the narrative and its characters, and engages them instead in a relation of "proximity without intimacy" (415).

But no attention has yet been paid to how the trilogy's extensive reflections on the act of looking contribute to the relation it seeks to establish with readers, and the consequences that these reflections have for the work's implicit commentary on the ethical. Especially in the first volume, *Auschwitz et après* frequently emphasizes the difficulties deportees have looking at their surroundings in the camps, and calls on readers, in turn, to look at the terrible things that make so many deportees flinch. Deportees recoil in fear like nearly all of us would when they come across dead bodies. When they watch prisoners being loaded into trucks to be sent to the gas chambers, it becomes an overwhelming experience because of how often it happens day in and day out. Internees turn their heads when the camp's SS officers train their dogs to attack mannequins because they know those dogs are being trained to kill them. And while the word *Muselmann* – or its female equivalent, *Muselweib* – never appears in Delbo's work, the plight of deportees who become unresponsive in these same ways is also a terrifying sight, primarily because their corpselike bodies move in ways that the relatively healthy can't initially understand.

Three short passages that occur in succession towards the end of the trilogy's first volume *Aucun de nous ne reviendra* – the only such sequence in the trilogy – clearly suggest that challenging readers to look at these same gruesome images of the human is a primary concern of *Auschwitz et après*. An examination of these will serve as my point of departure for analysing the trilogy's implicit theorization of the ethical. No more than a few lines long each and appearing on separate pages as self-contained images of camp life, they offer glimpses of three different flinch-inducing moments from Auschwitz, and all end with the same two-sentence refrain that dares readers to look at them: in Rosette Lamont's translation, "Try to look. Just try and see." However, this would better be rendered as "Try to look. I dare you to try," which more faithfully conveys the direct challenge Delbo issues to her reader in the original French: "Essayez de regarder. Essayez pour voir." The first passage provides a stark and spare description of a desecrated corpse with an open, eyelash-fringed eye and another eye eaten by a rat. The second provides a more detailed image of a male internee who is no longer able to keep up with the rest of his group yet continues to push forward, this in spite of the SS dog that has locked its jaws onto his bloody backside.

The third passage offers a comparatively elaborate description of a Jewish woman being abandoned to death by two camp inmates, the exact type of behaviour that Agamben stresses we not judge deportees for because of the lengths they had to go to in order to survive in such degrading conditions. The woman is being dragged by her fellow internees to block 25, the area of the women's camp where those who could no longer perform their daily tasks were held without food and water, sometimes for weeks, before being murdered in the gas chambers or dying from the block's miserable conditions, whichever came first. The passage reads (in its entirety):

> A woman dragged by two others, holding on to her arms. A Jewish woman. She does not want to be taken to block 25. She resists. Her knees scrape the ground. Her clothing, pulled up by the tug of her sleeves, is wound around her neck. Her trousers – men's trousers – are undone and drag inside out behind her, fastened to her ankles. A flayed frog. Her loins are exposed, her emaciated buttocks, soiled by blood and pus, are dotted with hollows.
>
> She is howling. Her knees are lacerated by the gravel.
>
> Try to look. Just try and see. (*Auschwitz and After* 86)
>
> [Une femme que deux tirent par les bras. Une juive. Elle ne veut pas aller au 25. Les deux la traînent. Elle résiste. Ses genoux raclent le sol. Son vêtement tiré aux manches remonte sur le cou. Le pantalon défait – un pantalon d'homme – traîne derrière elle, à l'envers, retenu aux chevilles. Une grenouille dépouillée. Les reins nus, les fesses avec des trous de maigreur sales de sang et de sanie.
>
> Elle hurle. Les genoux s'arrachent sur les cailloux.
>
> Essayez de regarder. Essayez pour voir.] (*ANR* 139)

The image that *Auschwitz et après* dares readers to look at here encapsulates the ethical complexities of Auschwitz that Agamben discusses in his work. Two deportees are literally dragging another to her death, and the deportee being dragged is resisting so intensely that her pants have nearly fallen off to expose her bloody, filthy, and emaciated buttocks. But, rather than see this woman as non-human because of a lack of dignity or self-respect – the kind of response Agamben presents as almost unavoidable in his work – this woman's desperate actions clearly humanise her for readers here, because, through Delbo's writing, we are led to see them as a testament to this woman's will to survive. The narrator presents her as someone resisting death with all her might by foregrounding the woman's will (she does not want to go to block 25) and her desire to fight (she is resisting) before then entering into the graphic details of the scene and offering a terse comparison of the woman's physical appearance to that of a "flayed frog." As a result, readers can't help but see her as someone who desperately wants to live, rather than someone whose physical state indicates that she has given up on life, has passed into a non-human state, and is ready to die.

But what is perhaps most notable in this – and, indeed, in all three of these short graphic passages – is the absence of any explicit moral or ethical commentary on the images that readers are being dared to look at. Unlike more famous concentration camp survivors like Primo Levi, Jorge Semprun, or Robert Antelme, Delbo does not offer theoretical digressions about the nature of her experience or elaborate new understandings of the human that she wishes us to grasp in these moments. A defining feature of Delbo's trilogy *Auschwitz et après* is its refusal to offer such explanations of the horrors of the Nazi camps, all while it bears witness to aspects of camp life that demolish our conceptualizations of the human. *Auschwitz et après* does not offer a masterful display of the horrific knowledge that a witness obtained in the camps, nor does it claim to impart definitive understandings about the experience of atrocity that we should all submit ourselves to.

Ross Chambers has argued that withholding explanation in such graphic moments and instead "flaunting" them to readers is a crucial rhetorical strategy that Delbo's trilogy uses in an act of fidelity towards the dead (225, 229). Explaining away the experience of survival in the camps, he reasons, would serve to deprive the dead of their power to haunt readers and disrupt their lives, because "the hauntedness of the survivors is exactly that which defines the difference between those who bear the memory of the dead" and those who, like the majority of people in postwar French society, live their lives smoothly, without disruption, and without regard to the spectres of the past (225). In order not to "lay the ghosts" of the camps – a central concern of Delbo's writing in Chambers' view – *Auschwitz et après* adopts this structure of a summation and summons, "calling up and calling back the dead and calling upon the living," in order to inculcate a shared sense of responsibility in readers for remembering the Auschwitz dead (225, xx).

However, the ordering of information and the level of detail in these three short passages also make the gruesome realities of the camp, and, in particular, the actions of deportees who, like the *Muselmänner*, are no longer able to perform their daily tasks, gradually more approachable for readers. *Auschwitz et après* may, as Chambers contends, flaunt these three graphic images at readers in order to honour the dead; but, in this portion of the text, each flaunt also provides a different kind of description than the previous one, and gradually leads us to a more refined understanding of the plight of deportees who some deem to be beyond help. The stark, flinch-inducing image that opens this sequence is followed by another shocking scene that provides a basic level of understanding that the first one did not, and is itself followed by a third moment from camp life that reads the desperate actions of the deportee described in it from the outset as signs of her resistance, her will, and, ultimately, her humanity. This trio of images does not lead us to judge or blame deportees like the two women dragging their comrade to block 25 because they fail to see and help others. Instead, it presents the horrors of the Nazi camps as forever horrifying – all of these images are atrocious and haunting – while also making it clear that all of these figures are human, and that we can come to see our responsibilities to them in spite of our fear and revulsion.[14]

Indeed, a defining feature of *Auschwitz et après* is the way it leads us to see the "non-human" as a form of humanity towards which we do not lose our sense of responsibility. But Delbo's writing guides us in this process much more delicately than Chambers's analysis would lead us to conclude. In other flinch-inducing moments that occur earlier in the trilogy's first volume, for instance, Delbo intervenes in the text to foreground the difficulties deportees themselves have bearing witness to their surroundings, and to offer reflections on her experience that are notable for their utter inadequacy. Unlike the "masterful" commentaries of a witness like Semprun – which assert his exemplarity as a witness and cultivate our dependency on the understandings he elaborates – Delbo's interventions serve to place the challenges of the camps within our reach and also, perhaps paradoxically, to keep us from thinking ourselves superior to or judging the camp's internees. A short narrative from early in the first volume titled "Les Mannequins" demonstrates this well. In it, the narrator continually interrupts descriptions of camp life to simultaneously exemplify and demystify a method people can use to remain engaged in their horrifying surroundings. Her commentary on this process occurs throughout an account of her comrades and herself coming face-to-face with a mass of naked, frozen corpses in the courtyard outside of block 25.[15]

After describing the mass of bodies, "Les Mannequins" flashes back to a moment from Delbo's childhood in which she saw a load of naked and disassembled mannequins delivered to a department store. The narrator then comments on the effect that looking at these mannequins had on her when she was a child:

> I looked. I was agitated by the nakedness of the mannequins. I had often seen mannequins in store windows, wearing a dress, shoes, a wig, their arms folded in affected gestures. I had never thought that they could exist naked, without hair. I had never thought that they could exist outside of their window displays, their electric lighting, and their gestures. To discover this gave me the same uneasy feeling as when seeing a dead person for the first time.[16]

> [Je regardais. J'étais troublée par la nudité des mannequins. J'avais souvent vu des mannequins dans la vitrine, avec leur robe, leurs souliers et leur perruque, leurs bras pliés dans un geste maniéré. Je n'avais jamais pensé qu'ils existaient nus, sans cheveux. Je n'avais jamais pensé qu'ils existaient en dehors de la vitrine, de la lumière électrique, de leur geste. Le découvrir me donnait le même malaise que de voir un mort pour la première fois.] (*ANR* 30)

Delbo reasons here that the feeling she has when looking at the "nakedness" of these department store mannequins as a child is caused by them appearing in an atypical context in which they aren't engaging in their typical, affected gestures, the same sensation that she experiences when seeing a dead body for the first time.[17] She further associates the word "fear" with this feeling in her final narratorial intervention of the passage, which reports her reaction when looking at a body in the mass of cadavers that still has some life in it. (Whether this reaction occurs in her past experience or the present of writing she leaves unclear.) "I look too" [Moi aussi je regarde (33)], Delbo states after describing one of her comrades who is staring wide-eyed at the still-living corpse, paralysed and unable to look away.[18] "I look at this corpse that moves but doesn't affect me. I'm grown up now. I can look at naked mannequins without being afraid"[19] [Je regarde ce cadavre qui bouge et qui m'est insensible. Maintenant je suis grande. Je peux regarder des mannequins nus sans avoir peur]. Delbo's commentary posits, in short, that fear, both inside and outside of the camps, is the effect of seeing something familiar in an unfamiliar context and engaged in an unfamiliar performance.

But what Delbo ultimately offers us throughout this passage is a conceptualization that presents confronting the horrors of the camps in a complex but accessible way for readers. While Delbo elaborates throughout her commentary a theoretical understanding of this experience that most of us would never come to on our own, she does so by drawing from non-camp experiences, and, thus, makes us as readers feel that we can confront these horrors thanks to past encounters of our own. The rhetorical effect of the narrator's intervention is equivalent to an invitation, one that demystifies the process of meaning-making and invites us to partake in it. You need to learn how to confront these horrors, Delbo seems to tell us, and learning how is not beyond you. Her commentary cultivates our belief in our own ability to make sense of the world of the camps rather than our submission to her theoretical frame.

And yet, the comparisons that the narrator makes throughout this passage also disrupt our ability to construct a neat or quick understanding of the event she describes because they discourage us from seeking to further refine her understanding or fill in its gaps. The ultimate point of Delbo's commentary in "Les Mannequins" is not to lead readers to classify this mass of dead bodies as nothing but a pile of department store mannequins or some other familiar image that we may personally associate with it. Rather, her remarks assert the absurdity of such an understanding, and of situations in which human beings are reduced to objects and treated with so little regard. This is an instance of verbal irony, one that calls our attention to the humanity of the people murdered in Auschwitz by bearing witness to the extent of their dehumanization. Delbo's writing gives voice here to a literal understanding that emerges from the camps (that human beings can be turned into mannequins) in order to communicate something quite different from that understanding (that human beings are not mannequins). One effect that Delbo's writing accomplishes through such irony is to make this scene approachable without in any way lessening its horror for readers. By offering an understanding that is so self-evidently absurd – the horror of seeing a pile of cadavers can be *compared* to seeing naked mannequins on the street but is certainly not *equivalent* to it – the narrator offers readers a way of getting a mental foothold in this encounter and of beginning to approach it. But, because her comparison is so inadequate, she also offers resistance to a less horrific understanding of the atrocities of Auschwitz coming to occupy its place. The obvious disparity between Delbo's commentary and the event that takes place before her eyes documents this moment as both terrifying and incomprehensible, which disrupts our impulse to claim to understand it, and keeps us engaged in the world of the camps in spite of our horror.

Yet another effect of this ironic stroke, then, is to break readers of their dependence on the knowledge about the camps that *Auschwitz et après* can relay to them. In contrast to the "masterful" metacommentaries that appear throughout Semprun's works, those offered in passages like "Les Mannequins" do not try to convince us that Delbo's vision of the camps is the one vision that we should all subject ourselves to, or that Delbo is an exemplary witness with definitive understandings to impart. In fact, disrupting fixed understandings about Auschwitz is an important goal of Delbo's writing throughout the trilogy, a point that a poem from the second volume of the trilogy highlights well. Delbo remarks in the final six lines of the poem titled "Ce point sur la carte" that

> Today people know
> have known for several years
> that this dot on the map
> is Auschwitz
> This much they know
> as for the rest
> they think they know. (*Auschwitz and After* 138)[20]

> [Aujourd'hui on sait
> Depuis quelques années on sait
> On sait que ce point sur la carte
> c'est Auschwitz
> On sait cela
> Et pour le reste on croit savoir.] (*CI* 37)

Knowing what name to associate with an atrocious event, Delbo reflects, leads people to the highly problematic assumption that they know everything else about the experience of atrocity. But, as the poetic "I" stresses earlier in the poem, *not* knowing where one is or what is really happening is central to the experience that victims have in relation to historically traumatic events; for millions, the poetic "I" stresses, Auschwitz was "un lieu sans nom" (which translates, literally, as "a place without a name"), and the people shipped there did not know where they were when they arrived or when they were murdered. The larger importance of resisting the neat understandings that readers may unintentionally construct, in other words, is that doing so brings us closer to the position that victims inhabit during the experience of atrocity.[21] Delbo's writing does this here from the outset by refusing to lump all of the different images it associates with Auschwitz – including fire, soot, blood, ashes, and the colours red and black – under one master image that encompasses and explains them all. The repetition of the phrasing "ce point" (this spot) and the association of all of these images with the place named Auschwitz insist instead on the instability of Auschwitz as a site, and reject the knowledgeable perspective and categorizations that a process like naming can facilitate.

Ironies are a key device that Delbo's writing uses both to disrupt these neat understandings and to bring readers face-to-face with the horrors of atrocity. However, rather than promote readers' retreat into themselves as do the narrative techniques analysed by Trezise, these ironies push us instead to look *outside* of ourselves and *towards* others in order to interpret the world of the camps – a disposition that mirrors the way Delbo and her comrades approach their experience throughout *Auschwitz et après*. This is especially apparent in a passage from the first volume titled "Le lendemain," which describes a special roll call that the women of the camp must endure in the middle of winter. A woman collapses during the ordeal, and Delbo comments on the reaction that she and her comrades have to it:

> At our feet, a woman sits down awkwardly in the snow. We hold ourselves back from saying to her: "Not in the snow, you'll catch cold." It's another reflex that comes from memory and former notions. She sits down in the snow and digs a place out for herself. A memory from reading as a child, animals making themselves their own death beds. The woman busies herself with minute and precise gestures, lies down. Her face in the snow, she moans gently. Her hands go limp. She goes quiet.
>
> We looked without understanding.[22]

> [À nos pieds, une femme s'assoit dans la neige, maladroitement. On se retient de lui dire: "pas dans la neige, tu vas prendre froid." C'est encore un réflexe de la mémoire et des notions anciennes. Elle s'assoit dans la neige et s'y creuse une place. Un souvenir de lecture enfantine, les animaux qui font leur couche pour mourir. La femme s'affaire avec des gestes

> menus et précis, s'allonge. La face dans la neige, elle geint doucement. Ses mains se desserrent. Elle se tait.
>
> Nous avons regardé sans comprendre.] (*ANR* 54–5)

Unlike in the "Mannequins" passage, the understandings that Delbo offers us here are neither absurd nor inadequate. Thanks to the animal image evoked, we, as readers, can understand what is happening to this woman in spite of the fact that Delbo and her comrades could not when they initially witnessed her collapse. Yet this use of dramatic irony exerts a similar effect on readers as the instance of verbal irony examined above, because it disrupts the conceptualizations we bring with us to this text and forces us to look more intently at the event taking place before our eyes. While we realize that this woman is just about to die, it is not in a way that we might be familiar with people dying. We recognize, in other words, both the limits of our understandings of human behaviour and that we need to make new associations in order to construct new ones. This woman isn't old, she isn't being shot, she doesn't have any visible wounds, she doesn't appear to have an illness or disease that we know of that is causing her to suffer, and she hasn't indicated to us that she is about to die by speaking her final words. Our understanding of this woman's plight depends, rather, on our openness to associating it with something that we have not associated with it before, an association that deportees themselves were unable to make during their past experience, and that only emerges over time, presumably in the present of Delbo's writing.

At the same time, though, Delbo's use of irony in this passage cultivates in readers the same approach that she and her comrades took to this woman while in the camps. Their reaction is to repress an ethical reflex that has been conditioned by conceptualizations that no longer make sense in Auschwitz – they restrain themselves from telling the woman not to lie down – and to instead "look without understanding" in order to record what is taking place. By employing dramatic irony here, Delbo's writing both intensifies our bond with the members of the Convoy of January 24th and helps us move beyond the lack of understanding that they – and, by extension, we as readers – initially experience when faced with this gruesome scene. We relate to these deportees because, like us, they are initially unable to comprehend the collapsing woman's behaviour. But we are discouraged from fully identifying with their blindness, and from confining ourselves to their limited vision of the camps because, unlike them, we can grasp what is happening to this woman. Submission to the Convoy of January 24th's interpretations of Auschwitz is not the effect that Delbo's ironies seek to produce. Rather, these ironies promote our attentiveness to the events of the camps, and combat the closure that results from us clinging to what we know.

Delbo reflects more explicitly on the importance of renouncing our relationship with knowledge of the ethical throughout the second and third volumes of the trilogy. In several key instances, the narrator directly calls upon readers' understandings of the human in order to demolish them, and then refuses to offer a fixed notion that would take their place. These interventions also disrupt the flow of each of the passages in which they appear, as Delbo interrupts her reflections on other aspects of camp life in order to issue them. For instance, while thinking through some of the differences between the living conditions of male and female political deportees interned in the Nazi system, and how these conditions affected deportees' mental faculties, the narrator breaks off her discussion to directly address readers:

> You will say that everything can be taken from a human being except the ability to think and imagine. You do not know. A human being can be made into a skeleton gurgling with diarrhea, the time and strength needed to think taken away. The imaginary realm is the first luxury that comes with having a body that gets enough food, enjoys a bit of free time, possesses the rudimentary things needed to cobble together dreams. In Auschwitz, people didn't dream, they were in a state of delirium.[23]

> [Vous direz qu'on peut tout enlever à un être humain sauf sa faculté de penser et d'imaginer. Vous ne savez pas. On peut faire d'un être humain un squelette où gargouille la diarhée, lui ôter le temps de penser, la force de penser. L'imaginaire est le premier luxe du corps qui reçoit assez de nourriture, jouit d'une frange de temps libre, dispose de rudiments pour façonner les rêves. À Auschwitz, on ne rêvait pas, on délirait.] (*CI* 90)

To disrupt readers' understandings of the human here, Delbo attaches the word "human being" to an image from camp life that falls outside of the categorizations she believes they bring with them to the text. Rather than classify a skeleton gurgling with diarrhea as non-human – the kind of response that serves as the point of departure for Agamben's rethinking of ethics after Auschwitz through the figure of the

Muselmann – she persists in using the word human for people who have passed into states not recognizable as human.

She disrupts the narrative and employs the word "human being" in a similar fashion in the third volume when explaining how the inhuman treatment deportees received in the camps stripped them of their ability to remember the past:

> You will say that everything can be taken from a human being except his or her memory. You do not know. When the quality "human being" is taken away, it's then that one's memory goes. One's memory peels off like tatters of burned skin. That one can survive in this stripped state is what you do not understand. It's what I don't know how to explain to you.[24]
>
> [Vous direz qu'on peut tout enlever à un être humain, tout sauf sa mémoire. Vous ne savez pas. On lui enlève d'abord sa qualité d'être humain et c'est alors que sa mémoire le quitte. Sa mémoire s'en va par lambeaux de peau brûlée. Qu'ainsi dépouillé il survive, c'est ce que vous ne comprenez pas. C'est ce que je ne sais pas vous expliquer.] (*MNJ* 44)

"Human being" is used here to refer both to an individual person and to a quality with which others endow that individual person. "Human being," that is, refers not just to a categorization, but also a kind of relation, one that, when not maintained with others, strips them of the characteristics that people recognize as human. Human beings must be *treated* as humans in order to *be* humans, Delbo tells us – this after her writing has already been guiding us, albeit covertly, to recognize as human those individuals who no longer fit into many people's categorizations.

For most readers, however, it is hard to feel directly called out by the narrator in these moments, because, throughout *Auschwitz et après*, we have already been so distanced from people who are incapable of recognizing humanity. In particular, through the ironies employed early on in the trilogy, Delbo's writing gradually guides us to see others as human by teaching us how to look while feeling terrified and repulsed. The narrator draws us into the world of the camps and makes us complicit in her way of looking at it before overtly demolishing any definitions of the human we may have. This makes us feel more aligned with her in these moments than it does with the "you" she denounces, which keeps us from withdrawing into ourselves or becoming defensive, and helps us remain open to the changes in our behaviours that Delbo's writing seeks to enact.

Auschwitz et après is, in fact, full of examples of deportees maintaining these kinds of human relations with people who no longer appear "human" and, in line with the rest of the text, their ability to do this is always presented as an ordinary feat. This, of course, is a crucial difference between Delbo's theoretical reflections on the camps and Agamben's. While Agamben confines the ability to treat others decently to a select group of dignified and faithful people whom he deems incapable of bearing witness to the reality of the camps, Delbo's writing makes readers see that being there for others – and bearing witness to others – is possible once we learn how to look at gruesome things. Being there for others is not about faith or strength or some other extraordinary capacity that all do not possess. The ethical is an ordinary response that each of us must improvise in our interactions with others. It depends on our attentiveness to victims and our engagement in the outside world, not on our mastery of any concept, our moral or physical strength, or our adherence to any idealized code.

But the point of Delbo's testimony is not to valorize deportees for their exemplary behaviour towards others or to demonize those who retreat into themselves. Rather, her writing endeavours to gain recognition for the strength and resolve of incomprehensible figures like the *Muselmänner*, and to make readers see protecting them as a matter of routine. These points are repeatedly emphasized in two short narratives from the trilogy in which she reflects on how extreme dehydration caused her to become one of the *Muselmänner* in the early stages of her internment in Auschwitz.[25] Titled "La soif" and "Boire," both describe the *Muselmann*'s experience in ways that directly contradict Agamben's reflections, and portray a deportee community that does not lose its sense of responsibility towards such figures. In "La soif," Delbo recounts how her face and her actions indicated to others that she was no longer capable of understanding what was required of her by the Nazi system:

> My comrades considered me mad. Lulu would say: "Take care of yourself. You know that here you must stay on your guard. You'll get yourself killed." I paid no attention. My friends never left me alone and they said to each other: "We must look out for C., she's crazy. She does not see the kapos, the S.S., the dogs. She just stands there, looking vague, instead of working. She doesn't understand when they shout, wanders off anywhere. They'll kill her." They were afraid for me, they were afraid to look at me with those crazed eyes I had then. They believed I was mad and probably I was. I can remember nothing about those weeks. (*Auschwitz and After* 72–3)

[Mes camarades me croyaient folle. Lulu me disait: "Fais attention à toi. Tu sais bien qu'ici il faut toujours être sur le qui-vive. Tu te feras tuer." Je n'entendais pas. Elles ne me quittaient plus et elles disaient entre elles: "Il faut veiller sur C., elle est folle. Elle ne voit pas les kapos, ni les SS, ni les chiens. Elle reste plantée, le regard vague, au lieu de travailler. Elle ne comprend pas quand ils crient, elle va n'importe où. Ils la tueront." Elles avaient peur pour moi, elles avaient peur de me regarder avec ces yeux fous que j'avais. Elles me croyaient folle et sans doute l'étais-je. Je ne me suis rien rappelé de ces semaines-là.] (*ANR* 119)

Unlike the descriptions of deportee behaviour that serve as the basis for Agamben's understanding of ethics after Auschwitz, Delbo's comrades become most attentive to others when they appear unresponsive to their environment. No doubt, the members of Delbo's group are disturbed by her behaviour and unable to understand it, but they respond by being afraid *for* her and moving to protect her, not recoiling in fear and turning a blind eye from her. Their reactions, of course, echo those that Delbo's writing promotes in readers through the confrontations it repeatedly stages with gruesome images of the human. *Auschwitz et après* ultimately guides us to participate in the kind of community that Delbo and her comrades formed while in the camps, but it does this by cultivating our attentiveness to others, not by presenting these women as exemplary models for us to imitate, emulate, and subject ourselves to.

Delbo's reflections on this period of her internment further make clear that the unresponsiveness of the *Muselmänner* results not – as the male deportees cited by Agamben conclude – because they lose their will to live, but rather because they become physically incapable of making their needs apparent to others.[26] Delbo characterizes her own experience of this as a state in which she could no longer make her body perform in ways that others could read as signs of her resolve. In the early stages of her dehydration, her inability to make her mouth muscles work so she could speak gave her the feeling "d'être morte et de le savoir" – which literally translates as "being dead and knowing it." Delbo's straightforward, minimal phrasing is rendered by Lamont's translation as "the full awareness of the state of being dead":

The others say: "She's mad. She's gone mad during the night." They summon words capable of recalling reason. An explanation is owed them, but lips decline to move. The muscles of the mouth want to attempt articulation and do not articulate. Such is the despair of the powerlessness that grips me, the full awareness of the state of being dead.[27] (*Auschwitz and After* 70)

[Les autres disent: "Elle est folle, elle est devenue folle pendant la nuit," et elles font appel aux mots qui doivent réveiller la raison. Il faudrait leur expliquer. Les lèvres s'y refusent. Les muscles de la bouche veulent tenter les mouvements de l'articulation et n'articulent pas. Et c'est le désespoir de l'impuissance à leur dire l'angoisse qui m'a étreinte, l'impression d'être morte et de le savoir.] (*ANR* 115)

At least for part of this experience, Delbo's mind is still capable of processing what's going on in her environment even though her body's movements don't seem to show it, and no amount of will on her part can make her body obey. In the later stages of her dehydration, her mental faculties become almost completely annihilated by her need for water, and she can only respond to her environment in instinctual ways. "Only the thought of water kept me alert" [Seule l'idée de l'eau me tenait en éveil (*CI* 44)], Delbo reflects (*Auschwitz and After* 143), and the sight of the smallest puddle was enough to make her go crazy and throw herself at it, even if SS guards and their dogs were waiting to attack. Yet while her comrades can understand none of this based on her appearance – unlike readers, who are led by Delbo's writing to see people in this position as fighting to survive, Delbo's comrades classify her as crazy at the time all this is happening – they continue to look at her and protect her, to treat her as human. It is a reflexive response that the group has to unresponsiveness, a reaction that keeps them from withdrawing into their ready-made concepts and keeps them turned towards others and engaged in their surroundings.

Delbo and Agamben clearly base their respective theorizations on the behaviour of two radically different groups, and two radically different witnesses, that were interned in Auschwitz.[28] But my analysis here suggests that there is more at stake in their differences than the fact that different survivors cannot be expected to see things in the exact same way. While Agamben's rethinking of the ethical recognizes that figures like the *Muselmänner* should not be excluded from our definitions of the human, it does not further recognize what is distinct about this state of being, and what is so problematic about the way the relatively healthy respond to it. People do not necessarily lose their will to live because they lose their ability to speak, and they are not necessarily beyond help when their bodies move in unfamiliar or "undignified" ways. As Agamben's work demonstrates, however, these are understandings that have been voiced by many concentration camp survivors in addition to Primo Levi.[29] But these are collective misunderstandings that cause us to ignore people in need, and to deny the reality of what they experience. *Auschwitz et après* stresses that these assumptions about unresponsiveness need to be corrected, just as we must correct the definitions of the human upon which they are based. The fact is that human bodies do not always obey a human's will, and our reflexive response cannot continue to be abandoning people who are most in need of our help because the sight of them makes *us* feel horror, disgust, or shame. Turning away from others may be an understandable reaction when faced with the horrors of atrocity. But to continue to declare that our responsibilities to others end with our conceptualizations is to condemn people in extreme states of suffering to a social death well before they have reached their physical point of no return, and to an agonizing solitude that no one should have to bear, especially when surrounded by ethically minded others. As much as we may feel for and admire the strength of survivors like Jorge Semprun, their actions abandon deportees like Maurice Halbwachs in the face of death, no matter how much their theoretical commentaries try to cover it up.[30]

Of course, *Auschwitz et après* acknowledges that being there for others is not something that everyone is in a position to do, and that deportees should not be condemned for their failures. Delbo painfully describes how her own extreme thirst, for example, causes her to lose sight of people in need, a fact that mortifies her when she comes back to her senses after her daily quest for water. Commenting on her blindness to the plight of a young woman in her convoy named Aurore who is also suffering from extreme thirst, Delbo writes:

> Lucidity returns, and my sense of sight – and I see little Aurore [...] She does not have the strength to go down to the stream [...] Every morning, she places herself near me. She's hoping I'll leave her a few drops in the bottom of my tin cup. Why would I give her any of my water? She's going to die no matter what. She waits. Her eyes beg and I do not look at her. I feel her thirsty eyes on me, and the pain in her eyes when I hook my tin cup back on my belt. Life returns to me and I'm ashamed. And every morning I do not feel the supplication of her look and of her lips that have been discolored by thirst, and every morning I'm ashamed after drinking.[31]

> [La lucidité revient, et le regard – et je vois la petite Aurore [...] Elle n'a pas la force de descendre au ruisseau [...] Chaque matin, elle se met près de moi. Elle espère que je lui laisserai quelques gouttes au fond de ma gamelle. Pourquoi lui donnerais-je de mon eau? Aussi bien elle va mourir. Elle attend. Ses yeux implorent et je ne la regarde pas. Je sens sur moi ses yeux de soif, la douleur à ses yeux quand je remets la gamelle à ma ceinture. La vie revient en moi et j'ai honte. Et chaque matin je reste insensible à la supplication de son regard et de ses lèvres décolorées par la soif, et chaque matin, j'ai honte après avoir bu.] (*ANR* 118–19)

But while, to paraphrase Agamben, *Auschwitz et après* bears witness to Delbo's shame and disorder in a moment like this, it also makes clear that her behaviour is not exemplary or something to model our own after. We are discouraged throughout Delbo's writing from looking at deportees as extraordinary models to follow, and *Auschwitz et après* never seeks to excuse Delbo's behaviour, nor to valorize her for it. However, Delbo's writing also makes clear that, unlike the relatively healthy deportees who retreat into themselves at the sight of the non-human, her blindness to others in this context is caused by physiological factors that are beyond her control. Delbo's irresponsibility occurs because her senses are annihilated by her extreme dehydration, not because, like Agamben's witness, she sees someone else's undoing as the occasion for her own.[32]

Male deportees are, in fact, the only group that *Auschwitz et après* routinely depicts as incapable of helping others in the Nazi system. And several passages indicate that this is because the experience of the camps confronts them with the failure of their conceptualizations of the ethical, which causes all of them to withdraw from the outside world. A series of short narratives titled "Les hommes" that are placed throughout the first two volumes offer particularly haunting and heartbreaking examples of the impotence and closure that takes hold of the men interned in Auschwitz. Like it does when confronting readers with gruesome images of the human, Delbo's writing bears witness to the men's courage and resolve, and offers no explicit commentary on the morality of their actions. In the first of these passages, the men of Auschwitz refuse to look at anyone in Delbo's group when they cross paths on their way to and from the marshes they all work in every day. In another, we see that the men also cannot look at each other during their collective punishments: they all stand in silence and avoid eye contact with each other while waiting to be castrated, each one of them with a look of revolt and resignation in his eyes, each one of them alone.

Delbo believes their blindness and paralysis to be a result of how much they suffer from not being able to act in heroic and individualistic ways, an explanation she offers at the beginning of *Une connaissance inutile*:

> They experienced, more than anything else, the feeling of being diminished in strength and of not being able to perform their duty as men, because they couldn't do anything for the women. If we suffered from seeing them unhappy, famished, deprived, they suffered even more from no longer being in a position to protect us, to defend us, to assume full responsibility for destiny on their own.[33]
>
> [Ils éprouvaient, plus aigu que tout autre, le sentiment d'être diminués dans leur force et dans leur devoir d'hommes, parce qu'ils ne pouvaient rien pour les femmes. Si nous souffrions de les voir malheureux, affamés, dénués, ils souffraient davantage encore de ne plus être en mesure de nous protéger, de nous défendre, de ne plus assumer seuls le destin.] (*CI* 10)

The men of Auschwitz are too physically weak to perform the "duties of men" by themselves, as individuals – something unavoidable given the miserable conditions of their internment – and they respond to this fact by closing themselves off to everyone around them. But this turning inward reduces everyone's chances of survival, a fact that hits home in descriptions of the chaos that ensues after Delbo and her comrades toss them pieces of bread during one of the brief moments in which they pass by each other. "They capture the bread, fight over it, grab it away from each other. They have eyes like wolves. Two of them roll in the ditch, the bread falling out of reach./ We watch them fight and we cry [...] They did not turn their heads towards us"[34] [Ils attrapent le pain, se le disputent, se l'arrachent. Ils ont des yeux de loup. Deux roulent dans le fossé avec le pain qui s'échappe./ Nous les regardons se battre et nous pleurons [...] Ils n'ont pas tourné la tête envers nous (*ANR* 36)].

The final passage of *Auschwitz et après* invokes the memory of these men and specifically links their closure to an understanding of the ethical that was shattered by the camp experience. In a poem titled "Envoi," the narrator takes up a line about a man's duty to others spoken by the Beggar of Jean Giraudoux's play *Électre*[35] – one of several works that Giraudoux authored in the interwar period that heavily influenced the ethics of the French Resistance – and calls on the Beggar never to say it again:

> *A man ready to die for another*
> *that's something to look for*
> don't say this any longer Beggar
> don't say it
> there are thousands
> who stepped forward for all the others
> for you too
> Beggar
> so that you can salute the dawn
> the livid dawn
> of all the Mont Valériens
> and now
> it is called break of day
> Beggar
> this dawn stained by their blood. (*Auschwitz and After* 354)[36]
>
> [*Un homme qui meurt pour un autre homme*
> *cela se cherche*
> ne dis plus cela Mendiant
> ne le dis plus
> ils sont des milliers
> qui se sont avancés pour tous les autres
> pour toi aussi
> Mendiant
> pour que tu salues l'aurore
> l'aube était livide
> aux matins des mont-valérien
> et maintenant
> cela s'appelle l'aurore
> Mendiant
> c'est l'aube avec leur sang.] (*MNJ* 214)

We recognize again here the summation and summons structure identified by Chambers as a way *Auschwitz et après* calls upon the living and pays tribute to the dead. Delbo asks Giraudoux's Beggar to remember the sacrifices people made so that he could live to "salute the dawn" – specifically, the sacrifices of the men who died at Mont Valérien, a fortress near Paris where men of the Resistance, including Delbo's husband Georges Dudach, were executed throughout the Occupation[37] – but she also commands the Beggar to renounce his belief in people dying for others because this does not bring about the ideal world that they envision. The clunky phrasing in the last line of the poem marks the end of this and all neat conceptualizations by insisting on a demystified vision of the present moment, and suggests, in the process, that we approach the ethical differently in the post-Auschwitz world. The present moment is called a "dawn," but it is also "l'aube avec leur sang" which, more literally translated, would be "daybreak with their blood," not "dawn stained with their blood." This phrasing distances the poem's final line, and its overall objectives, from the ideological connotations that the word "dawn" [*aurore*] had for communist militants in the Resistance, who conceived of their aim in the fight against fascism as bringing about a "new dawn" [*nouvelle aurore*].[38] The replacement of the word "*aurore*" with "*aube*" implies a rejection of the idealized and politicized notion of a "dawn," and, moreover, that we must not neatly cover up the past with these idealized visions if we are to remember the dead and acknowledge their suffering. The way Delbo's writing makes Giraudoux's Beggar confront this fact further echoes the process employed throughout the trilogy to lead readers to share in her understanding of responsibility. To see responsibility you must see beyond the limits of your knowledge, and respond to the gruesome by including its disorder in your vision.

This characterization *Auschwitz et après* offers of men who retreat within themselves when faced with the limits of their conceptualizations can further be seen as analogous to the potential response Delbo's writing seeks to ward off in readers. The strategies employed to open us up and place the challenges of the camps within our reach seem intent on not making us feel like failures for not initially knowing how to respond. *Auschwitz et après* does not directly call us out for our inadequacies, but rather guides us past them, which keeps us from withdrawing into ourselves or succumbing to paralysis. There is no shame in finding ourselves in situations that confront us with our limits. But we can only come to see where our responsibilities lie if, like the women of Delbo's convoy, we look at others rather than retreat from them when inhabiting this unstable position.

2 Witnessing

There is a connection between Agamben's understanding of the *Muselmann*'s importance for ethics after Auschwitz and the ethically problematic behaviour recorded in Jorge Semprun's works that bears consideration. Both cases confront us with approaches to the Nazi camps that exclude the experiences of less privileged deportees from their theoretical visions. The narrators of Semprun's texts claim to articulate theoretical understandings of the shared experience of *all* survivors (a claim that most critics have not challenged). But, in passages that contain less articulate or relatively less healthy deportees, his texts themselves continuously expose the limits of these theories and the limits of their narrators as "masterful" witnesses to the camps. Events like the "death" of Maurice Halbwachs (see chapter 1 pp. 45–53) and interactions with survivors like Manuel Azaustre (see chapter 2 pp. 71–4), for example, demonstrate that Semprun's narrators retreat into theory in order to distance themselves from aspects of their experiences that they do not know how to face. The effect of this approach is that it exerts a sort of conceptual and epistemic hegemony that represses and denies the existence of experiences that fall outside of its bounds. When something or someone does not fit into the narrator's conceptualizations in one of Semprun's texts, he wipes it out, forgets it, or turns a blind eye. He does this because of the anxiety he feels at not knowing how to respond to atrocity, both in his past experience and when confronting it after the camps, through memory.

We see the same epistemic habit at work in Agamben's understanding of our ethical obligations to others that emerges from his work on the witness-*Muselmann* relation. While Agamben recognizes the shortcomings of the understandings that deportees entered the camps with in a way that Semprun's narrators do not, the solution he proposes – elaborating a new, more total concept of the human through Levi's acts of witnessing – sets us up to always lose sight of our responsibilities to others when we are exposed to the limits of our conceptualizations of the human. One consequence of Agamben's model is that, whenever we do not have a *definition* of the human to motivate our ethical responses, we reach a zone in which behaving responsibly is no longer possible – "the inhuman and human enter into a zone of indistinction," Agamben writes, "one in which it is impossible to establish the position of the subject" and, as such, to assume our responsibilities towards others (*Remnants* 120).[39] To this, Agamben further adds a totalizing and nihilistic understanding of precisely how we react to the failure of our concepts: in these limit moments, we respond by closing ourselves off in shame and withdrawing from helping unresponsive others, because if *one* piece of our understanding of the ethical breaks, then *all* of our ethical reactions and practices break as well.[40]

Though in different ways and for different reasons, both Agamben and Semprun unwittingly institutionalize the practice of turning a blind eye when our frameworks fail: Semprun's narrators do this by claiming that everything fits into their theories even when it does not, and Agamben does this by arguing that while a better conceptualization that can account for what does not fit is being formed, turning away from our responsibilities is an unavoidable outcome.[41] I have been arguing here that Delbo's *Auschwitz et après* shows us the destructive consequences that hegemonic conceptions of the ethical like Agamben's and Semprun's exert on the deportee community through its implicit critique of the men of Auschwitz. By teaching us to look at and see our responsibilities towards gruesome forms of the human, Delbo's trilogy further strives to dismantle our desire to filter our surroundings, and less privileged others within them, through a universalizing and exclusionary ethical conception.

A rigid and reductive approach to the experience of the camps is not simply a theoretical concern. We can see it play out in concrete reality in postwar France. Ironically, though the camp experience has generally been identified with the Jewish experience of Auschwitz since the 1970s in France, postwar memory initially coalesced around the accounts of deported Resistance fighters. While Auschwitz was the largest killing centre of the Holocaust, and the camp where approximately 75,000 Jews from France were murdered,[42] Buchenwald – the destination for the vast majority of France's political deportees – was at the centre of the nation's understanding of the camp experience in the decades immediately following the Second World War. This status was due, in part, to the fact that the French state backed totalizing understandings of the French experience of the war that would help to unify a divided nation.[43] Henry Rousso, in particular, has shown that the French government first did this by not acknowledging the significant differences between what political deportees and Jews experienced at the hands of the Nazis, and then, beginning in the mid-1950s, by promoting the myth of the majority of the nation's heroic Resistance to Nazi Germany. The French state's response to the emergence of Jewish memory in the 1970s has provided yet another universalizing response – the ethical "devoir de mémoire" that dominates the public sphere to this day.[44]

But survivor testimonies have contributed in their own way to the monolithic constructions that have gripped French society. As Annette

Wieviorka has noted, upon liberation, the well-organized communists of Buchenwald offered accounts of the camps that appealed to the needs of an audience whose country had recently been ravaged by war, occupation, and collaboration (*Auschwitz* 175). While they were not the only deportees speaking out, Buchenwald returnees were the dominant members of the survivor community, and their narratives offered heroic visions of resistance to the Nazis that the French public was eager to identify with, and that the French state was eager to disseminate.[45] Accounts of the Jewish experience of the camps have served a similar function since the emergence of Auschwitz as the primary site of memory in the 1970s. French society has come to identify the plight of Europe's Jews as a universal symbol of suffering, Bruno Chaouat has observed,[46] and all citizens – including former political deportees – routinely identify their own experiences of humiliation and shame with the Jewish experience of the camps instead of recognizing the differences between them and their particularities.[47]

While Michael Rothberg has argued that Delbo's testimonial writings seek to challenge the French state's "hegemony in controlling meaning" in order to "shape the terrain of politics" in postwar society ("Between Auschwitz and Algeria" 171, 162),[48] scholars have thus far ignored how Delbo's works combat the repressive ethics of the deportee community itself. Perhaps this is because Delbo's most obvious criticisms – and, in fact, those that open *Auschwitz et après* – are of people other than camp inmates who turn a blind eye to disaster victims. Two poems that appear just pages into *Aucun de nous ne reviendra* specifically identify Christians and "those who know" as groups who fail to acknowledge the suffering of others because of their rigid filters. "You who have wept two thousand years/for one who agonized three days and three nights," the poetic "I" declares in the first poem, "what tears will you have left/ for those who agonized/far more than three hundred nights and far more than three hundred days" (*Auschwitz and After* 10) [Vous qui avez pleuré deux mille ans/un qui a agonisé trois jours et trois nuits/quelles larmes aurez-vous/pour ceux qui ont agonisé/beaucoup plus de trois cents nuits et beaucoup plus de trois cents journées (*ANR* 20)]. Like Christians – who are incapable of feeling for deportees because of one fixed image of suffering that they recognize – the poetic "I" proposes on the following page that "those who know" turn a blind eye because language groups and binds distinct experiences of suffering under one single term. "[T]here is only one word for dread/one word for anguish," the poetic "I" tells "those who know" (*Auschwitz and After* 11) [il n'y a qu'un mot pour l'épouvante/qu'un mot pour l'angoisse] (*ANR* 21). But, as she goes on to state, "la souffrance n'a pas de limite" and "l'horreur pas de frontière" – the suffering and horrors of atrocity resist the limits and constraints that knowledge seeks to impose (*ANR* 22).

However, the same exclusionary dispositions identified in these early passages are also at work in the deportee community – specifically, among the men of Auschwitz and the Resistance – as portrayed later in the trilogy. *Auschwitz et après* advances a broad critique of the blindness that results from seeking out rigid forms of understanding, but it does this in part, I argue, in order to divert readers' attention from the fact that groups other than those named are also its targets. Denouncing the behaviour of other groups allows Delbo's writing to address the faults of deportees without putting readers on the defensive, because it points out the more obviously problematic behaviour of non-deportees, and does not deny camp internees the recognition they deserve. This further lays the groundwork for the critique that is implicit throughout *Auschwitz et après*, and helps to open readers up to the changes that Delbo's ironies seek to enact.

And yet modifying the responses that male political deportees offer to atrocity poses a particular set of challenges. As the works of Delbo and Semprun demonstrate, because they recognize that their knowledge has not prepared them to respond, the men of the camps become paralysed and withdrawn when faced with the horrors of the camps. This closure is further exacerbated by the fact that, within their communities, acting in the interest of others actually depends on being able to confirm pre-established understandings that all of their participants share. The classic way in which the major political movements of the twentieth century aroused their members' desire to engage in a given cause, Jacques Rancière observes, was to deploy images of what they deemed intolerable about the state of the world, which would provoke a crisis of conscience in militants that would move them to change it (*Emancipated* 103). But, for this effect to be generated, militants need to already be convinced that what they are seeing is, in fact, intolerable (84–5). Put somewhat differently, what political militants share as a community is a particular way of reading the intolerable, where they seek to confirm meanings that they already associate with it and can only act upon such confirmation.

Auschwitz et après clearly leads us to see that the experience of the camps exposed the limits of this way of reading and responding to "the intolerable." As the final passage of Delbo's trilogy points out, the conceptualizations of ethical action that male political deportees brought with them to the camps no longer made sense in the Nazi order of things – actions like dying in the place of another were hardly possible in the camps because the Nazis would kill both people in such a situation, and did not bring about the objectives and the idealized worlds that those sacrificing their lives hoped would be the result of their struggle. Moreover, the forms of intolerable suffering that deportees witnessed with their own eyes in the camps actually resisted the larger meanings they wanted to find in them, leaving them in a position in which they felt called on to help others but despairing at not knowing how. A passage from the first volume of *Auschwitz et après* titled "Un jour" that documents the death of a Jewish woman after she breaks rank, falls into a ditch, and is mauled to death by an SS dog during roll call because of life-threatening dehydration – a woman, in other words, who has become one of the *Muselmänner* – illustrates all of these crises well. A close consideration of it will lead us back to our discussion of how the trilogy frames the question of responsibility in the camps and after.

"Un jour" describes two distinct attempts on Delbo's part to bear witness to this woman's horrifying ordeal – the first resulting in Delbo turning a blind eye, the second in her forging a connection with the dying woman – as well as the destabilizing effects of finding herself confronted with the intolerable and not knowing how to respond. Her narration uses different subject pronouns – "on" (one), "nous" (we), and "je" (I) – to register various, conflicting understandings that traverse her gaze in this encounter, two of which – "on" and "nous" – influence her initial attempt to bear witness. The first responses to appear in the passage belong to the subject "on," whose reading is juxtaposed with descriptions of the woman trying to crawl out of the ditch:

> She was taut from her index finger to her toes but every time she lifted a hand to cling to something higher and try to climb up the embankment, she would fall. Her body became slack and pitiful. Then she would lift her head and *one could follow on her face the mental work being done inside of her in order to readjust her body parts for another try* [...]
>
> Each of her movements was so slow and awkward, so glaringly weak, that *one wondered how she was even able to move*. At the same time, *one found it difficult to grasp that she needed to put such an enormous effort into the entire enterprise, which seemed so out of proportion given that her body must have weighed almost nothing*.[49] (my emphasis)

> [Elle était arc-boutée de l'index à l'orteil mais chaque fois qu'elle soulevait une main pour s'agripper plus haut et essayer de gravir le talus, elle retombait. Son corps devenait flasque, misérable. Puis elle relevait la tête et *on suivait sur son visage le travail mental qui se faisait au-dedans d'elle-même pour réajuster ses membres à l'effort* [...]
>
> Chacun de ses gestes était si lent et si maladroit, si criant de débilité, *qu'on se demandait comment elle pouvait seulement bouger*. En même temps, *on comprenait mal qu'il lui fallût se donner une peine aussi disproportionnée à l'entreprise, aussi disproportionnée à ce corps qui ne devait rien peser*.] (*ANR* 40–1; my emphasis)

"On"'s immediate response to this woman is to attempt to imagine her "mental work" and "effort." Delbo's description of the scene switches to the present and attempts to narrate the woman's thoughts:

> She turns her head as though to assess the route, looks upward. One sees a growing bewilderment in her eyes, in her hands, in her contorted face.
>
> "What are all of those women doing looking at me in that way? Why are they there and why are they lined up in close ranks and why do they stay standing there immobile? They are looking at me and they seem not to see me. They cannot see me, they wouldn't just stand there otherwise. They would help me get up. Why don't you help me, you who are there, so close? Help me. Pull me up. Lean towards me. Hold out your hand. Oh, they won't move."[50]

> [Elle tourne la tête comme pour mesurer le chemin, regarde vers le haut. On voit grandir l'égarement dans ses yeux, dans ses mains, dans son visage convulsé.
>
> "Qu'ont-elles toutes ces femmes à me regarder ainsi? Pourquoi sont-elles là et pourquoi sont-elles rangées en lignes serrées et pourquoi restent-elles là immobiles? Elle me regardent et elles semblent ne pas me voir. Elles ne me voient pas, elles ne resteraient pas ainsi plantées. Elles m'aideraient à remonter. Pourquoi ne m'aidez-vous pas, vous qui êtes là si près? Aidez-moi. Tirez-moi. Penchez-vous. Tendez la main. Oh, elles ne bougent pas."] (*ANR* 41–2)

In light of reflections advanced elsewhere in *Auschwitz et après,* this interior monologue projected by "on" testifies to a lack of understanding of the *Muselmann*'s struggle as Delbo's testimony conceives of it. "On" reads the look on the woman's face as indicative of a mounting sense of despair at her fellow inmates' failure to help her, however Delbo consistently describes the *Muselmänner* as figures who are desperately fighting on their own to survive.

The passage then shifts to a description of the group of female deportees who are looking at the woman's ordeal from their position within rank at roll call. The second understanding that traverses Delbo's gaze is an effect of this collective order – an understanding associated with the subject pronoun "nous." Delbo's writing emphasizes her community's own struggle to remain upright in the freezing cold before returning to its account of the woman's plight:

> We were all there, several thousand of us, standing up in the snow ever since morning – that's what night is called here, since morning starts at three AM. Daybreak had lit up the snow just like the snow lit up the night – and the cold grew even more bitter.
>
> Immobile since the middle of the night, we were becoming so heavy on our legs that we were sinking into the earth, into the ice, unable to do anything to fight off the numbness [...]
>
> We were there, immobile, several thousand women who spoke all the languages of the world, packed tightly one against another, lowering our heads under the bursts of stinging snow.
>
> We were there, immobile, reduced to nothing but the beating of our hearts.
>
> Where is she going, the one who has broken rank? She's walking like a disabled or blind person, a blind person who looks around. She heads straight for the ditch as though walking on wooden legs. She's on the edge, crouches down to lower herself in. She falls. Her foot slipped on the collapsing snow. Why does she want to go in the ditch? She left our ranks without the slightest hesitation, without hiding herself from the SS officer standing stiff in her black cape, stiff in her black boots, who is watching over us. She took off as though she were somewhere else, in a street where she would be crossing from one sidewalk to another, or in a garden. To evoke a garden here is laughable. Perhaps better, one of those crazy old women who scare children in public parks. She's a young woman, almost a girl. Such frail shoulders.[51]

> [Nous étions là toutes, plusieurs milliers, debout dans la neige depuis le matin – c'est ainsi qu'il faut appeler la nuit, puisque le matin était à trois heures de la nuit. L'aube avait éclairé la neige qui jusque-là éclairait la nuit – et le froid s'était accentué.

Immobiles depuis le milieu de la nuit, nous devenions si lourdes à nos jambes que nous enfoncions dans la terre, dans la glace, sans pouvoir rien contre l'engourdissement [...]

Nous étions là immobiles, quelques milliers de femmes de toutes les langues, serrées les unes contre les autres, baissant la tête sous les rafales de neige qui cinglaient.

Nous étions là immobiles, réduites au seul battement de nos cœurs.

Où va-t-elle, celle-ci qui quitte le rang? Elle marche en infirme ou en aveugle, un aveugle qui regarde. Elle se dirige vers le fossé d'une démarche en bois. Elle est au bord, s'accroupit pour descendre. Elle tombe. Son pied a glissé sur la neige qui s'éboule. Pourquoi veut-elle descendre dans le fossé? Elle a quitté le rang sans hésiter, sans se cacher de la SS droite dans sa pèlerine noire, droite sur ses bottes noires, qui nous garde. Elle s'en est allée comme si elle était ailleurs, dans une rue où elle changerait de trottoir, ou dans un jardin. D'évoquer un jardin ici peut faire rire. Peut-être une de ces vieilles folles qui font peur aux enfants dans les squares. C'est une femme jeune, une jeune fille presque. Des épaules si frêles.] (*ANR* 42–3)

In stark contrast to the "mental work" that "on" projects onto this woman's struggle, "nous" responds by paying attention solely to her actions and her body and does not attempt to portray her inner thoughts. "Nous" raises questions about the woman's behaviour – indeed, expressing bewilderment at them – and associates it with figures that act in similar ways outside of the camp while presenting them in a manner that emphasizes the uncertainty of her interpretations. The woman broke rank "as if" [*comme si*] she were somewhere else and is "maybe" [*peut-être*] like a crazy old woman, neither of which becomes a definitive explanation for what Delbo is witnessing or serves as an endpoint to her attempt to understand.

Still, *not* understanding the woman's behaviour while also feeling called on to help her causes Delbo to feel increasingly anxious, which eventually causes her to look away and withdraw from the entire scene:

I no longer look at her. I no longer want to look at her. I want to change places, no longer see. No longer see those holes at the bottom of her eyesockets, those staring holes. What does she want to do? Does she want to reach the barbed wire fence? Why is she staring at us? Isn't she pointing me out? Imploring me? I turn my head. Look elsewhere. Elsewhere.[52]

> [Je ne la regarde plus. Je ne veux plus la regarder. Je voudrais changer de place, ne plus voir. Ne plus voir ces trous au fond des orbites, ces trous qui fixent. Que veut-elle faire? Veut-elle atteindre les barbelés électriques? Pourquoi nous fixe-t-elle? N'est-ce pas moi qu'elle désigne? Moi qu'elle implore? Je tourne la tête. Regarder ailleurs. Ailleurs.] (*ANR* 44)

Delbo's attempt to bear witness ends with her interrupting the passage to refer to the context in which her present act of writing takes place. "And now I am in a café writing this story – for it becomes a story"[53] [Et maintenant je suis dans un café à écrire cette histoire – car cela devient une histoire (*ANR* 45)].

Delbo's account of her struggle to understand and her subsequent retreat into herself in this portion of the passage offers crucial insights into the problematic behaviours within the deportee community that *Auschwitz et après* strives to change. Most obviously – and to return to Agamben's reflections on the question of responsibility in the camps – Delbo clearly does not withdraw from her surroundings in this instance because she abandons her responsibilities to others. Rather, her closure results from being unable to negotiate feeling called on to help while also recognizing that this confrontation demolishes her understandings of the intolerable. We see throughout the passage that "on" fails to grasp what the *Muselmänner* experience and that Delbo is aware of it – the questions Delbo asks herself when she eventually looks away call attention to her failure to comprehend – and that the descriptive and questioning response "nous" offers is unable to repair "on"'s deficiencies. However, in stark contrast to Semprun's testimonies or Agamben's theorization of witnessing, Delbo's writing does not seek to conceal her inadequacies or her incapacities when responding to this woman's suffering. Instead, it documents the destabilization of Delbo's frameworks and acknowledges the anxiety that she experiences because of the conflicting readings that traverse her gaze. The challenge for witnesses, in other words, is to inhabit this space between an understanding that is unravelling and one that is not yet formed, and to remain engaged in their surroundings in the face of such instability.

Moreover, Delbo's insistence on this event's status as a story clearly links her act of witnessing to the act of reading, and implies, in so doing, that her attempt to bear witness here allegorizes the challenges that readers also encounter throughout *Auschwitz et après* – a text which, I have been arguing, seeks to divest readers of their desire for rigid and stable meanings. This collapses the distinction between the acts of witnessing and reading in the trilogy and further highlights a way in which Delbo's writing strives to combat the exclusionary responses of the deportee community. Delbo's writing registers the failure of both "on" and "nous" to account for the woman's experience, but it also encourages us to relate differently to the way each approaches the act of witnessing – and, by extension, the act of reading. "On" immediately reads this woman's struggle based on the assumption that it understands what she is going through: "on" cannot look at this woman without simultaneously reading her actions as signs of her inner thoughts and attempting to give voice to them, seeking to confirm and project understandings that it has already formed about her state in a way that echoes the militant way of reading as described by Rancière. In contrast, "nous" reads the woman's movements without assuming that it already understands: "nous" reads only what it can perceive from its exterior perspective, and tries to figure out what the woman is doing by raising questions and making associations. While neither "on" nor "nous" can account for her behaviour, "nous" does not claim to understand her experience or to speak in her place as "on" does, but rather approaches her situation as something singular and unknown that must be witnessed and recorded. Delbo's writing allows readers to see for themselves how "on"'s reading fails by gradually revealing "on"'s inadequacies, which keeps us from reducing this woman's experience or denying its existence because it falls outside of knowledge's bounds. This encourages us, in the process, to adopt "nous"'s open and searching disposition and to abandon "on"'s reductive one, which ultimately makes us more attentive to the woman that the passage describes, and less apt to seek confirmation of meanings we have already established. Delbo's writing seeks, in short, to cultivate "nous"'s epistemic habits as a witness in its readers while simultaneously distancing us from "on"'s mode of witnessing – that is, reading – atrocity.

"Un jour" further distances us from our desire for stable and definitive understandings of atrocity in its account of Delbo's second act of witnessing. In it, Delbo negotiates three different responses, and begins by adopting "nous"'s descriptive approach. Her narration underscores the atemporal nature of her act of witnessing, further linking her own position to the one readers occupy in relation to the camps:

> A flash. Is it afternoon? We have lost all sense of time. The sky appears. Very blue. A forgotten blue. Hours have passed since I succeeded in looking away from the woman in the ditch. Is she still there? She has reached the

top of the embankment – how was she able to? – and she has stopped there. Her hands are drawn to the glittering snow. She takes a handful of it and brings it to her lips in an exasperatingly slow gesture that she must be trying infinitely hard to make. *She sucks the snow. We understand why she broke rank, that resolute expression on her face. She wanted clean snow for her swollen lips.*[54] (my emphasis)

[Une éclaircie. Est-ce l'après-midi? Nous avons perdu le sentiment du temps. Le ciel apparaît. Très bleu. D'un bleu oublié. Des heures se sont écoulées depuis que j'ai réussi à ne plus regarder la femme dans le fossé. Y est-elle encore? Elle a atteint le haut du talus – comment a-t-elle pu? – et elle s'est arrêtée là. Ses mains sont attirées par la neige qui scintille. Elle en prend une poignée qu'elle porte à ses lèvres avec un geste d'une lenteur exaspérante qui doit lui coûter une peine infinie. *Elle suce la neige. Nous comprenons pourquoi elle a quitté le rang, cette résolution sur ses traits. Elle voulait de la neige propre pour ses lèvres tuméfiées.*] (*ANR* 45; my emphasis)

"Nous" is finally able to construct an understanding of the woman's experience once her actions are completed; "nous" understands that the woman is suffering from dehydration after seeing her put snow in her mouth, a conclusion that can easily be drawn by anyone who is able to look at her and remain engaged. A second understanding emerges when Delbo links the woman's actions to a memory from her own childhood in which she witnessed her family dog's death – an association that recalls her description of the collapsing woman in "Le lendemain":

She sucks her snow but she seems to no longer want it. Snow doesn't quench your thirst when you have a fever. All of that work for a handful of salt. Her hand drops, her neck buckles. A fragile stem that should break at any minute. Her back hunches, with her shoulder blades protruding through the worn fabric of her coat. It's a yellow coat, the yellow of our dog Flac who had become so thin after his sickness, and whose entire body curved to look like the skeleton of a bird in a museum just before he died. This woman is going to die.[55]

[Elle suce sa neige mais elle semble n'en avoir plus envie. Cela ne désaltère pas, la neige, quand on a la fièvre. Tous ces efforts pour une poignée de sel. Sa main retombe, sa nuque ploie. Une tige fragile qui devrait se casser. Son dos s'arrondit, avec les omoplates qui ressortent sous l'étoffe mince du manteau. C'est un manteau jaune, du jaune de notre chien Flac qui était devenu tellement maigre après sa maladie et dont tout le corps s'arrondissait en squelette d'oiseau du muséum au moment qu'il allait mourir. La femme va mourir.] (*ANR* 45–6)

Delbo's writing becomes more disruptive and unstable towards the end of the passage as it records the competing visions that "on," "nous," and "je" all offer of the dying woman's plight. Each narratorial voice persists in its particular way of seeing: "on" projects a monologue onto the woman in which she is calling out to Delbo and her comrades for help and criticizing them for not acting; "nous" keeps describing the woman's movements without attempting to speak in her place, but now also categorizes her as someone who has passed into a state of physical degradation from which she can no longer be saved; "je"'s commentary draws deeper parallels between Delbo's childhood dog, Flac, and the woman dying before her eyes. Their contrasting visions are all documented in the text as Delbo and her comrades watch the woman go into convulsions, break rank for a second time, stagger directly towards an SS officer with her body so bent and arched that she appears she is about to fall, and be killed by his dog. Delbo's descriptions of the woman's final moments begin with "on"'s projected monologue and end without insisting on one single vision of the event:

"Why are you surprised that I'm walking? Didn't you hear him call me, him, the SS officer who is in front of the gate with his dog. You can't hear because you're dead."

The female SS officer in the black cape has left. Now it's a male SS officer in green who is in front of the gate.

The woman steps forward. *One would think she is obeying.* Right in the face of the SS officer, she stops. Her back shakes all over in endless shudders, her back is hunched with her shoulder blades protruding from beneath her yellow coat. The SS officer has his dog leashed. Did he give an order, make a sign? The dog lunges at the woman – without growling, without panting, without barking. It's silent like a dream. The dog leaps onto the woman, sinks its fangs into her neck. And we do not budge, stuck in something viscous that keeps us from making the slightest gesture – as in a dream. *The woman cries out. A shattering scream. A single scream that tears apart the immobility of the plain. We don't know if the scream comes from her or us, from her punctured throat or ours. I feel the dog's fangs at my throat. I scream. I howl. Not a sound comes out of me.* The silence of a dream.

The plain. The snow. The plain.

The woman collapses. One last jerk and it's over. Something snaps. The head in the muddy snow is nothing more now than a stump. Eyes make dirty wounds.

"All these dead women who are no longer looking at me." Mom, Flac is dead. He agonized for a long time. Then he dragged himself to the stoop. There was a moan that wasn't able to escape from his throat and he died. *One might have said that someone strangled him.*[56] (my emphasis)

["Pourquoi vous étonnez-vous que je marche? N'avez-vous pas entendu qu'il m'a appelée, lui, le SS qui est devant la porte avec son chien. Vous n'entendez pas parce que vous êtes mortes."

La SS en pèlerine noire est partie. Maintenant c'est un SS en vert qui est devant la porte.

La femme s'avance. *On croirait qu'elle obéit.* Face au SS, elle s'arrête. Son dos est secoué de frissons, son dos arrondi avec les omoplates qui saillent sous le manteau jaune. Le SS tient son chien en laisse. Lui a-t-il donné un ordre, fait un signe? Le chien bondit sur la femme – sans rugir, sans souffler, sans aboyer. C'est silencieux comme dans un rêve. Le chien bondit sur la femme, lui plante ses crocs dans la gorge. Et nous ne bougeons pas, engluées dans une espèce de visqueux qui nous empêche d'ébaucher même un geste – comme dans un rêve. *La femme crie. Un cri arraché. Un seul cri qui déchire l'immobilité de la plaine. Nous ne savons pas si le cri vient d'elle ou de nous, de sa gorge crevée ou de la nôtre. Je sens les crocs du chien à ma gorge. Je crie. Je hurle. Aucun son ne sort de moi.* Le silence du rêve.

La plaine. La neige. La plaine.

La femme s'affaisse. Un soubresaut et c'est fini. Quelque chose qui casse net. La tête dans la boue de neige n'est plus qu'un moignon. Les yeux font des plaies sales.

"Toutes ces mortes qui ne me regardent plus." Maman, Flac est mort. Il a agonisé longtemps. Puis il s'est traîné jusqu'au perron. Il y a eu un râle qui n'a pas pu sortir de sa gorge et il est mort. *On aurait dit qu'on l'avait étranglé.*] (*ANR* 47–8; my emphasis)

"Un jour" ends by once more reminding readers that Delbo's act of witnessing takes place from a future position outside of the camps, and distancing us from the world of the camps: "And now I am in a café writing this"[57] [Et maintenant je suis dans un café à écrire ceci (*ANR* 49)].

None of the interpretations offered in this portion of the passage prove adequate in accounting for this woman's horrifying experience, and yet Delbo displays none of the paralysis or closure that define the genre of testimony in the works of Agamben and Semprun. Delbo remains attentive to her surroundings and identifies so completely with the woman's death in this act of witnessing that she feels as though she has the SS dog's fangs at her own throat – this in spite of the woman becoming more and more stripped of her "human" qualities in the course of her ordeal, and in spite of the numerous instabilities – of space, of time, of meaning, of framing – that Delbo negotiates as a witness throughout. In light of her failure to bear witness documented earlier in "Un jour," we cannot help but see the drastically different approach she initially takes here as a contributing factor to her presence and her engagement. Delbo does not proceed from the assumption that she can understand this woman's inner thoughts or that she can narrate the scene as though experiencing it from the woman's position. Delbo's objectives here, in other words, are not to display her understandings or to confirm them, but rather to watch this event and record it, to continue to look in spite of her uncertainty. This requires negotiating the conflicting visions that traverse her gaze and disrupt her vision while she looks at this woman's horrifying ordeal. For Delbo, bearing witness means occupying this unstable position – it is not a matter of disciplining or of reducing another's experience, or of creating new conceptual spaces when confronting suffering. *Auschwitz et après* guides its readers, in turn, to approach victims in this humble and grounded way, and to pay attention to their suffering without subjecting it to the meanings or defensiveness that would exclude its singular nature.

For Delbo, then, bearing witness also means inhabiting a radically different "I" when faced with another's struggle than the "masterful" one in the works of a witness like Jorge Semprun. Fragmented and inadequate, Delbo's "I" asserts the impossibility of any one "I" offering a definitive account of incomprehensible human suffering. Her writing here and throughout the trilogy promotes a humbler approach to the act of witnessing, one that keeps us from losing sight of the people around us when their experiences do not coincide with the meanings we have elaborated in theory. The childhood memory she associates with this woman's suffering serves to separate the act of looking from understanding – what knowledgeable adult let alone child could claim to definitively understand the dying thoughts of a beloved family dog? Yet it further insists on her own, distinct position as a witness when confronting figures such as the *Muselmänner* – not, as Agamben insists, on a "zone of indistinction" in which her position as witness cannot be separated from theirs. Indeed, Delbo's horror when witnessing this woman's death comes not from *understanding* it but rather from *knowing that she does not know*, the kind of horror we may feel when we know that a loved one is suffering but cannot gain access to their thoughts or feelings. Delbo's is not an exemplary witness who claims to understand what the camps were all about. It is, rather, an *engaged* witness, one who refuses to reduce others to a category or definition or to look away from them because of his or her inadequacies.

Cultivating "dispositions of the body and mind where the eye does not know in advance what it sees and thought does not know what it should make of it," Jacques Rancière argues, is one way that works depicting intolerable events can modify the problematic responses of political militants and produce a new sense of community among them (*Emancipated* 105). "The issue is knowing the kind of attention prompted by some particular system," Rancière remarks, and resisting the meanings and effects that a certain community's members anticipate finding based on their shared beliefs (99). But my analysis here of the defensive retreat of the male political internees of *Auschwitz et après* points us towards some additional factors to consider when seeking to alter the behaviour of an ethically minded community and to guide them towards this open disposition. Most obviously, this group of militants experienced their inability to confirm meanings when faced with the intolerable as indicative of their personal shortcomings rather than the failure of their shared understandings. This resulted in their closure to the outside world, a reaction motivated by their desire to cover up their inadequacies from the community members they believed to have failed. To paraphrase Rancière, *inattention* is the attention they offer to those things they do not know what to make of in advance. This turning inward is one response that witness writing must anticipate when addressing an audience of ethically oriented individuals, and not knowing is a response that such readers must be made to feel they can share with their community.

Moreover, and to return to the succession of monolithic understandings and responses that have defined the Nazi camps in the French public sphere, the writing of a survivor like Delbo also leads us to see the broader social and political effects that witnesses can exert by striving to modify the way people who acknowledge their responsibilities to others approach the act of reading. By resisting the urge to confirm pre-established meanings or to articulate new, more masterful understandings about the horrors of the Nazi camps, we readers also offer resistance to neat and codified visions of the past that normalize the experiences of victims, that remember as a way to exclude, and that can be employed to reinforce pernicious political ideologies. Witness writing such as Delbo's shows us ways to remain open during our moments of vulnerability, failure, and ignorance in order to acknowledge the messy, chaotic, and variegated nature of the experience of atrocity. This writing dares us to look and, in the process, to try to be human.

4 Irony and Community

In a passage from Delbo's *Mesure de nos jours* titled "Marie-Louise," two Auschwitz survivors – Charlotte and Marie-Louise – talk about their lives in France since the end of the Second World War. Years have passed, and they have not seen each other since their time in the camps. Charlotte is visiting Marie-Louise in her new house, and they both speak of the different ways they have remade their lives and reintegrated into French society.

Like any good hostess, Marie-Louise gives her guest a tour upon her arrival. She accompanies Charlotte from room to room and comments on the details that an outsider's eyes might miss. The order of things in the household allows Marie-Louise to quickly perform her daily tasks – "because, you know, you should spend as little time on housework as possible," she explains [parce que le ménage, tu comprends, il faut n'y passer que le moins de temps possible (83)].[1] Old pieces of furniture that were in the attic of her previous home fit neatly into the rooms of her new one. Colours blend harmoniously from one room to the next. There is even a peaceful little home office – "the most peaceful room in the house," Marie-Louise tells Charlotte (84) – where the survivor reads nearly every text published about the Nazi camps and writes about her own experience of Auschwitz. Marie-Louise's loving husband Pierre, who was not deported to the camps, reads everything his wife writes, and they constantly talk about her traumatic past. "My memories have become his," Marie-Louise reflects [Mes souvenirs sont devenus les siens (88)]. "So much so that I often have the feeling he was there with me. He remembers everything, better than me even" [À tel point que souvent j'ai l'impression qu'il était avec moi là-bas. Il se rappelle tout, mieux que moi, même]. Her voice is as peaceful as her household while she tells Charlotte about her post-Auschwitz life. "She spoke in a low, soft voice that fit in perfectly with the soft hues of the drapes, with the pale colour of her dress, with the light filtered by the gathered tulle of her curtains and by the foliage of a tree that covered the window," the passage's narrator, Delbo, comments [Elle parlait d'une voix feutrée qui s'accordait aux teintes douces des tentures, à la couleur pâle de sa robe, à la lumière filtrée par des tulles froncées et par le feuillage d'un arbre qui remplissait la fenêtre (85)]. Everything seems to be in order for the couple – "you see, I'm not lacking anything," says Marie-Louise calmly [tu vois, il ne me manque rien (83)] – and the survivor states that she is happy.

In *Fast Cars, Clean Bodies*, Kristin Ross notes that the ideal of the happy couple played a crucial role in the reorganization of French social space in the years after the Second World War. In the 1950s and 1960s, representations of ideal couples diffused by the mass media in France presented the husband-wife relation as a unit in which no one maintained his or her individuality and as the site for nearly all of a person's emotional ties to the world (127, 133). Along with state-led modernization efforts of French households after the Second World War, Ross argues that such representations inspired middle-class couples to withdraw from political life into their clean and comfortable domestic existences, to cease believing that they were linked to any entity larger than themselves, and to close themselves off from the outside world rather than focus their attention on contemporary social and political struggles such as the Algerian War (133). This movement inward paralleled the state's attempts to create a clean break with France's colonial history during this same period and, in the process, it facilitated the exclusion of France's colonial past from its modern identity formations (11). By thus encouraging couples to perform activities simultaneously replicated by others throughout the nation, a model of national identity was forged in France around the ceremonies of everyday life, one which diverted people's attention from the tumultuous social and political events that were unfolding before their eyes (145).

I propose to explore here a different kind of exclusion that the ideal of the happy middle-class couple facilitated in postwar France, one whose dynamics are laid bare in the "Marie-Louise" passage of *Mesure de nos jours*. I want to suggest that this conceptualization of coupledom further contributed to the normalization and denial of Nazi camp memory in the years after liberation. The narrative configurations that the ideal couple uses to speak about Auschwitz seek to erase the uncontrollable and disruptive dimensions of the event and the individuality of camp survivors, and this serves to close off the past and reinforce repressive and exclusionary social visions. To combat the destructive effects that these kinds of narratives and relations exert in the aftermath of disaster, *Mesure de nos jours* attempts to educate its audience, ironically, in a reading practice that continuously revives the past and seeks out new modes of contact with others, a practice that rejects the forms of social and historical closure sought by the French state. Witness writing can offer resistance to the instrumentalization of atrocity, that is, by presenting the social as a space of disruption and improvisation in which connections with others are never ideal, and the self unravels and is never complete.

1 The Couple

Witnesses often stress the near impossibility of returning to their previous lives after their traumatic experiences. Auschwitz survivor Primo Levi describes his attempt to return to a peaceful and orderly existence after the camps as a "deception of the senses" that is frequently interrupted by a "dream full of horror" that haunts him in the aftermath (*The Reawakening* 207). "I am alone the center of a grey and turbid nothing," Levi reflects, and "I *know* what this thing means … I am in the Lager once more, and nothing is true outside the Lager" (emphasis in original). As Susan Brison observes, these uncontrollable interruptions of memory occur because traumatic events forever haunt survivors' minds and remain in their bodies' senses, ready to resurface whenever something triggers a reliving of the past (x). "In the aftermath, trauma survivors experience the physical intrusions of visceral traumatic memories," Brison explains, which makes recovery a matter of learning to incorporate what she calls the "awful knowledge" of trauma into one's life in order to carry on living (48, 21). Returnees can never completely rid themselves of trauma's disruptions or completely master its intrusive aftereffects. Rather, they must learn to live with them, a task that they must undertake on a day-by-day basis.

Mesure de nos jours tells the story of deportation, internment, and return from the perspectives of different concentration camp survivors, including Charlotte Delbo, who live in France in the decades following liberation. Though the disruptions that traumatic memory causes in each of their lives vary in frequency and severity, nearly every survivor who testifies in the volume offers a chilling vision of life after Auschwitz, the kind of haunted and disjointed existence described by Brison. A woman named Marceline tells of her "typhoid fever anniversary" – a fever she is stricken with at the same time every year and that paralyses her for weeks each time (183). Delbo describes a nightmare that she personally suffers from once a year in which she is given permission to leave a prison or a concentration camp in the morning, only to return to it of her own free will every evening. A survivor named Mado even adopts the rather extreme position that for deportees to try to rid themselves of their trauma in any way is unethical, because it disrespects the memory of the people who did not survive the camps.

However, the chorus of voices that speak out in *Mesure de nos jours* also calls attention to the extreme pain that many non-deportees – including survivors' loved ones – experienced when confronted with others' trauma after the war. Upon learning what camp inmates witnessed and what they lived through, readers and listeners who were not themselves returnees withdrew and distanced themselves from witnesses and their narratives in problematic ways. As one poem in the text declares:

Do not say they cannot hear us
they hear us
they want to understand
obstinately
meticulously
the edge of their being wishes to understand
a sensitive border at their edge
but their deepest self
their inner truth
remains remote
flees as we think we're catching it
retracts contracts escapes
do they withdraw and fall back
because they hurt
where we no longer hurt... (*Auschwitz and After* 269)[2]

[Ne dis pas qu'ils ne nous entendent pas
ils nous entendent
ils veulent comprendre
obstinément
méticuleusement
une frange d'eux veut comprendre

une lisière sensible à la frange d'eux-mêmes
c'est leur eux du fond
leur vérité
qui reste loin
qui fuit quand nous croyons l'atteindre
qui se rétracte et se contracte et échappe
n'est-ce pas parce qu'ils ont mal
là où nous n'avons plus mal
qu'ils se retirent et se replient ...] (68)

The way the poetic "I" addresses readers here is an important characteristic of all of the testimonies assembled in *Mesure de nos jours* with the exception of "Marie-Louise." In them, different Auschwitz survivors speak to an unnamed interlocutor with the informal "tu" while recounting, in monologue form, the ways in which trauma disturbs and disrupts their daily lives. These acts of witnessing are first addressed within the text to its narrator, Delbo, and, by extension, to readers, who are invited to occupy the place that Delbo inhabited in the original conversations that *Mesure de nos jours* records. The poetic "I" suggests that these people are well-intentioned, and want to engage and understand survivors' testimonies, but they possess "deep selves" with a lower threshold for pain than those of traumatized camp returnees. They embark on their experience "obstinately" and "meticulously," but, because their deep selves are pained by learning what survivors went through, they retreat into themselves and withdraw from the act of witnessing. The ellipsis at the end of the poem (an end that is not an end) implies both that this listening and reading practice persists as a problem long after the end of the war and that such a dilemma has no easy or definitive solution. But how does this retreat of non-deportees' pained, deep selves – the deep selves of readers and listeners, that is, who genuinely want to immerse themselves in survivor testimonies – affect witnesses in the aftermath?

Mesure de nos jours in fact presents the problematics of the normalization and denial of Second World War memory as a matter of readers and listeners not knowing how to engage witnesses and their testimonies *in spite of* their desire to understand.[3] And the survivors who testify throughout the text repeatedly reflect in particular on how the misguided ways their spouses respond to the ghosts of the camps harms witnesses upon their return. The ethically minded Mado explains that she never speaks to her "nice" husband about her

Auschwitz trauma because of the calm and reassuring reaction he would offer:

> I never wonder whether he understands because I know he doesn't and I've known since the moment I met him that my explanations would elude him. Could I even explain? He would say, in a quiet, reassuring voice: "I know what you've been through. I know that one doesn't return from there without scars that rip back open at the lightest touch. That's why I never speak to you about it. I want to help you forget. Speaking hurts. One must not speak if one wants to forget." You see, everything is wrong. Those who love us want us to forget. They don't understand, first, that it's impossible, and, moreover, that forgetting would be atrocious.[4]
>
> [Je ne me demande jamais s'il comprend parce que je sais qu'il ne comprend pas et je sais depuis que je le connais que mes explications lui échapperont. Suis-je seulement capable d'expliquer? Il dirait tranquille, rassurant: "Je sais par où tu es passé. Je sais qu'on ne revient pas de là-bas sans garder des cicatrices qui se redéchirent au moindre effleurement. C'est pour cela que je ne t'en parle jamais. Je veux t'aider à oublier. Parler fait mal. Il ne faut pas parler si on veut oublier." Tu vois, tout est faux. Ceux qui nous aiment veulent que nous oubliions. Ils ne comprennent pas, d'abord que c'est impossible, qu'ensuite, oublier ce serait atroce.] (63–4)

Mado's husband is, of course, full of good intentions in wanting to help his wife forget her pain. But his response denies the simple fact that – as Brison demonstrates and Mado emphasizes in her testimony – the wounds of a traumatic past can never be fully healed, and that acknowledging them is essential for one to go on living. Mado believes that being married to a fellow camp survivor would make her life easier – she believes that she would at least be able to speak to him about her hauntedness because, having had a similar experience, he would be able to understand her daily struggles and the depths of her pain.

But even those survivors from *Mesure de nos jours* who married other deportees after the war eventually came to experience serious problems with their husbands. A woman named Louise, for example, married a Buchenwald returnee and, in the beginning, she and her husband had all of the same references, and even spoke the same coded language because of their traumatic experiences. She notes that years later, though, her husband seems to be the only one in their house who has the "right" to be sick anymore. As Louise puts it:

> After twenty years of marriage, there is only one deportee in this household. The deportee, it's him [...] He must take care of himself, he must monitor himself, he must keep from overexerting himself [...] He was deported, so he must follow a strict diet [...] Granted, it's of course true that he isn't in perfect health. None of us returned unharmed. But he's the only one who has the right to be sick. At any rate, we wouldn't both be able to be sick at the same time.[5]
>
> [Après vingt ans de mariage, il n'y a plus qu'un déporté dans le ménage. Le déporté, c'est lui [...] Il faut qu'il se soigne, il faut qu'il se surveille, il faut qu'il se ménage [...] Il a été déporté, il doit suivre un regime [...] Remarque, c'est sans doute vrai qu'il n'a pas une santé à toute épreuve. Aucun de nous n'est rentré indemne. Mais il n'y a que lui qui ait le droit d'être malade. De toute façon, nous ne pourrions pas être malades tous les deux en même temps.] (176–7)

Louise is able to speak to her husband about the Deportation thanks to their shared identity as camp survivors. But because they cannot both be sick at the same time (even though they both are), she must shoulder the burden of their daily existence as a couple. Their shared experience of the camps does not lead to a postwar existence in which they share in the tasks of everyday life.

Yet the most troubling couple dynamic that appears in *Mesure de nos jours* – and the one that Delbo's writing clearly singles out in the work – is that of the self-proclaimed "happy couple" who appear to share everything, Marie-Louise and Pierre. The passage devoted to their story obviously stands apart from the other narratives in the text, a fact that previous studies have attributed to the couple's problematic handling of Marie-Louise's Auschwitz trauma. As Patricia Yaeger notes, Pierre "acts like the perfect trauma listener" and tries to experience the "unreachable anguish" of what his wife went through in the camps (401). But one is disturbed when reading this passage because Pierre seems to want to carry his wife's trauma "upon his capable shoulders." Lawrence Langer proposes in *The Age of Atrocity* that "Marie-Louise" is one of the most unsettling narratives in the entire volume because the survivor's ability to recover so completely from her traumatic experience seems to "betray" the ethical duty she has to the Auschwitz dead (238, 235).

Although Marie-Louise speaks less than any other witness about her post-traumatic symptoms, the rest of *Mesure de nos jours* is "so full of failure" to escape Auschwitz that "the momentum of the narrative" forces readers to recognize that there is something abnormal about the happy life she lives with her husband (238, 236).

Scholars have failed to note, however, that "Marie-Louise" is also the first of five passages in *Mesure de nos jours* that tells the story of an *imaginary* survivor who was deported on the Convoy of January 24th and imprisoned in Auschwitz. Though based on conversations that Charlotte Delbo had with her fellow convoy members while she was working on the collective biography *Le convoi du 24 janvier* in the early sixties, the passages "Marie-Louise," "Gaby," "Louise," "Marceline," and "Françoise" actually contain fictional protagonists, and the women who bear witness in them did not really exist.[6] This fictionalization clearly highlights the importance of these passages for Delbo's overall project in this volume of her trilogy. It also suggests that she is speaking more directly to readers through them and seeks to distance her witness writing even further from pure reportage. All of these narratives with imaginary protagonists, in fact, reflect at length on a common theme: the dynamics of couples in the aftermath. This is a subject that Delbo reflects on throughout her writings, and her treatment of it is heavily influenced by her relationship with her own husband, Georges Dudach, who was executed by firing squad by the Nazis for his activities in the French Resistance several months before she was deported to Auschwitz. Delbo was imprisoned at the same time as her husband – the two were captured in the same raid of their apartment and incarcerated in the Paris prison at La Santé – and she was taken to see him on the morning he was to be murdered. Their final moments together in his prison cell haunt Delbo's works not just due to the utter devastation caused by knowing that she was seeing her husband for the last time and him knowing the same. The experience also led Delbo to rethink the understanding of love that had governed her relation with her husband, the dynamics on display in their final interaction, and the political ideals that led to both of them being imprisoned. A brief analysis will lead us back to our discussion of the disruptive "Marie-Louise" and the social and reader-text relations it implicitly criticizes.

The glimpses that *Auschwitz et après* offers of Delbo's relationship with Dudach paint a romantic and tragic portrait of their last interaction that highlights Delbo's concern with honouring the memory of the man she loved. Appearing as the last short narrative in *Mesure de nos jours,*

"Françoise" offers a fictionalized account of the final day of Dudach's life that emphasizes its shattering effects on the woman who lived on after him. "When I was called that morning," Françoise reflects, "something in me stopped, and nothing could get it back working again, like a watch that stops when the person wearing it stops living"[7] [Quand j'ai été appelée, ce matin-là, quelque chose en moi s'est arrêté, et rien ne peut le remettre en marche, comme la montre qui s'arrête quand celui qui la porte s'arrête de vivre (206)]. She stresses the impossibility of remaking her life after such a loss – "Starting your life over again, what an expression," she repeats throughout, a remark that echoes the text's prevailing views on trauma recovery – and she explains that she primarily goes on living because her husband, Paul, made her promise that she would when she saw him for the last time. Not allowing the world to forget her husband's fire and his commitment to bringing about a better world motivates her as well. "With me dead, who will remember the fire he wanted to set to the world in order for a new dawn to rise?" [Moi morte, qui se souviendra du feu dont il voulait embraser le monde pour que monte une nouvelle aurore? (210)] she asks, citing a well-known phrase communist militants associated with their actions in the fight against fascism.[8] Passages from the second volume, *Une connaissance inutile*, adopt a similarly poetic and memorializing tone in their treatment of Delbo's final exchange with Dudach. "He was made beautiful by his death becoming more and more visible each second./ It's true that it makes you beautiful/ death," Delbo writes in a poem towards the end of the volume about their final moments together [Il était beau de sa mort à chaque seconde plus visible./ C'est vrai que cela rend beau/ la mort (158)].[9] "I'll never forget his smile," she simply states a few pages earlier [Je n'oublierai jamais son sourire (156)].

Elsewhere in her writings, though, Delbo reflects on these heartbreaking final moments and the effects of her husband's execution through a more critical – but no less devastating – lens. In the one-act play devoted to this encounter that again features the imaginary couple of Françoise and Paul, *Une scène jouée dans la mémoire*, Françoise overtly criticizes her husband's politics in several asides that she addresses to the audience when reliving the scene through memory.[10] Throughout their conversation, Paul looks to reassure his wife about the larger importance of his death through a series of ideological assertions – he assures her that victory is near and that she will live to see it, that his death will not be in vain and will be avenged by others, that all combatants know when they engage in a struggle that not everyone will live to see the end of their fight for freedom, justice, and human dignity, all ideas that, when speaking to her husband for the last time, Françoise admits to having believed before they were arrested.

But Françoise – and, ultimately, the play as a whole – actually adopts a more critical attitude towards Paul's ideological understanding of commitment and the way he interacts with his wife in these moments before his execution. Especially towards the end of their final conversation, Françoise secretly disputes everything she and Paul had previously said and believed, including how the two of them understood their love and their politics, a fact that she shares with her audience but not with her husband:

> PAUL: What kind of flavour would there be to life if all one did was bore or distract oneself throughout one's stay. What meaning does love have if one only lived to preserve it at all cost, out of reach, outside of reality, like a fragile plant afraid of the air, that doesn't expose itself, that doesn't live?
>
> FRANÇOISE: (Aside: what she adds when reliving this scene): I thought that I would have preferred to keep him, the man I loved, whose arms were so soft, lips so soft, his warm chest, I would have preferred to keep him no matter what the price. (Return to the scene, to Paul) Yes, Paul, I know all that. We thought ourselves so rich that we risked everything we had. Everything.[11]

> [PAUL: Quel goût aurait la vie si on ne faisait qu'y séjourner en s'ennuyant ou en se distrayant. Quel sens l'amour si on ne vivait que pour le garder à tout prix, hors d'atteinte, hors de la réalité, comme une plante fragile qui craint l'air, qui ne s'expose, qui ne vit pas?
>
> FRANÇOISE (A parte: ce qu'elle ajoute quand elle revit cette scène): Moi je pensais que j'aurais préféré le garder, lui, l'homme que j'aimais, aux bras si doux, aux lèvres douces, à la poitrine chaude, j'aurais préféré le garder à n'importe quel prix. (Retour à la scène, à Paul) Oui, Paul, je savais tout cela. Nous nous sentions si riches que nous risquions tout ce que nous avions. Tout.] (34–5)

Françoise also calls our attention to the inaccurate assumptions both she and Paul had at the time about what awaited female political militants at the hands of the Nazis. "Could he have foreseen that I would have to pass through Auschwitz and Ravensbrück, wait three years, to see victory?" she asks herself in another aside [Pouvait-il prévoir qu'il me faudrait encore passer par Auschwitz et Ravensbrück, attendre trois ans, pour voir la victoire? (41)]. "We thought then that women didn't have to fear for their lives, we didn't know what deportation was" [On croyait alors que les femmes n'avaient pas à craindre pour leur vie, on ne savait pas ce qu'était la deportation]. She voiced none of these remarks to her husband at the time – she did not want him to know of her unbearable pain or that she would have preferred he betray his ideals for them to spend one more day together, a realization that, being herself a dedicated militant, caused her great shame. And, of course, one cannot help but also wonder what secret thoughts Paul might be hiding behind his ideological statements because of his love for Françoise and his powerlessness to change his fate. But his final words and stated belief in the symbolic importance of his death are all the more crushing for Françoise in light of the atrocities committed by communist regimes that she (and so many others) only discovered after the Second World War. "I've lost my taste for that new dawn," she explains in her testimony in *Mesure de nos jours* [J'ai perdu le goût de cette nouvelle aurore (210)]. "Without him, what does it matter? And now that the lie has been unmasked?" [Sans lui, à quoi bon? Et maintenant que le mensonge a été démasqué?].

I want to suggest here that the imaginary "Marie-Louise" echoes these criticisms of what couples share and repress in their interactions because of their politics and their love advanced in *Une scène jouée dans la mémoire*. This short passage from *Mesure de nos jours* also, moreover, points to the broader social harms that such relations can cause in the aftermath of trauma. However, in contrast to a text like *Une scène jouée dans la mémoire*, I want to propose that Delbo's writing in *Mesure de nos jours* – and, indeed, throughout the trilogy *Auschwitz et après* – transmits these ideas and seeks to combat them not through explicit statements or overt addresses to its audience, but, rather, through its use of *irony*, a device that it uses to modify these relational dynamics without completely alienating those readers who are the targets of its criticisms. In all of *Mesure de nos jours*, Marie-Louise is the only survivor who insists that it is possible to completely heal from trauma and to confine her experience to the past. As Wayne Booth notes in *A Rhetoric of Irony*, when a character's speaking style departs notably from the dominant way of speaking in a text as Marie-Louise's does, it is a direct clue to readers that "stable irony" is at work and that we must reject what a passage states literally (67, 7). Stable irony invites us instead to *reconstruct* meanings in order to discover the different messages that authors intentionally hide beneath the surface of their texts (7). It increases the rhetorical force of the ideas authors are trying to transmit because readers must become deeply involved in a given text in order to understand why an author rejects its literal meanings (40, 42).

Yet stable irony is also less alienating than non-ironic statements attempting to transmit the same critical messages because all readers – even those who are attacked through an author's ironic strokes and disagree with his or her conclusions – are invited to share in the task of constructing new meanings and discovering what an author's ironic messages are. Thus, Booth suggests, the predominant emotion when we read stable ironies is often

> that of joining, of finding and communing with kindred spirits. The author I infer behind the false words is my kind of man, because he enjoys playing with irony, because he assumes *my* capacity for dealing with it, and – most important – because he grants me a kind of wisdom; he assumes he does not have to spell out the shared and secret truths on which my reconstruction is to be built. (28; emphasis in original)

Stable irony may cause us to distance ourselves and pull back from a text, but it also draws us in and establishes a kind of communal bond between us readers and the authors who have faith in our intellectual capacities. We must first be engaged and then remain involved if we are to understand the criticisms a text advances ironically. Such ironies may disrupt the experience we readers have of a given text, but they do not cause us to completely retreat or withdraw from the act of reading.

I have been arguing throughout my analyses of Delbo that well-intentioned individuals, such as political deportees and their loved ones, are an important readership singled out by her trilogy *Auschwitz et après*. By using irony to advance its critique of these readers, Delbo's writing is both less alienating for them and more compassionate towards them, because it grants them the recognition they deserve for the sacrifices they have made for others. Political militants like Françoise's husband Paul and dedicated husbands like Pierre desire to be there for others and want to be good people who help and support their loved ones no matter what the cost. *Mesure de nos jours* would risk losing its readers by criticizing the actions of such ethically minded individuals outright. In the case of postwar France, such people were among the few who paid attention to the plight of survivors at all and they must be engaged with this broader context in mind. But the actions of these well-meaning people harm returnees and obscure camp memory, a fact that "Marie-Louise," I argue, makes abundantly clear. Irony is a key device for criticizing an audience of loved ones because it creates an inclusive environment that acknowledges their efforts and their pain all while modifying their problematic modes of engagement.

My intention here, then, is to reconstruct some of the harsh critical messages about well-meaning people like Marie-Louise and Pierre that are transmitted ironically through "Marie-Louise" and, in so doing, to explicate the approach to reading that *Mesure de nos jours* as a whole seeks to cultivate in its audience. The numerous thematic differences between "Marie-Louise" and the other return narratives will serve as my point of departure. Perhaps the most obvious example emerges when Pierre and Marie-Louise reflect on the difficulties she had when readapting to life immediately after the war. According to the couple, Marie-Louise's life was as disjointed and haunted as any survivor's when she returned, but since this time she has managed to overcome trauma's disruptions and to rid herself completely of her Auschwitz ghosts. They describe how Marie-Louise was initially too "mentally tired" to return to her former job, how she became paralysed in social interactions with her friends and family and how she was so terrified when interacting with people at the post office or supermarket that she trembled and stammered when she spoke.

When Pierre witnessed his wife's erratic behaviour, he even wondered if Marie-Louise would ever become a "normal person" again. His commentary offers the first detailed description of some of the techniques he used to cure his wife of her "awful knowledge":

> I wondered if she would manage to readapt to life. When I saw her picking up wilted, yellowing cabbage leaves that had fallen from a crate, at the produce stand, I wondered if she would ever become a normal person again. She'd wake up in the middle of the night, she jumped out of bed because she thought it was morning. I'd do the same so that she didn't feel lost with everyone else asleep. She got over the cabbage leaves quickly enough. Afterwards, she was content to stare at them with a look of regret. She slowly examined every leaf when peeling a head of lettuce, trying to make full use of the large outer ones. As for waking up, that took longer. We've actually never managed to get back to the time we used to wake up.[12]
>
> [Je me demandais si elle parviendrait à se réadapter à la vie. Quand je l'ai vue ramasser des feuilles de choux jaunies qui étaient tombées d'un cageot, chez le marchand de légumes, je me suis demandé si elle redeviendrait une

personne normale. Elle se réveillait au milieu de la nuit, elle sautait du lit parce qu'elle croyait que c'était le matin. Je faisais comme elle afin qu'elle ne se sente pas perdue dans la maison endormie. Pour les feuilles de choux, cela a passé assez vite. Après, elle se contentait de les regarder comme avec regret. Elle épluchait la salade en examinant chaque feuille lentement, en essayant de tirer parti de grosses feuilles du tour. Pour le réveil, cela a été plus long. D'ailleurs, nous n'avons jamais repris l'habitude de nous lever à notre heure d'avant.] (89)

Pierre describes here a process by which he would imitate Marie-Louise's disruptive behaviour so that she would feel less isolated, but the fact that the couple has never managed since Marie-Louise's return to wake up at the time they did before her deportation calls into question the efficacy of his resocialization methods. Of course, it is obvious that Pierre is only trying to be a loving husband for a wife who is desperately in need of his help. But it is also evident that *Mesure de nos jours* as a whole indicates that the possibility of a complete return to the "normal" person one was before Auschwitz is an illusion. When reading Pierre's reflections, readers are forced to raise a whole series of questions about the horror that lurks beneath the surface of this happy couple's life, a horror that the couple refuses to acknowledge, to open up about or to share. Does Marie-Louise heal from her trauma thanks to the loving efforts of her husband, or does the couple patiently and "meticulously" cover it up? Do they rid Marie-Louise of her ghosts, or do they train her not to speak of them? What horrors resurface in Marie-Louise's mind when she wakes up so early every day?

When Marie-Louise comments on how her husband helped her relearn the gestures of "normal" life, it becomes clear that his resocialization techniques lovingly repress her trauma rather than cure it. Marie-Louise compares the way her "nice" husband treated her when she returned from the camps to the way parents teach their children to walk and talk:

For a long time, Pierre kept taking care of everything around the house. I can't explain to you how he did it: he put me back into life without me noticing it. "Like how one teaches children to speak," he said to me once. "One speaks to them, one shows them how to move their lips, they imitate you and one day they finally speak." I personally think it's more like how one teaches them to walk. I have a nice husband, you know.[13]

[Pendant longtemps, Pierre a continué à s'occuper de tout à la maison. Je ne peux pas t'expliquer comment il s'y est pris: il m'a remise dans la vie sans que je m'en aperçoive. "Comme lorsqu'on apprend à parler aux enfants," m'a-t-il dit une fois. "On leur parle, on leur montre comment on bouge les lèvres, ils vous imitent et un beau jour ils parlent." Moi, il me semble que c'est plutôt comme on leur apprend à marcher. J'ai un mari gentil, tu sais.] (87)

In light of every other survivor's story of a disjointed life upon return, it is disturbing for Marie-Louise to insist that Pierre "put her back into life" without her being aware of it. She displays no awareness of the normalizing forces of postwar society and immerses herself totally in her husband's world. Comments she makes later in the conversation paint a more detailed portrait of her husband's reassuring parenting methods:

Like one does with children when they learn to walk [...] You let go of them and squat in front of them with your arms open wide. Little by little, you step back, all while keeping your arms wide open. And when you see that they are standing solidly on their feet, you wait for them on the other side of the room and let them come by themselves. Pierre did the same with me. When it was my turn, at the post office or in a store, he'd step back. As soon as he let go of my arm, I had the feeling I was drowning, so he would come a bit closer and speak in my place. After a while, he would leave me to manage by myself, all while standing within arm's reach. You can't imagine how nice he was.[14]

[Comme on fait avec les enfants quand ils apprennent à marcher [...] On les lâche en se tenant accroupi devant eux les bras ouverts. Petit à petit, on s'écarte, tout en gardant les bras ouverts. Et quand on les voit assurés sur leurs jambes, on les attend à l'autre bout de la pièce et on les laisse venir tout seuls. Pierre a fait pareil avec moi. Au moment où c'était mon tour, au guichet de la poste ou chez un commerçant, il s'écartait. Dès qu'il me quittait le bras, j'avais l'impression de me noyer, alors il se rapprochait un petit peu et parlait à ma place. Puis, il m'a laissé me débrouiller toute seule, tout en restant à portée de ma main. Tu ne peux pas te figurer ce qu'il a été gentil.] (92–3)

Like a father teaching his toddling daughter to walk, Pierre used his love to guide Marie-Louise throughout her return by holding it out as a reward for her successful performances. Put somewhat differently, to help Marie-Louise readapt to life in French society, Pierre imitated his traumatized wife's disturbing behaviour to calm her and then steadied her social performance by having her imitate him. Marie-Louise attributes the fact that her "faculties" came back to her "little by little" after the war to this doubly-imitative process:

> I was so tired that I thought I would never recover. And then, little by little, everything worked itself out. All of my faculties came back to me. Thanks to Pierre. If he hadn't been there to help me, I never would have been able to readapt. With him, it was easy, but as soon I was in the presence of other people, even friends, everything became blurred and confused. I could no longer find the right words, I'd start trembling, sweating. If Pierre hadn't been there, I would have been buried, totally withdrawn.[15]
>
> [j'étais tellement fatiguée que je croyais ne jamais pouvoir me remettre. Et puis, peu à peu, cela s'est arrangé. Toutes mes facultés me sont revenues. Grâce à Pierre. S'il n'avait pas été là pour m'aider, je n'aurais jamais pu me réadapter. Avec lui, je n'avais pas de difficultés, mais dès que j'étais en présence d'autres gens, même des amis, tout se brouillait. Je ne trouvais plus mes mots, je me mettais à trembler, à transpirer. Si Pierre n'avait pas été là, je me serais enfouie dans une retraite totale.] (86)

The use of reflexive verbs to describe how Marie-Louise "brings herself back" to normal life "thanks to Pierre" clearly implies that the mental faculties she recovers after her traumatic experience are not the result of returning to her pre-Auschwitz self. Rather, they are an effect of her husband's imitative techniques, and a result of her submitting little by little to the unrelenting pressure to be normal like him. It is nice to think that a husband's love could have the power to return his wife to the person she once was. And, again, it is also obvious that Pierre has nothing but good intentions and genuinely wants to help his ailing wife. But the contrast between this couple's peaceful life and the haunted existences of every other survivor in *Mesure de nos jours* causes readers to see their marriage as a cover-up. It refuses to acknowledge Marie-Louise's trauma, denies her of any individuality, represses her uncontrollable memories, and dominates her through its constant reassurance.

The harmful effects that this happy couple's behaviour has on Auschwitz memory fully emerge in the passage when Pierre and Marie-Louise tell Charlotte about a trip that they took to Auschwitz together.

Pierre describes how the information he had extracted from his wife's testimonies before their trip guided and controlled his experience – a visit that he describes as a kind of "pilgrimage" in which he set out to identify the important sites of his wife's internment:

> It was one of the first pilgrimages. Marie-Louise had described to me so well the blocks, the marshes, the area where your block stood for roll call, the sentry post at the entrance, everything, that I immediately recognized the sites: the place where you endured that endless roll call in front of block 25 ten days after your arrival, the field where you stood stock-still all day in the snow and the circuit you ran when Madame Brabander and Alice Viterbo were caught [...] Naturally, it couldn't be the same. It was nice out, I was wearing good shoes. But in thinking of the snow, of your make-shift shoes, the dogs, the wind, of your fatigue, I understood well enough.[16]
>
> [C'était l'un des tout premiers pèlerinages. Marie-Louise m'avait si bien décrit les blocks, les marais, la place où votre block se tenait pour l'appel, la guérite à l'entrée, tout, que j'ai tout de suite reconnu les lieux: l'endroit où vous avez fait cet appel interminable devant le block 25 dix jours après votre arrivée, le champ où vous êtes restées plantées toute la journée dans la neige et la course où madame Brabander et Alice Viterbo ont été prises [...] Naturellement, ce ne pouvait pas être pareil. Il faisait beau, j'étais bien chaussé. Mais enfin, en pensant à la neige, à vos godasses, aux chiens, au vent, à votre fatigue, je me suis assez bien rendu compte.] (96–7)

While Pierre recognizes that his own experience of Auschwitz could not have been like his wife's, his insistence that he was able to understand "well enough" what it was like for internees by thinking of the differences between the conditions they faced during their imprisonment and those that he experienced makes any reader question his initial claim. His offhand way of listing the atrocious features of camp life seems to deny their annihilating force and brutality, and to collapse the differences between two experiences that are, quite clearly, not the same.

The problems with this "pilgrimatic" approach become even more evident when Pierre tries to use the information he obtains from his wife to correct her faulty memory in the years after the war. The couple explains to Charlotte that, while they were visiting Auschwitz, Marie-Louise could not remember which bunk she slept in when she was interned in the camp. Marie-Louise attributes the memory lapse to the different physical conditions of the space when she and her husband visited it. The reactions of all three characters, beginning with Marie-Louise's, are registered in the passage:

– You know, it changes things to see the block empty and, with the roof half-caved in, there's light inside now. And, it was also summer. With the sun …

– She no longer knew if she was on the right or the left. In any event it was in the second bunk since you could see the courtyard of block 25 from your spot.

– It was on the right, in the second bunk," I said. By chance, I remembered.

"You see, I was right. When you explained to me that you could see the courtyard of block 25 but not the door, I told you it had to be on the right. I took pictures."[17]

– Tu sais, cela change de voir ce block vide et, comme le toit est à moitié écroulé, il y fait clair maintenant. Et puis, c'était l'été. Avec le soleil …

– Elle ne savait plus si elle était à droite ou à gauche. En tout cas c'était dans la deuxième travée puisque vous voyiez la cour du 25 de votre place.

– C'était à droite, dans la deuxième travée," ai-je dit. Par chance, je m'en souvenais.

"Tu vois, j'avais raison. Quand tu m'as expliqué que vous voyiez la cour du block 25 mais non la porte, je t'ai dit que c'était surement à droite. J'ai pris des photos." (96–7)

Pierre clearly demonstrates here how he remembers the camps "better than his wife" does, but the way he quickly interrupts her to fill in her memory gap points to yet another humble way that he constantly covers up and denies her experience. How often does he correct Marie-Louise before she can finish her thoughts? His information is factually accurate, and how much he loves and wants to help his wife is evident. But, in the process, he seems to be imprisoning Marie-Louise in a set vision of the past, and he closes both of them off from the new ideas about Auschwitz that can and should emerge over time.

In fact, by the time Charlotte is visiting Marie-Louise and Pierre after the war, the closure of this happy couple is so complete they almost never leave their house, state-sponsored commemoration ceremonies being one of the only events that can draw them out. "We rarely go out," Marie-Louise pleasantly explains to Charlotte [Nous ne sortons guère (98)].[18] "We're so well off at home, just the two of us, but we go to all of the ceremonies. First of all, because it's a duty, and also because it always makes us happy to see comrades again" [Nous sommes si bien chez nous, tous les deux, mais nous allons à toutes les cérémonies. D'abord, parce que c'est un devoir, et puis cela nous fait toujours plaisir de revoir les camarades]. The rest of Delbo's comrades are of course less convinced of the efficacy of these official occasions to remember. The criticisms Mado levels against them echo the implicit critique of loved ones petrified by their good intentions that is advanced throughout "Marie-Louise":

> What can be done to ensure that Mounette didn't die for nothing? Nothing. Because nothing is what these ceremonies for remembering are, these commemorations, these reassuring parodies for people that we give the chance to feel pity for us once a year, to have a clean conscience. Whatever we do, it does nothing.[19]

> [Que faire pour que Mounette ne soit pas morte pour rien? Rien. Car ce n'est rien que ces cérémonies du souvenir, ces commemorations, ces parodies rassurantes pour les gens à qui nous donnons l'occasion de s'apitoyer une fois l'an, l'occasion d'avoir bonne conscience. Quoi que nous fassions, cela ne sert à rien.] (60)

The happy couple has retreated from the outside world, seeking out only relations that are officially sanctioned or that reassure. The ghosts of Auschwitz have been normalized on the surface of their aftermath life, and the state's exclusionary visions reinforced through their denial of Marie-Louise's trauma and the calm, orderly narrative they have built about their life.

2 Reading

Constructing narratives that assume the heritage of the past only to deny it is one of the techniques that French society uses to insert moments of social rupture into its pre-existing systems and to instrumentalize them for its own exclusionary purposes. As Kristin Ross argues in *May '68 and Its Afterlives*, the narrative configurations that dominate the nation's social space often strive to restrict the temporal and geographical nature of an event – in the case of May '68, a political movement that was built throughout the 1960s and in all of France became reduced afterwards to the actions of students in the Latin Quarter that occurred in the space of one month – and to fix that event in a way that legitimates the configurations of power of a given era. "Forgetting, just as much as remembering, is made possible by the work of various narrative configurations," Ross explains, "narratives that model the identity of the protagonists of an action at the same time as they shape the contours of events" (4). These accounts seek to reconfigure, obscure, or erase the past to serve the needs of the present, and to reinsert moments of rupture into a social system so as to reinforce its exclusionary identity formations.[20]

The ideal of the happy couple pursued by the imaginary couple of *Mesure de nos jours* lays bare a humble and pernicious way in which the state's projects can be reinforced throughout French social space. Marie-Louise and Pierre only seek to fix the experience of the camps in an effort to control the havoc it wreaks in their aftermath lives. But by attempting to confine the spectres of Auschwitz to their past, they unknowingly facilitate the closure of this moment of rupture and its instrumentalization by broader power structures at work in society. For her part, Delbo insists that her literary texts be considered weapons that can fight configurations of power. "In our time, power has become more and more powerful, more and more extensive and wide-ranging," she explains:

> Even in the remotest parts of the countryside, one cannot escape it … I don't like gratuitous or formal literature. I don't write for the sake of writing. I use literature as a weapon, because the threat seems too massive to me […] I consider the language of poetry to be the most effective – for it stirs readers in their secret depths – and the most dangerous for the enemies that it fights.[21]
>
> [À notre époque, le pouvoir est de plus en plus puissant, de plus en plus étendu. Même dans la campagne la plus reculée, on ne saurait lui échapper … Je n'aime pas la littérature gratuite ou formelle. Je n'écris pas pour écrire. Je me sers de la littérature comme d'une arme, car la menace m'apparaît trop grande […] Je considère le langage de la poésie comme le plus efficace – car il remue le lecteur au secret de lui-même – et le plus dangereux pour les ennemis qu'il combat.] ("Je me sers" 25–6)

The ironic "Marie-Louise" further calls our attention to how our practices as readers of witness literature can facilitate such an erasure of the past and, in the process, broader forms of exclusion and denial. The reactions that each character offers to Marie-Louise's memory lapse in the passage cited above clearly allegorize the harmful effects that readers can exert on concentration camp memory when approaching deportee narratives like Pierre does. Pierre conceives of survivor testimonies as a source of facts about Auschwitz and constantly uses those facts to guide his understandings, but he fails to recognize the new ideas about the site that emerge over time. By recognizing only what the *facts* of the past allow them to see, such readers risk stabilizing the meaningful inconsistencies that can also be found in the memories of survivors. The gap in Marie-Louise's memory while she and her husband were visiting Auschwitz clearly points to an idea about the physical conditions of a space and one's experience of it. But Pierre is too eager to help his wife remember historical facts and her previous testimonies to be open to the new understandings of her experience and of Auschwitz itself that her memory lapses may reveal.

"Marie-Louise" also calls our attention, then, to how our social interactions can harm others when they seek to stabilize and contain the past. For Pierre, this conversation offers the occasion to confirm pre-existing meanings about the camps and to share in that confirmation with survivors, both practices that close him and others off from anything new. Charlotte clearly approaches this encounter differently. It is not an opportunity for her to recycle old memories or to reinforce her identity as a camp returnee, nor to expose her trauma or hauntedness to others – undoubtedly in part because, like the readers of her story, she recognizes that the happy couple is living a calm life of denial. The fictional and satirical nature of the people and events described within the passage further implies that this is an important message about returning to the French social order that the text transmits ironically to readers: because some returnees succumb, albeit unknowingly, to society's loving but normalizing forces, even survivors from the same convoy cannot always completely reveal what ails them in their interactions with each other in the aftermath.

But there is more to it than this. As the implicit critique of the men of the Resistance advanced throughout *Auschwitz et après* makes clear, Delbo's writings display a deep, general concern for the destructive consquences of closing ourselves off and turning inward to cope with the horrors of atrocity. Her play *Ceux qui avaient choisi* reflects much more overtly on the phenomenon in a way that specifically emphasizes the disastrous repercussions it has in society at large. A brief analysis offers crucial insights into the kind of relation that *Mesure de nos jours* ultimately seeks out with its readers. The play consists of an extended dialogue between an Auschwitz survivor, Françoise, and a German citizen, Werner, who cross paths at a café while separately vacationing in Greece more than a decade after the end of the Second World War. They speak to each other about their experiences during the Nazi era – Françoise's story is recognizable as a fictionalized version of Delbo's own, while Werner spent the war as a soldier stationed in Athens who saw no combat. Werner largely worked on producing maps for the German army, had enough free time to visit archaeological sites, and displays throughout the play how genuinely guilty he feels for not having been more socially and politically engaged or aware at this point in his life.

When their discussion turns to the period before the war, Françoise voices her most biting criticisms of her interlocutor: that he was closed off and distracted from the events of his time, and even after the war lives in a dream world that makes him blind. "[T]he racial laws, the glorification of physical force and of blood, the war-cries, the falsifications of science in schoolbooks, it wasn't enough to draw you out of yourself, to put you outside of yourself?" [(L)es lois raciales, l'exaltation de la force et du sang, les cris de guerre, les falsifications de la science dans les manuels, ce n'était pas assez pour vous sortir de vous-même, pour vous mettre hors de vous?"] Françoise asks while Werner strives to explain his lack of involvement in the world around him, something he attributes to his total immersion in his university studies and the blindness caused by falling in love with his future wife (59–60).[22] She ultimately believes this closure affects his way of interacting with her as well, which she makes clear in the final criticisms she voices before parting ways with him at the end of the play:

FRANÇOISE. All of your life, you have been blind. You believe that you've recovered your sight today because you see me. But what's happening around you, what's going on in the world, do you see it? If the National Socialists or something like them were to reappear, would you see them?

WERNER. I believe that I would see them. I see them already.

FRANÇOISE. And what are you doing? Are you better armed today than yesterday? No. You continue to dream your life. And what you are proposing I do is to enter into your dream. You dream of seeing me make your dream real. You are mistaken. I am the dream of no one.

[FRANÇOISE. Toute votre vie, vous avez été aveugle. Vous croyez aujourd'hui que vous avez recouvré la vue parce que vous me voyez. Mais ce qui se passe autour de vous, ce qui se passe dans le monde, le voyez-vous? Si les nationaux-socialistes ou engeance d'espèce voisine réapparaissent, les verriez-vous?

WERNER. Je crois que je les verrais. Je les vois déjà.

FRANÇOISE. Et que faites-vous? Êtes-vous mieux armé aujourd'hui qu'hier? Non. Vous continuez de rêver votre vie. Et ce que vous me proposez, c'est d'entrer dans votre rêve. Vous rêvez de me voir donner réalité à ce rêve. Vous vous trompez. Je ne suis le rêve de personne.] (73–4)

Françoise's remarks here echo the critique advanced in the ironic narrative about Marie-Louise and Pierre and resituate it more explicitly in relation to one's present socio-political context. While Pierre is closed off to anything new about the past and, along with his wife, has retreated outright from most contact with the outside world, Werner's closure results from the way he approaches his interactions with others and looks for them to correspond with a dreamed-up vision he imposes on them. In both cases, Delbo's writing proves critical towards people who are incapable of engaging others as real, distinct individuals – individuals who articulate their own positions, voice their own thoughts, and who do not correspond exactly with the images others construct of them because their identities and ideas may change over time – and towards the harmful social and political effects that these closed ways of being in humble interactions ultimately exert in society at large.

The formal differences between "Marie-Louise" and the rest of the survivor narratives that appear in *Mesure de nos jours* bear witness to the distance that Delbo's writing seeks to establish between its readers and these closed off individuals. As the gap-filling interaction shows, unlike every other return story in the volume, "Marie-Louise" is not a monologue narrated in the first-person singular, but a dialogue narrated from the perspective of Delbo – the listener addressed as "tu" by the passage's title character. Readers are not offered unhindered access to the "tu" position originally occupied by Delbo in this (wholly imaginary) conversation, which interrupts the formal flow of the text and further disrupts the kind of intimate relation we are invited to maintain with the survivor who bears witness in it. Unlike in every other account of return, moreover, Delbo intervenes in the narrative to provide her own commentary even before the problems with Pierre and

Marie-Louise's relation emerge. The passage's opening lines are telling in this regard:

> "You see, I'm lacking nothing. I'm happy." She took me from one room to another, drawing my attention to the details of the arrangements that made her household tasks easier – "because, you know, you should spend as little time on housework as possible" – a colour that harmonized well with the others, a piece of furniture that came from the old attic and completed this corner room so well.[23]

> ["Tu vois, il ne me manque rien. Je suis heureuse." Elle me conduisait d'une pièce à l'autre, me faisait remarquer des détails d'installation qui rendaient sa tâche plus facile – "parce que le ménage, tu comprends, il faut n'y passer que le moins de temps possible" – une couleur qui s'harmonisait heureusement avec les autres, un meuble qui venait de l'ancien grenier et qui complétait si bien cette pièce d'angle.] (83)

As she does in several of her other interventions in the passage, the narrator describes here the "complete" space in which Marie-Louise resides, and the actions that Marie-Louise performs while she tells Charlotte about her "easy" post-Auschwitz existence. But the tranquil images of post-camp life evoked in the separate commentaries of Marie-Louise and the narrator contrast starkly with the narrative's messy form; the narrator's intrusion into Marie-Louise's testimony disrupts its "harmonious" flow, and suggests a disjointed relationship between the two convoy survivors from the beginning of their interaction. Although the character Charlotte clearly participates and remains engaged throughout her conversation with the normalized couple, the first-person narrator speaks to the distance that separates Charlotte from her interlocutors. Long before all of the thematic differences between "Marie-Louise" and the rest of *Mesure de nos jours* fully emerge in the passage, the narrative structure marks a difference between Marie-Louise's return to French society and everyone else's.

However, for readers of *Mesure de nos jours*, these formal differences between "Marie-Louise" and the other survivor narratives ultimately change the kind of relationship that they are invited to establish with every other witness in the text as well. Appearing as the fifth return narrative in the volume, "Marie-Louise" alters and disrupts the more intimate bond created by the work's earlier testimonies, in which survivors bear witness to their disjointed and haunted lives. It is impossible, in short, to immerse oneself completely in the witness narratives placed after "Marie-Louise" in the same, unhindered way as those placed before it. Yaeger notes that changing the tempo on readers and making us "experience the text's refusal to draw near" is a defining feature of the kind of ethical relation that *Auschwitz et après* as a whole ultimately elicits from its readers (422). She suggests that we conceive of the reader-text relation the trilogy cultivates as one of "proximity without intimacy," which the trilogy creates through its use of various figures of speech that evoke readers' empathy only to "burn it away" (415). Taking readers through such a process further leads them to shed their "comforting illusions" about what it means to empathize with another's experience and creates instead a strange, "discompassionate" relationship that causes us to step back from the intimate one we initially seek out with the people and events described in the work (410, 402).

But Delbo's other works indicate that it is the nature of any and all social relations – not just ethical ones such as empathy and compassion – that the writer interrogates and seeks to modify through her *ironic* strokes in *Auschwitz et après*. From guilt-ridden Werner to politically committed Paul, Delbo's writing is consistently critical of those who totally immerse themselves in a relationship or lose themselves in a cause, and of the disastrous political repercussions these closed ways of being exert in society at large. "Marie-Louise" extends this critique to include loved ones of victims and victims themselves, and offers resistance to any reassuring ordering of social relations in the aftermath through its ironic tone. Interactions worth having with others – including those between fellow survivors – do not reinforce visions of oneself or illusions one has about who we or other people were or are. They consist, rather, of unending negotiations and improvisations – a messy, rather than idealized, practice in which definitive meanings never emerge and connections with everyone are never total or complete.

That said, Delbo's writing in *Mesure de nos jours* clearly cultivates our compassion for the well-intentioned people that the happy couple of Marie-Louise and Pierre represent. As the gap-filling interaction demonstrates, Delbo's writing includes such individuals in the community it constructs, and does not ask readers to completely avoid contact or ignore the accounts of the camps that these people provide. In spite of the normalizing effects Pierre's behaviour has on Marie-Louise and on Auschwitz memory, Charlotte's behaviour in the passage actually makes clear that the kind of factual information he provides is important in some contexts, because it can help non-deportees cope with the loss of their loved ones. During her visit with the couple, Charlotte mentions to Marie-Louise and Pierre that a young woman came to her in search of information about her mother who died in Auschwitz, and that she was unable to tell the woman anything at all:

> I don't know how she got my address or who sent her to me; one of us, no doubt. She'd learned that I was in the same convoy as her mother and she wanted me to talk to her about her mother. Unfortunately I was incapable of telling her anything. I didn't know her mother. In any case, I don't remember her, I didn't even recall her name. I asked Mado, who has the best memory of all of us. She doesn't remember her either.[24]

> [Je ne sais comment elle a eu mon adresse ni qui l'a envoyée chez moi; l'une d'entre nous, sans doute. Elle avait appris que j'étais du même convoi que sa mère et elle voulait que je lui parle de sa mère. Malheureusement j'ai été incapable de rien lui dire. Je n'ai pas connu sa mère. En tout cas, je ne me la rappelle pas, je n'avais pas même retenu son nom. J'ai demandé à Mado qui, de nous toutes, a la mémoire la plus sûre. Elle ne s'en souvient pas non plus.] (94)

For the family members of those who perished, the information they can obtain from survivor narratives plays a crucial role in their attempts to mourn the loss of the people they loved. Ironically, the pilgrimatic Pierre is best able to remember the woman's mother – he immediately recalls a whole list of facts about her, including the name and age of her daughter who contacted Charlotte – which shows that, in certain situations, his practices serve an invaluable function even though they do harm to his wife and, ultimately, to himself.

Similarly, in a story that appears later in *Mesure de nos jours*, the fictional character Marceline describes how a witness's testimony helped her mother move on after her husband's death in the camps:

> My mother, she didn't want to believe it. She hoped to see him again for a long, long time. And long afterwards, when she would say that she no longer hoped, when her lips said that she no longer hoped, her eyes still had hope in them […] How tenacious hope can be! How desperate hope can be! There were stories about prisoners and deportees in Russia, that they were stuck in Odessa waiting for a ship, or hospitalized, or even that they were wandering here or there … In Poland, in Hungary, in Romania … Do you remember all of the legends that were formed? Up until one

of my father's comrades who was unable to come earlier because he was sick, and no doubt because he also didn't have the courage, up until this comrade came to see us, my mother kept hoping. And how many times did she repeat the same question: "Did you see him dead? Did you see him dead with your own eyes?" The poor man was nearly tortured.[25]

[Ma mère, elle, ne voulait pas le croire. Elle a espéré le revoir longtemps, longtemps. Et longtemps après, quand elle disait qu'elle n'espérait plus, quand ses lèvres disaient qu'elles n'espéraient plus, ses yeux gardaient de l'espoir [...] Que l'espoir peut être tenace! Que l'espoir peut être désespéré! On racontait qu'il y avait des prisonniers et des déportés en Russie, qu'ils étaient bloqués à Odessa dans l'attente d'un bateau, ou bien hospitalisés, ou encore qu'ils erraient, par là ... En Pologne, en Hongrie, en Roumanie ... Tu te souviens, toutes ces légendes qui se forgeaient? Jusqu'à ce qu'un camarade de mon père qui n'avait pas pu venir plus tôt parce qu'il était malade, et sans doute aussi parce qu'il n'en avait pas le courage, jusqu'à ce que ce camarade vienne nous voir, ma mère persistait dans son espoir. Et combien de fois n'a-t-elle pas répété sa question: "Vous l'avez vu mort? Vous l'avez vu mort de vos propres yeux?" Le malheureux était au supplice.] (179–80)

Survivors' ethical obligation to the memory of the dead entails this additional obligation to the living, because returnees are the only ones who possess the information that loved ones so desperately need to move on. As such, deportees need to remain connected to each other and their shared past in the aftermath because, as a collective, they can bear witness to these facts better than any one person with a limited vision can.[26] Their task, in short, is larger than any one survivor can accomplish alone. But Marceline's story also points to the harmful effects that loved ones, in their quest for understanding, can exert on witnesses in the aftermath. The awful information that camp survivors relate is painful for them to relay, and, of course, painful for loved ones to hear. However, like Marceline's mother, people may end up taking out their pain on traumatized survivors, and in so doing, punishing the very witnesses who allow them to grieve.

Pierre of course is also one of these loved ones who harms survivors because of how he deals with his pain. Marie-Louise was arrested, imprisoned, and deported to a concentration camp, and after an absence of more than two years, she returned to him reduced to the social state of a child. Who wouldn't be crushed to see the person they love crippled by trauma and unable to fend for him or herself? Misguided though they may be, Pierre's dedicated efforts to return Marie-Louise to her "normal" pre-Auschwitz self, and to help her remember everything about the camps, clearly speak to the depths of his love. And, as Marie-Louise states herself, without Pierre, she may be closed off in different ways from the rest of the outside world.

But, in the end, "Marie-Louise" illustrates how well-meaning and loving people like Pierre can go horribly wrong when trying to cope with unimaginable pain. The passage clearly links this harmful behaviour, moreover, to these people trying to understand Auschwitz by recognizing only the facts they have retained from the past when engaging others in the present. Pierre wants to see the world through his wife's eyes, but – as his initial exchange with Charlotte demonstrates – his behaviour also seeks to erase the differences between his experiences and those of Marie-Louise. Delbo's narratorial intervention at the moment Charlotte first meets Pierre offers an implicit critique of his way of recognizing and sharing in things. Marie-Louise introduces them to each other:

"Pierre, we have a visitor. Guess who. Charlotte.

– Ah! Charlotte! I'm so happy to finally see you. I don't say to meet you; I've known you for a long time.

– You know each other very well. I also spoke about you a lot to Charlotte, over there, didn't I?

– Yes, in fact, we know each other.

– Embrace like old comrades."

He was like I imagined given what his wife had told me. A bit older, with a melancholy look in his eye that he most likely did not have at the time she was telling me about him.[27]

["Pierre nous avons une visite. Devine qui. Charlotte.

– Ah! Charlotte! Que je suis heureux de vous voir enfin. Je ne dis pas de faire votre connaissance; je vous connais depuis longtemps.

– Vous vous connaissez très bien. J'ai aussi beaucoup parlé de toi à Charlotte, là-bas, n'est-ce pas Charlotte?

– Oui, en effet, nous nous connaissons.

– Embrassez-vous comme de vieux camarades."

Il était comme je l'imaginais d'après ce que m'avait dit sa femme. Un peu vieilli, avec un regard un peu mélancolique qu'il n'avait sans doute pas à l'époque où elle me parlait de lui.] (88)

Given Pierre's pilgrimatic behaviour that is revealed later in the passage, it is no surprise that he and Marie-Louise insist here that he "knows" Charlotte like a comrade in spite of having never met her before. Yet Charlotte's reaction – "Yes, in fact, we know each other," she replies – does not completely reject the idea that she and Pierre can be acquainted with each other thanks to the stories that Marie-Louise has told. As Delbo's narratorial remarks make clear, Pierre largely resembles the person Charlotte imagined from the things Marie-Louise told her about him. He may be older, and have a "melancholy" look in his eyes that he did not have before his wife's internment in Auschwitz, but he is ultimately recognizable thanks to Marie-Louise's stories.

What distinguishes Charlotte from Pierre – and, for that matter, from characters like Werner and Paul – though, is that she clearly hesitates when having recourse to any descriptions or imagined notions and looks to compare them with what she can see with her own eyes. Information gleaned from Marie-Louise's testimonies may traverse Charlotte's gaze, but, unlike Pierre, her approach to the present is not limited to what these testimonies reveal. Charlotte also does not proceed from the assumption that she can really ever share in either of her interlocutors' pain – even the pain of a fellow deportee who faced the same traumatizing horrors as her. Her relations with others are all disjointed, undoing and disrupting those formed with them before. This undoing extends to her own identity as well, which unravels and reforms and never stabilizes into any kind of whole. Delbo's disruptive and ironic writing in *Auschwitz et après* cultivates a similar disposition in its readers. It seeks to modify, that is, how we *initially* approach relating to others, and to reconfigure our desire to immerse ourselves in or to identify completely with the limited visions anyone constructs of the world.

In light of all this, the disruption caused by the painful "Marie-Louise" exerts a different kind of "communitarian" effect on Delbo's implied readers than would Booth's "stable irony" and its feeling of communing with a kindred spirit. This interruption distances readers from the reassured lovers presented in the passage, but the critical messages that Delbo asks readers to reconstruct all underscore the importance of remaining engaged in any and all acts of communication, and of seeking out the new, and different, understandings and forms of social contact that emerge from them. Jean-Luc Nancy's understanding of the kind of communication that takes place in the social formation he calls "community" suggests something similar. In *The Inoperative Community*, Nancy argues that community resists Pierre-like connections that erase differences between people. As opposed to "communions," which group people around shared characteristics and close the collectives they form off from the outside world, communities open up spaces in which people communicate with each other by "exposing" their limits, recognizing each other in their difference, and sharing in their lack of identity (60–1). This "sharing" of community

> is not a communion, nor the appropriation of an object, nor a self-recognition, nor even a communication as this is understood to exist between subjects. But these singular beings are themselves constituted by sharing, they are distributed and placed, or rather *spaced*, by the sharing that makes them *others*: other for one another, and other, infinitely other for the Subject of their fusion, which is engulfed in the sharing, in the ecstasy of the sharing: "communicating" not by "communing." These "places of communication" are no longer places of fusion, even though in them one *passes* from one to the other; they are defined and exposed by their dislocation. Thus, the communication of sharing would be this very dis-location. (25; emphasis in original)

According to Nancy, this constant exposure and sharing of their limits keeps members of a community always looking beyond whatever qualities they may share, which disrupts the kinds of fusional bonds with others and with "superior" forms of identity and subjectivity that totalitarian societies in particular seek to cultivate in their citizens. "On all sides the interruption turns community toward the outside instead of gathering it in toward a center," Nancy writes (60). "[W]e understand only that there is no common understanding of community, that sharing does not constitute an understanding (or a concept, or an intuition, or a schema), that it does not constitute a knowledge" (69). One of the messages that Delbo transmits to her readers through "Marie-Louise" proposes something similar: it asks readers to look beyond their fixed ways of being with others and what they may already understand, and to seek out new ideas and relations that emerge during any act of communication.

However, while this passage ultimately demands such a disjointed, outward-looking relation from its *readers*, it also outlines an additional, and quite different, mode of contact in social interactions with deportees and their well-meaning loved ones. Charlotte does not share her limits with Marie-Louise and Pierre, and her behaviour on the surface of this encounter does not disrupt the fusional relation that they seek out with her. Rather, she tries to seek out and share in the singularity that each member of the couple does not, indeed *cannot*, reveal themselves – a sharing that she herself conceals in this encounter, perhaps to keep Marie-Louise and Pierre from retreating further into their reassured selves. Charlotte engages the couple, in other words, with her obligations to others, and with the larger social context in which survivor narratives circulate, both clearly in mind. Idealized notions of coupledom may facilitate the projects of a social order that morphs, reconfigures, and codifies memory. But even the narratives produced by normalized witnesses can potentially contribute to our memory of the dead and help loved ones to mourn and, ultimately, move on. Nancy's "community" is too utopian a concept to account for the demands placed on survivors in messy situations like these. Such encounters require activating outmoded concepts and their engulfing bonds to include people like Marie-Louise and Pierre in our communities and to draw them out of their "selves." They require us, that is, to read in two ways at once: one that is attentive to our own undoing and another turned outward and imagining the singularity others hide.

In the end, though, *Mesure de nos jours* also quite obviously rejects the idea that a peaceful, orderly, or "normal" life is possible after a collective experience of trauma like Auschwitz. Through the wholly fictional "Marie-Louise," the text ironically transmits the harsh and extreme message that loving people who have nothing but good intentions deny the ghosts of Auschwitz with their reassurance. Delbo's narratorial intervention at the conclusion of the passage – "I left them in the doorway of their pretty house at the end of the pathway made cool and shady by pine trees," she reflects [Je les ai laissés sur le seuil de leur jolie maison au bout de l'allée que les sapins faisaient fraîche et sombre (99)][28] – marks the distance that anyone should ultimately maintain from the normalizing communion in which couples like Pierre and Marie-Louise engage. And, in the end, this also means that readers must learn to proceed with caution in any interaction in which someone, even an old comrade, addresses them intimately; the reflective behaviour of Charlotte/Delbo in "Marie-Louise" teaches readers not to open themselves completely to anyone's familiar calls. *Mesure de nos jours* makes its readers recognize the limits of the interpretive approaches that they reflexively bring to a text, and to be wary of their own Marie-Louise-like submission to the pull of any text's flow. Only then can we ethically negotiate the new contexts in which we find ourselves, and discover what lies beyond what we already know.

Conclusion: This Has Been for These People

Those who we tell about this now
do not understand that so many of us
died so quickly. Our explanations do not
make them understand.

– Charlotte Delbo

[Ceux à qui nous racontons cela maintenant
ne comprennent pas que tant d'entre nous
soient mortes si vite. Nos explications ne le
leur font pas comprendre.]

L'Album d'Auschwitz is a collection of photos that depicts the experience of arrival, selection, and departure for the gas chambers of several convoys of Hungarian Jews. Between 15 May and 9 July 1944, more than 400,000 Jews were deported to Auschwitz II-Birkenau from Hungary. Roughly 350,000 of them were gassed in assembly-line fashion hours after their arrival. In spite of a general prohibition against taking photographs in the camp, the trajectory of several of these convoys was documented by an SS photographer.[1] Reprinted in France in 2005 for the sixtieth anniversary of the liberation of Auschwitz, the album is a shocking testament to one of the most atrocious campaigns in the Nazi attempt to exterminate Europe's Jews.[2]

When I first came across *L'Album d'Auschwitz*, I did not know much about the plight of the Hungarian Jews. I picked up the text because I had never seen photos depicting the experience of arrival in Auschwitz and because I wanted to know more about how people from different nations were treated by the Nazis. The photos assembled in the album confirmed much of what I already knew from my research on France. I extracted a few new pieces of information from the text's introductory chapters about the layout of Auschwitz, the specificities of the Hungarian experience of the Second World War, and the story of the photo collection's discovery in postwar Poland; but nothing really struck me about the photos themselves. Seeing what I already knew as a fact – that masses of people were calm and obedient while the Nazis mechanically marched them to the gas chambers – was admittedly disturbing, but anyone who researches mass death grows familiar with such feelings.

My experience changed abruptly when I came to the section of *L'Album d'Auschwitz* immediately following the original photo collection. In it, historians Marcello Pezzetti and Sabine Zeitoun comment on sixteen enlarged photos from the album that represent the major steps through which people gassed upon arrival in Auschwitz had to pass. A picture that I had previously overlooked made me stop. Photo number 112 captures three Jewish men and a woman standing in a wooded area with four SS guards behind them (figure 1). I guessed that the woman was engaged in some sort of struggle with the three men, but I couldn't say for sure. What, I wondered, is going on here? The caption to the photo written by Pezzetti and Zeitoun explained:

> These people are in front of the entrance of Crematorium V's undressing room. Behind them, the path that separates the two crematoria, in the birch forest (*Birkenwald*), was called the *Ringstrasse*.
>
> This photo and photo 128 are exceptional because they provide us with documentation of the next-to-last step before people were put to death. In the background, we see a large portion of Crematorium IV, which was operating to its full capacity at the time. Both the upper and lower portions of the building are visible. (emphasis in original)[3]

> [Ces personnes sont devant l'entrée de la salle de déshabillage du *Krematorium* V. Derrière eux, la route qui sépare les deux *Krematorium*, dans le *Birkenwald*, était appelée la *Ringstrasse*.
>
> Cette photo et la suivante (photo 128) sont exceptionnelles car elles témoignent de l'avant-dernière étape avant la mise à mort. À l'arrière-plan, on peut voir une grande partie du *Krematorium* IV dans une période où il est en pleine activité. Sont ici visibles tout à la fois la partie haute et la partie basse du bâtiment.] (133; emphasis in original)

I looked back at the photo. Who could guess that the nondescript building in the background contained gas chambers, or that these people were standing in front of the doorway to one of the camp's crematoria? The caption continues:

> Crematoria IV and V are identical and symmetrical. Crematorium IV was in operation from 22 March 1943 to 7 October 1944, the date of the *Sonderkommando* revolt that partially destroyed it. Unlike Crematoria II and III, Crematorium IV's installations were located exclusively on the ground floor. There were eight cremation ovens as well as a large room that was used both for undressing people and as a morgue. There were also three gas chambers. Another way in which this building differed from Crematoria II and III was that it had two chimneys, each of which was more than 16 meters tall. Zyklon B tablets were poured into the gas chambers through small openings that were hermetically sealed. Crematorium V was in operation from 4 April 1943 to 18 January 1945, when it was destroyed by the Nazis. However, the gas chambers were only used until November 1944. An order from Himmler suspended the extermination of the Jews en masse at this time.
>
> In the beginning of the summer of 1944, the Nazis had five large pits dug next to Crematorium V. In these, they burned the cadavers of people gassed in Crematorium V in the open. They did this because the Crematorium was able to kill people at a faster rate than it could liquidate their bodies in its cremating ovens.
>
> At this time, the Nazis had not yet camouflaged these two crematoria. They were soon to be surrounded by a fence of tree branches. (emphasis in original)

> [Les *Krematorium* IV et V sont identiques et symmétriques. Le *Krematorium* IV a fonctionné du 22 mars 1943 au 7 octobre 1944, date de la révolte du *Sonderkommando* qui l'a détruit partiellement. À la différence des *Krematorium* II et III, les installations du *Krematorium* IV se trouvaient exclusivement au rez-de-chaussée, où la salle des fours crématoires (au nombre de huit) avait été aménagée, ainsi qu'une grande salle. Celle-ci était utilisée soit pour le déshabillage, soit comme morgue. Dans la partie la plus basse, il y avait trois chambres à gaz. Également à la différence des *Krematorium* II et III, ce bâtiment était doté de deux cheminées mesurant chacune plus de 16 mètres de haut. Les cristaux de Zyklon B étaient versés à travers de petites ouvertures fermant hermétiquement. Le *Krematorium* V a fonctionné du 4 avril 1943 au 18 janvier 1945, date de sa destruction par les nazis. Cependant, ses chambres à gaz n'ont été utilisées que jusqu'en novembre 1944. En effet, à partir de cette période, l'extermination de masse des Juifs avait été suspendue sur ordre d'Himmler.

> À côté de ce *Krematorium*, au début de l'été 1944, les nazis firent creuser cinq vastes fosses pour brûler les corps en plein air, car la capacité de mise à mort était supérieure à celle de la liquidation des cadavres dans les fours.
>
> À cette époque, les nazis n'avaient pas encore camouflé ces deux *Krematorium*, qui seront par la suite ceinturés d'une palissade constituée de branches d'arbres.] (133; emphasis in original)

Again, I looked back at the photo. Pezzetti and Zeitoun's explanations gave me a more detailed understanding of the scene, but something here wasn't right. The caption made clear how and when these two crematoria functioned and how their appearance changed over time, but there was no mention of the four people in the foreground. The crimes that the Nazis perpetrated in this space had become more readable, but the figures that had initially drawn me to the photo had been reduced to nothing more than "these people," mere incidental scenery. They are the visual subject of the photograph, but Pezzetti and Zeitoun focus on the building in the background and the one, off-frame, that the victims are about to enter.

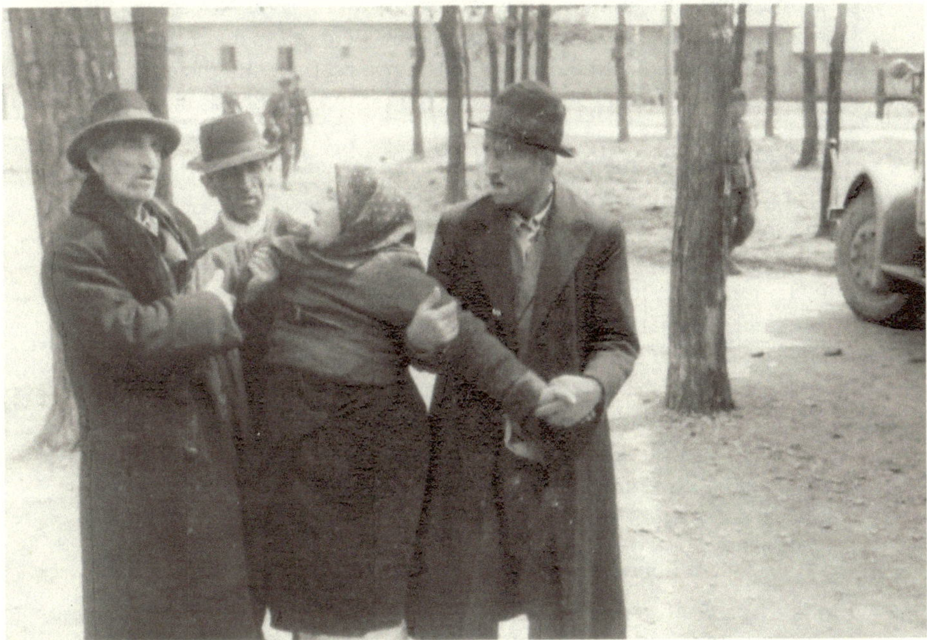

Figure 1: Photo 112 from *L'Album d'Auschwitz*

I quickly reread the caption, thinking I must have missed something. Pezzetti and Zeitoun explain that the next enlarged photo testifies to the same "exceptional" step in the extermination process as Photo 112, so I turned the page hoping to find more information there. Photo 128 also captures a group of people outside of a crematorium's doorway, but here I saw something completely different. A group of women and children are looking calmly at their SS photographer (figure 2). As one of my friends put it when I showed him the photo, they look like they are on their way home from a trip.[4] Pezzetti and Zeitoun explain:

> This group of women and children, coming from the *Hauptstrasse* (the principal route in the camp), are entering the courtyard of Crematorium II. A large portion of Crematorium III is visible in the background. Its deceptive appearance hides beneath it an enormous room containing four cremation ovens.
>
> Situated opposite Birkenau's entrance, at the end of the ramp, Crematoria II and III were the largest and most sophisticated killing centres that the Nazis created for exterminating the Jews. Crematorium II began operating on 14 March 1932 and Crematorium III on the following June 25th. Identical and symmetrical, they were both in operation until November 1944. The portions of the building in which people were put to death were in the basement, the room with the ovens on the ground floor and the quarters of the members of the *Sonderkommando* on the second. (emphasis in original)
>
> [Ce groupe de femmes et d'enfants, venant de la *Hauptstrasse* (route principale du camp), entre dans la cour du *Krematorium* II. Une grande partie du *Krematorium* III est visible à l'arrière-plan. Sous une apparence trompeuse, ce bâtiment cache une énorme salle dans laquelle se trouvent quinze fours crématoires.
>
> Situés à l'opposé de l'entrée de Birkenau, au fond de la rampe, les *Krematorium* II et III étaient les installations de mise à mort les plus perfectionnées et les plus vastes que les nazis aient mises en place pour exterminer les Juifs. Le *Krematorium* II était entré en fonction le 14 mars 1943 et le *Krematorium* III le 25 juin suivant. Identiques et symétriques, ils ont fonctionné tous les deux jusqu'en novembre 1944. Les locaux de mise à mort étaient au sous-sol, la salle des fours au rez-de-chaussée et le logement des membres du *Sonderkommando* au premier étage.] (135; emphasis in original)

I looked back at the women and children in Photo 128. If they know they are about to enter one of the largest and most efficient killing centres

Figure 2: Photo 128 from ***L'Album d'Auschwitz***

constructed by the Nazis, they are doing a good job of hiding how terrified they must be. I read the rest of Pezzetti and Zeitoun's description:

> From the courtyard, the victims took a set of stairs that sank into the ground and led to the large undressing room that was about fifty metres in length. With an unassuming appearance, the room was outfitted with benches and coat racks. The Nazis "advised" the Jews to be sure to remember the number of their coat rack, and to lace their shoes together so as to find them more easily after the "shower." Then, the victims entered the gas chambers, first the women with the children, then the men. With a total capacity of more than 1500 people, this room was equipped with fake showers. When it was almost entirely full, the last few men were violently stuffed in. The door could then be shut.
>
> The SS doctor who oversaw operations was the person who carried out the selection on the ramp immediately prior. He gave the order to the sanitation staff (*SS Sanitätsdienstgrade*), who were supplied with gas masks, to

pour Zyklon B crystals through the openings that had been made in the ceiling. These openings lead to columns throughout the room from which mortal fumes emanated. Ten minutes was all it took for everyone to be dead. At that point, air extractors were turned on to allow for the men of the *Sonderkommando* to enter the room twenty minutes later to extract the cadavers from the gas chamber. Then, they cut the women's hair and pulled out gold teeth. They next placed the cadavers on the freight elevator that served the room with the cremation ovens on the ground floor. Their ashes were thrown into the river, either the Sola or the Vistule. Like Crematoria IV and V, Crematoria II and III were not yet camouflaged at the moment this picture was taken. They were shortly after, by means of an enclosure consisting of piled up tree trunks. (emphasis in original)

[De la cour, les victimes empruntaient un escalier qui s'enfonçait sous terre et débouchait dans la grande salle de déshabillage, longue d'une cinquantaine de mètres. Cette salle, à l'aspect neutre, était équipée de bancs et de portemanteaux. Les nazis "conseillaient" aux Juifs de bien retenir leur numéro de portemanteau, et de lacer leurs chaussures entre elles afin de les retrouver plus facilement après la "douche." Ensuite, les victimes entraient dans la chambre à gaz, d'abord les femmes avec les enfants, puis les hommes. Cette salle d'une capacité de plus de 1500 personnes était dotée de fausses douches. Lorsqu'elle était presque entièrement remplie, il fallait y entasser avec violence les derniers hommes. La porte pouvait alors être fermée.

Le médecin SS qui dirigeait les opérations était celui qui avait, au préalable, effectué la sélection sur la rampe. Il donnait l'ordre au personnel de service sanitaire (*SS Sanitätsdienstgrade*), muni de masques à gaz, de verser des cristaux de Zyklon B par des ouvertures ménagées dans le plafond. Celles-ci donnaient sur des colonnes d'où s'échappaient, à travers la salle, des émanations mortelles. Dix minutes suffisaient pour que tout le monde soit mort. Alors, des extracteurs d'air étaient mis en route afin de permettre, vingt minutes après, aux hommes du *Sonderkommando* d'y entrer pour extraire les cadavres de la chambre à gaz. Puis, ils tondaient les cheveux des femmes et arrachaient les dents en or. Ils mettaient ensuite les cadavres sur le monte-charge qui desservait, au rez-de-chaussée, la salle des fours crématoires. Leurs cendres étaient jetées dans la rivière, la Sola, ou dans la Vistule. Comme les *Krematorium* IV et V, les *Krematorium* II et III n'étaient pas encore camouflés au moment de la prise de vue. Il l'ont été peu de temps après, à moyen d'une clôture constituée de troncs d'arbres empilés.] (135; emphasis in original)

The magnitude of the figures and the precision of the process Pezzetti and Zeitoun describe is shocking. However, nearly seventy years after the end of the Second World War, we are prepared for this shock: in spite of the vast scale of the atrocities Pezzetti and Zeitoun detail, the massive and efficient cruelty of the Nazis is no longer a revelation. Does anybody – aside from Holocaust deniers – approach photographs of the concentration camps and not expect to find images testifying to the evils of the Final Solution?

Again, I assumed that I missed something explained elsewhere. I turned back to the page immediately preceding Photo 112. There I saw a picture of a large group of men, women, and children in a wooded area (figure 3). All of them look like they are waiting for something to happen. Pezzetti and Zeitoun explain:

> Before entering the gas chambers in Crematoria IV and V, people judged "unfit for work" often had to wait their turn in the birch forest (*Birkenwald*) where these installations were located. They were promised that, after "disinfection," they would be transferred to a family camp. There, they would be reunited with their family members when they returned from work. As a result, people remained calm and felt reassured. After a difficult journey, children could play outside, old people could relax, and women could talk among themselves. (emphasis in original)

> [Avant d'entrer dans les chambres à gaz des *Krematorium* IV et V, les personnes jugées "inaptes" devaient souvent attendre leur tour dans le *Birkenwald* (le bois de bouleaux) où se trouvaient ces installations de mise à mort. On leur avait promis qu'après la "désinfection," ils seraient transférés dans un camp regroupant les familles. Là, ils retrouveraient leurs proches quand ces derniers rentreraient du travail. Par conséquent, ils demeuraient confiants. Après un voyage pénible, les enfants pouvaient jouer dans la nature, les vieillards se reposer, les femmes discuter entre elles.] (131; emphasis in original)

I wondered if I was looking at the same photograph as Pezzetti and Zeitoun. The children in the photograph are not playing, the old people are not relaxing, and the women are not conversing. Although this might have been the intention of the SS, this most certainly is not what's going on here. There are tense knots of old men in the background, and worn-out and wary women and children in the foreground. Pezzetti and Zeitoun report what the Nazi gaze wants to see, and not what the photograph actually depicts.

Figure 3: Photo 138 from *L'Album d'Auschwitz*

Pezzetti and Zeitoun pay scant attention to the *people* in these photographs. But the people are what draw me in, the people are what I want to know about. This is the source of my bewilderment: the captions are not describing what I'm seeing with my own eyes. Instead, Pezzetti and Zeitoun's captions tell me about the scale and efficiency of the slaughter, how buildings in the camp functioned, the deceptive strategies that the Nazis employed, and how the Nazis expected their victims to behave. What I don't find in these captions is information about who these people were, what they might have been thinking in these moments, and the complex individual histories that brought each of them to this point.

Though surely unintentionally, Pezzetti and Zeitoun have "massified" the Jewish experience of arrival in Auschwitz. They lump the people in these photos into a mass, and deny the particularities that each photograph depicts. Pezzetti and Zeitoun's historical commentary gives us a detached, depersonalized view of this ordeal. If you had only the captions, you would hardly realize that these photos depict people at all.

Of course, as historians, their objective was undoubtedly to make these scenes as readable as possible from the documents they had amassed at the time. But, in the process, they have constructed a monolithic narrative about these scenes that massifies the individual stories they're composed of, and washes out the differences between what each person went through. Were all of these people "confident" and "calm" after they exited the trains, or were they playing the roles that people with guns told them to? Were they deceived until the moment Zyklon B tablets were poured into the fake showers they had been forced to enter, or did they have an inkling of what was in store and see no way out of it? Pezzetti and Zeitoun have made the scenes in these photographs more historically readable, but their descriptions echo the massifying gaze through which the Nazis originally saw all of these people.

Nearly anyone will recognize that there is more going on in Photo 112 (figure 1) than what Pezzetti and Zeitoun tell us. "These people" are obviously not just standing outside of one of Auschwitz's crematoria. And the fact that Pezzetti and Zeitoun's caption does not address what I find striking in this struggle makes me want to construct my own narrative about it. The woman does not want to move forward, and at least two of the men accompanying her are pulling her in that direction. The man on her left has his mouth open and either is saying something or is going to say something – I imagine it's something reassuring, like "Calm down, it's OK" – and he's looking at the man on the woman's right who is helping him to restrain her. The man on the woman's right is staring blankly in the direction of the crematorium, with a distant, nearly expressionless look on his face. To him, the building he's looking at is probably as unrecognizable as *Krematorium* IV was to me when I first looked at this photo. These two men are literally forcing this woman and themselves to move towards death. To look at Photo 112 with this fact in mind makes what's going on between these four people horribly absurd.

I began to ask other kinds of questions as I looked more closely at Photo 112. What happened to cause these four people to be engaged in this struggle? What happened or is happening that is causing this woman to resist, and these men to try to calm her down? Knowing that this photo was taken after the selection process in which women, young children, the elderly, and the disabled were separated from people who entered the camp as forced labourers, I could only assume that she's resisting because she's just been separated from someone she knows. She's trying to break free and go back to this person, and these men are keeping her from going there. Based on their body language, she must know or at least trust the man on her left. He's using his right arm to restrain her beneath her left armpit, but the two are delicately holding hands. These calm hands add an eerie stasis to the entire scene.

This added something to my reading of Photo 112: the men restraining the woman were probably trying to reassure her that she would see the person she is missing soon enough if she would just do as she were told. And maybe that's what the people in Photo 128 were thinking (figure 2). But the more I think about it, the whole scene nauseates me. I know from my future position what the Nazis did to Jews in Auschwitz, and these men should be following this woman's example, not telling her to follow their own. Maybe they were waiting until an opportunity presented itself in which they could act, and break free from their oppressors. Or maybe they just didn't know, like I do, that they were being deceived and manipulated. Maybe none of them knew that they were going to die minutes after they entered the camp's familiar-looking buildings. Maybe some of them did.

No one can know for sure what's going on in the moments captured in any of these photographs. All of the people in them were murdered before they could tell us – the singular experiences that they had are forever lost. All that remains as a testament to them are these SS photographs. The fact that these images exist will always remind us that, whatever was going on, it happened to *these people*. This is what the struggle captured in Photo 112 led me to see: encountering a photograph that did not conform to my expectations about arrival in Auschwitz led me to examine it and the other photographs more closely, and to see that they really didn't fit with what I was expecting to find, either. This caused me to question the information I was being fed by the historical commentary in *L'Album d'Auschwitz*, and to rethink what I thought I already knew about these events. And it has also made me realize that, when placed in this extreme context, our everyday behaviour looks horrifyingly absurd.

In his influential study of photography, *La chambre claire*, Roland Barthes explains that two elements – the "studium" and the "punctum" – co-occur in every photograph that interests him. The studium encompasses the culturally coded ways in which Barthes initially views photographs; through the studium, he takes a generalized interest in and is somewhat moved by whatever a photograph depicts, but these same cultural filters mute his emotional responses. The punctum disrupts the reactions of the culturally coded studium, and evokes his intense interest in photographs. "[I]t is not I who seek it out (as I invest the field of the *studium* with my sovereign consciousness)," Barthes describes, "it is this element which rises from the scene, shoots out of it like an arrow, and pierces me" (26; emphasis in original)[5] [(C)e n'est pas moi qui vais le chercher (comme j'investis de ma conscience souveraine le champ du *studium*), c'est lui qui part de la scène, comme une flèche, et vient me percer (48–9)].

Historical photographs exert a particular version of the intense punctum effect on Barthes: they horrify him because they point towards the future death of the subjects depicted in them. Commenting on a photograph of nineteenth-century death row inmate Lewis Payne, Barthes writes:

> I now know that there exists another *punctum* (another "stigmatum") than the "detail." This new *punctum*, which is no longer of form but of intensity, is Time, the lacerating emphasis of the *noeme* (*"this-has-been"*), its pure representation.
>
> In 1865, young Lewis Payne tried to assassinate Secretary of State W.H. Seward. Alexander Gardner photographed him in his cell, where he was waiting to be hanged. The photograph is handsome, as is the boy: that is the *studium*. But the *punctum* is: *he is going to die*. I read at the same time: *This will be* and *this has been*; I observe with horror an anterior future of which death is the stake. By giving me the absolute past of the pose (aorist), the photograph tells me death in the future. What *pricks* me is the discovery of this equivalence [...]
>
> This *punctum*, more or less blurred beneath the abundance and the disparity of contemporary photographs, is vividly legible in historical photographs: there is always a defeat of Time in them: *that* is dead and *that* is going to die. (96; emphasis in original)
>
> [Je sais maintenant qu'il existe un autre *punctum* (un autre "stigmata") que le "détail." Ce nouveau *punctum*, qui n'est plus de forme, mais d'intensité, c'est le Temps, c'est l'emphase déchirante du noème (*"ça-a-été"*), sa représentation pure.
>
> En 1965, le jeune Lewis Payne tenta d'assassiner le secrétaire d'État américain, W.H. Seward. Alexander Gardner l'a photographié dans sa cellule; il attend sa pendaison. La photo est belle, le garçon aussi: c'est le *studium*. Mais le *punctum*, c'est: il va mourir. Je lis en même temps: cela sera et cela a été; j'observe avec horreur un futur antérieur dont la mort est l'enjeu. En me donnant le passé absolu de la pose (aoriste), la photographie me dit la mort au futur. Ce qui me point, c'est la découverte de cette équivalence [...]
>
> Ce *punctum*, plus ou moins gommé sous l'abondance et la disparité des photos d'actualité, se lit à vif dans la photographie historique: il y a toujours en elle un écrasement du Temps: cela est mort et cela va mourir.] (148–50; emphasis in original)

Barthes explains here that historical photographs make available a dual perspective on the moment of death. From his present position, he already knows that the subjects depicted in the photographs are dead. But the photograph allows him to adopt another perspective simultaneously, one from which those deaths are still in the future. The effect of this dual perspective is a warping of time that makes much more vivid the basic message that Barthes retains from any photograph – the message "this has been" (148) [*ça-a-été* (176)].

Viewing the photographs in *L'Album d'Auschwitz* through Barthes's theoretical apparatus, it would appear that their horror lies in the simple fact that we realize that the people captured in them "are dead and are going to die." However, given that the album depicts the events leading up to one of the largest slaughters in Auschwitz's history, viewers approach these photographs already knowing the fate of the people in them. These photos point us towards death on a massive scale, but we expect to find images of countless anonymous people slowly making their way towards death. This flattening of time does not exert an intense punctum effect on us because – Holocaust deniers aside – we have prepared ourselves to experience it. In the seventy years since Auschwitz's liberation, knowing that the people in these photographs are dead and are going to die has become our studium, the message that we consciously seek out whenever the word "Holocaust" is brought up.[6] And, because of the extent to which information about the Holocaust and the Nazi camps justifiably saturates our culture, it follows that our emotional responses to them have inevitably become muted along the way. We take a generalized interest in these events as subjects. But, because we think we know so much about them, their horrors can no longer affect us in an intense, punctum-like way.[7]

And yet, these photographs *do* exert a horrifying punctum effect on us – but not because we discover that all of the people in them are moments away from being murdered en masse. Instead, these photos horrify us today because we can see the similarities between our everyday actions and those of the people captured in them; we are horrified because this everyday behaviour has been, and we know that it largely still is. "It is the details of everyday life – the portrait of a woman who saved her single ration of bread for her children, or that of a man who volunteered for forced labor because his wages were promised to his family," Lenore J. Weitzman and Dalia Ofer observe, "that restore individuality and humanity to the victims" (14). It is these same kinds of details that horrify and wound us from our present perspective because they connect us, as individuals and as humans, to the everyday behaviour of victims of atrocity. How many of us would react just like these people if faced with a similar ordeal? How many of us would hide our terror, or reassure our loved ones into moving forward (if, indeed, this is what's going on in these photographs)? How many of us would find very good reasons for allowing ourselves to be mechanically marched to an atrocious death? How many of us fail to recognize the horrific absurdity of how we act and how we engage others in our everyday lives?

History and memory are steadily becoming accepted as complementary ways of understanding the Holocaust in spite of their past rivalry.[8] As Aleida Assmann has explained, "[w]hile memory is indispensable, as a view from the inside, to evaluating the events of the past and to creating an ethical stance, history is needed, as a view from the outside, to scrutinize and verify the remembered events" (263–4).[9] Assmann suggests that, in light of this, we should give up looking for a "clear and unanimous solution" for how best to represent the Holocaust, and instead reflect on the merits and shortcomings of the plurality of approaches we can use to understand it (272). By considering, rather than dismissing, multiple and contradictory readings and by leaving ambiguities unresolved, Marianne Hirsch similarly observes, we can

> broaden the boundaries of our understanding and tap into a deeper register of intergenerational transmission. We gain access to what the images and stories about this past do not readily reveal – the emotional fabric of daily life in extreme circumstances, its aftereffects in the process of survival. (*Generation* 76)

Hirsch proposes that the reading and viewing practices of the children of survivors be considered modes of engagement that can help us gain access to this emotional fabric because they resemble the reactions that their family members had to the trauma of the past (63).[10] The projection of needs and desires from the present onto the past that characterizes the "postgeneration's" response to the Holocaust may serve, problematically, to mask many aspects of the event, Hirsch explains. Yet, "for better or worse," these affiliative and identificatory reactions can also be likened to how the "the protective shield of trauma" also functions in survivors: they absorb the shock, filter and diffuse the impact of trauma, and ultimately diminish its harm (48). They can be seen, in this sense, as analogous responses that reinforce the "*living* connection" between the generation of witnesses and survivors and the generation after, responses that also offer insights into the experience of everyday life in the midst of massive historical trauma (emphasis in original).

But the photographs examined above and the witness narratives analysed throughout this book suggest that some of the connections well-meaning people seek out with survivors, and some approaches that political deportees take to the camps, can also serve to exclude, ignore, and deny the experiences of victims rather than broaden our understanding of them as a whole. Indeed, both *L'Album d'Auschwitz* and the testimonies of survivors like Delbo and Semprun, expose the problems and limitations of our ethical responses in the face of atrocity, and remind us that no matter how much we think we may know, the singular experiences that millions of people had will always remain unknown. Neither the discipline of history nor survivor memory – nor any interpretive framework – can ever tell us what is going on in the minds of these people in these moments. This is not to say that the experiences of Jews and political deportees were ultimately the same in the Nazi camps, or can be reduced to what a few, exemplary testimonies show us. My contention is, in fact, the opposite: that, when engaging witness testimony and the horrors of atrocity, we must proceed from the assumption that our understandings are inadequate, and that the experiences of victims are inherently singular, different, and irreducible. To paraphrase Barthes, we must never lose sight of the idea that *this has been for these people*. These people's stories will never be told, and we must respect the massive void that engulfs their experiences. We must view this as one of our ethical tasks that emerges from the experience of collective catastrophe, and resist the urge to stabilize, to codify, or to claim to know.

What we need is to change how we approach the horrors of the Nazi camps. What we need is to try to imagine what Auschwitz may have looked like from the perspective of the victims *in spite of* the inadequacies of whatever we can imagine. "In order to know, we must imagine for ourselves" [Pour savoir il faut s'imaginer], Georges Didi-Huberman tells us in a study of four photographs taken clandestinely by Auschwitz internees in the same year as the mechanized slaughter of the Hungarian Jews:

> We must attempt to imagine the hell that Auschwitz was in the summer of 1944. Let us not invoke the unimaginable. Let us not shelter ourselves by saying that we cannot, that we could not by any means, imagine it to the very end. We *are obliged* to that oppressive imaginable. It is a response that we must offer, as a debt to the words and images that certain prisoners snatched, for us, from the harrowing Real of their experience. So let us

> not invoke the unimaginable. How much harder was it for the prisoners to rip from the camps those few shreds of which now we are trustees, charged with sustaining them simply by looking at them. Those shreds are at the same time more precious and less comforting than all possible works of art, snatched as they were from a world bent on their impossibility. Thus, images *in spite of all*: in spite of the hell of Auschwitz, in spite of the risks taken. In return, we must contemplate them, take them on, and try to comprehend them. Images *in spite of all*: in spite of our own inability to look at them as they deserve; in spite of our own world, full, almost choked, with imaginary commodities. (*Images In Spite of All* 3; emphasis in original)

> [Nous devons tenter d'imaginer ce que fut l'enfer d'Auschwitz en été 1944. N'invoquons pas l'inimaginable. Ne nous protégeons pas en disant qu'imaginer cela, de toutes les façons – car c'est vrai – nous ne le pouvons, nous ne le pourrons pas jusqu'au bout. Mais nous le *devons*, ce très lourd imaginable. Comme une réponse à offrir, une dette contractée envers les paroles et les images que certains déportés ont arrachées pour nous au réel effroyable de leur expérience. Donc, n'invoquons pas l'inimaginable. Il était tellement plus difficile, pour les prisonniers, de soustraire au camp ces quelques lambeaux dont nous sommes à présent dépositaires, dans la lourdeur de les soutenir d'un seul regard. Ces lambeaux nous sont plus précieux et moins apaisants que toutes les œuvres d'art possible, arrachés qu'ils furent à un monde qui les voulait impossibles. Images *malgré tout*, donc: malgré l'enfer d'Auschwitz, malgré les risques encourus. Nous devons en retour les contempler, les assumer, tenter d'en rendre compte. Images *malgré tout*: malgré notre propre incapacité à savoir les regarder comme elles le mériteraient, malgré notre propre monde repu, presque étouffé, de marchandise imaginaire.] (*Images malgré tout* 11; emphasis in original)

The photos that Didi-Huberman refers to here were taken in 1944 by members of the *Sonderkommando* to show others the process by which murders were taking place on a massive scale in Auschwitz, and were smuggled out of the camp to the Polish resistance movement as a testament to it. They depict bodies burning in the open air outside one of Auschwitz's crematoria and also a group of women running naked from the woods outside of a crematorium to its gas chamber. Not trying to imagine what this particular set of images represents amounts to denying the relation the clandestine photographers sought out with others themselves – they wanted those looking at them to imagine what they symbolized – and to ignore the tremendous effort and determination to resist to which the hasty, off-kilter compositions of their photos attest. "We must know how to look like an archaeologist" [Il faut savoir regarder comme regarde un archéologue], Didi-Huberman writes (*Écorces* 61).[11] "And it is through such a mode of looking – such a mode of questioning – at what we see that things begin to look at us from their buried spaces that time has left behind" [Et c'est à travers un tel regard – une telle interrogation – sur ce que nous voyons que les choses commencent de nous regarder depuis leurs espaces enfouis et leurs temps enfuis].

But how should our reading change when approaching photographs taken from the *Nazi* perspective like those from *L'Album d'Auschwitz*? How can we get closer to the victim's perspective when they are captured by the gaze of their killers? What resistance can we offer now, as people engaging these images from the future, to the massifying and murderous gaze through which the Nazis saw these people, and through which perpetrators continue to see people? Even now – especially now – resisting this gaze matters, as does acknowledging and paying tribute to the largely anonymous victims that we can see through it.[12] Didi-Huberman suggests that imagining the humanity of the victims and their own *inability* to imagine what awaited them upon their arrival in the camp, is one possible mode of engagement. Commenting on a visit he made to Auschwitz and his own experience as a tourist on the arrivals platform depicted in the photos of the Hungarian Jews, Didi-Huberman writes:

> I looked, it was unimaginable and so simple at the same time. By discovering, over there, the selection platform – with a group of visitors scattered throughout the pathway facing it – I felt the unimaginable of the now gone reality (the tragedy of the selections) as well as the unimaginable of the now gone viewpoint (the observation, in front of the same window, of the smooth functioning of things by the SS guard). The unimaginable was the impossibility, for the victims, of accessing a clear representation of the minutes that would follow, that would consummate – consume – their destiny. Or else it was the refusal, on the part of the SS guard, to imagine the humanity of these men, of these women, of these children, that he observed from above and far away. But today, for me on this page, for anyone in front of a history book or on site at Auschwitz, it is the necessity to not remain at this impasse of imagination, this impasse that was precisely one of the great strategic strengths – via its lies and brutality – of the Nazi extermination system.

> [J'ai regardé, c'était inimaginable et si simple en même temps. En découvrant, là-bas, la rampe de sélection – avec un groupe clairsemé de visiteurs sur le chemin d'en face – j'ai bien éprouvé l'inimaginable de la réalité passée (la tragédie des sélections) comme l'inimaginable du point de vue passé (l'observation, devant la même fenêtre, du bon fonctionnement des choses par le SS de garde). L'inimaginable, ce fut l'impossibilité pour les victimes d'accéder à une claire représentation des minutes qui allaient suivre, qui allaient consommer – consumer – leur destin. Ou bien c'était le refus, pour le SS de garde, d'imaginer l'humanité de ces hommes, de ces femmes, de ces enfants, qu'il observait de haut et de loin. Mais aujourd'hui, pour moi sur cette page, pour n'importe qui devant un livre d'histoire ou sur le territoire d'Auschwitz, c'est la nécessité de n'en pas rester à cette impasse de l'imagination, cette impasse qui fut précisément l'une des grandes forces stratégiques – *via* les mensonges et les brutalités – du système d'extermination nazi.] (*Écorces* 30–1)

Reading the Holocaust in a distanced and detached way, or from the position of one who knows, reproduces the way of seeing exploited by the Nazis in the extermination process, Didi-Huberman explains, because it fails, like the Nazis, to imagine the humanity of the victims or what the experience of arrival may have looked like from their unknowledgeable perspective. We can never know what these victims thought, knew, or felt, but we can certainly try to imagine what their experience may have been like as people who could not have understood everything about their situation.

However, we must also recognize the fundamental inaccessibility of these people's experiences as part of our approach, and persist in engaging images of victims – and, indeed, the horrors of the Holocaust and the Nazi camps as a whole – in spite of their ultimate inaccessibility. As Didi-Huberman puts it:

> To study an image of the Shoah is not "to pretend to regain hope in front of the image that grows distant." It is to persist in approaching it *in spite of all*, in spite of the inaccessibility of the phenomenon. It is to *not* console oneself in abstraction; it is to seek to understand *in spite of all*, in spite of the complexity of the phenomenon. It is to tirelessly ask the question of *how*: "After continuously considering the Nazi crimes as unrepresentable, and the massacre of millions of innocent beings as definitively unintelligible, we end up no longer asking *how* the camps functioned," writes Wolfgang Sofsky. It is not a matter of unilaterally positing the unsayable and the unimaginable of

> this story; rather, it is a matter of working *with* it, yet *against* it: by making the sayable and the imaginable into infinite tasks, necessary yet inevitably lacunary. (*Images In Spite of All* 155; emphasis in original)
>
> [Étudier une image de la Shoah, ce n'est pas "feindre de reprendre espoir devant cette image qui s'éloigne." C'est persister dans l'approche *malgré tout*, malgré l'inaccessibilité du phénomène. C'est ne pas se consoler dans l'abstraction, c'est vouloir comprendre *malgré tout*, malgré la complexité du phénomène. C'est poser inlassablement la question du *comment*: "À force de considérer les crimes nazis comme irreprésentables et le massacre de millions d'innocents comme définitivement inintelligible, on a fini par ne plus se demander *comment* fonctionnaient les camps," écrit Wolfgang Sofsky. On ne pose pas unilatéralement l'indicible et l'inimaginable de cette histoire, on travaille *avec*, c'est-à-dire *contre*: en faisant du dicible et de l'imaginable une tâche infinie, nécessaire quoique forcément lacunaire.] (*Images malgré tout* 194; emphasis in original)

Working *with* the unimaginable is one way of working *against* it, that is, of engaging in the infinite task of trying to speak of the camps and imagine victims' experiences in spite of the inadequacies of what we imagine. This, after all, brings us closer to the victims' perspective, especially their perspective when they arrived in the camps – a perspective defined, in part, by its lack of access to knowledge and understanding. We of course will never completely understand any of it – claiming to do so would be reductive and ethically atrocious. But we cannot let the complexity of the Nazi camps and the Holocaust – and the complexity of the task we face as readers of them – be a barrier to engaging these events in the first place.

Yet the testimonies I have analysed throughout this book indicate that some major obstacles stand in the way of us truly adopting this destabilized approach to the experience of atrocity. The defensive ethics of the male deportee community and of survivors' loved ones illustrates the tremendous pressure many of us feel to act as though we know and to display this knowledge to others. Failed understandings and past modes of relationality are also reassuring and comforting forces because they offer us ways of responding that have been deemed appropriate by others before. But these rigid codes and sets of behaviours codify neat and exclusionary modes of contact that deny the particularities of others' experiences and reinforce the repressive moral gestures of social orders that ignore victims' ideas and concerns. These set ways of being mean, in short, not drawing near the experiences of victims at all, and not approaching them as fundamentally singular, as fundamentally human, as different and evolving through time. This does not mean celebrating our incapacities and weaknesses or transforming them into some new idealized ethical code. It means, rather, no longer hiding them, and liberating us all from the constraints of ethical knowledge and the limits it places on our interactions with others and, ultimately, on our ourselves.

What we can never know about the photographs in *L'Album d'Auschwitz* is how these people experienced the singular moments captured within them. What we cannot know is, precisely, my initial question about Photo 112 (figure 1): what is going on here? No matter how many documents we consult – testimonies, historical narratives, other photographs – we will never be certain of the answer to this question. What we say about the singular experiences captured in the images in *L'Album d'Auschwitz* will always, and necessarily, miss the mark. Let's face it: your guess is as good as mine. But we can recognize this together, and that there is always more going on than any reconstruction can ever tell us about the experiences that these people had in these moments. And, as a community, we can approach reading Nazi camp testimonies and the Holocaust as a whole with the complexity and inaccessibility of these phenomena always in mind. We can inhabit this unstable space together and engage each other knowing that, while what we say and imagine will always be inadequate, doing so is an essential act that brings us closer to the victims, and distances us, in the process, further from the perpetrators. We can thus conceive of the ethical as, quite literally, this kind of *stance*, one that requires our responses to others to be continuously improvised according to the demands of the encounter at hand.

In the end, this is also an essential point that my inquiry into the ethics of reading witness literature points us towards. By changing our habits as readers of survivor testimonies, we can promote less exclusionary ways of engaging atrocity, and cultivate a humbler, more grounded approach to being there for others that does not lose sight of victims and their concerns. And by recognizing the fundamental inadequacies of our readings, we forever acknowledge a basic fact about atrocities that can never be forgotten – that *this has been for these people*. These horrific moments happened and continue to happen, and we must recognize that millions of people had, and have, singular experiences of them that no one will ever fully understand. Let's work to ensure that no one ever denies that.

Notes

Introduction

1 All ellipses in brackets in this book denote where portions of the original texts have been eliminated. Ellipses without brackets occur in the original texts.

2 As many scholars have noted, Rosette Lamont's English translation of Delbo's *Auschwitz et après*, *Auschwitz and After*, is problematic in places because of its prosaic transformations of Delbo's original French text, its occasional disrespect of the original spacing of poetic passages, and, in some cases, its complete omission of entire sentences from the original. In this translation of "O you who know," for example, Lamont's rendering of the line "que le soir on a peur" as "and in the evening you fear it" inappropriately confines the fear deportees feel to a fear of death, rather than a feeling of fear in general that deportees feel every night (a fear, of course, that would include a fear of death, but not be limited to it). A better translation that is more loyal to the original French would read, more straightforwardly: "that at night you are afraid." Similarly, the translation of the lines "Saviez-vous que la souffrance n'a pas de limite/l'horreur pas de frontière" as "Did you know that suffering is limitless/that horror cannot be circumscribed" distorts the minimalism, the severity, and the rhythm of Delbo's style. A better rendering of these lines would be: "Did you know that suffering has no limit/horror no bound." When necessary, I include my own English translations of prose passages from *Auschwitz et après*, and have marked them thus throughout this book. I also include, when needed, my own alternate translations of poetic passages from *Auschwitz et après* in footnotes throughout.

3 The structure of this paragraph was inspired by the opening paragraph of Kristin Ross's *May '68 and Its Afterlives*.

4 Fassin elaborates these claims through analyses of, among other things, the distribution of financial assistance to the poor in France and the management of asylum claims by the French government during Chirac's presidency. See *Humanitarian Reason*.

5 Chambers further argues that the cultural function of witness literature is indexical, a reference to the second classification of the sign in Charles Sanders Peirce's work in semiotics. See *Untimely Interventions*.

6 In the seminal text *Testimony*, co-authored with Shoshana Felman, Laub specifically observes how these defensive reactions can arise in therapeutic contexts in order to protect therapists from trauma and its horrors, observations he bases on his years as a psychiatrist working with Holocaust survivors. Brison advances her ideas about these defence mechanisms in *Aftermath*, where she draws from her own experience as a survivor of sexual assault and attempted murder who became "the recipient of misguided attempts at consolation" on the part of the few people willing to acknowledge what happened to her after she was attacked (12).

7 For an excellent overview and detailed critique of these claims, see Trezise's *Witnessing Witnessing*.

8 Such questions have, of course, been subject to much debate in the fields of Holocaust studies and testimony and memory studies more broadly, and the bibliography on this subject is too extensive to cite fully here. Foundational works include Adorno's "Cultural Criticism and Society," Agamben's *Remnants of Auschwitz*, Blanchot's *L'écriture du désastre*, Felman and Laub's *Testimony*, and the numerous testimonial writings produced by Auschwitz survivor Primo Levi. Claude Lanzmann's landmark documentary *Shoah* has been at the centre of many of these discussions for its manner of representing the camp experience. For an overview, see Stuart Liebman's edited volume *Claude Lanzmann's Shoah*. For a more extensive bibliography of works pertaining to these areas of inquiry more broadly, see the bibliography of Trezise's *Witnessing Witnessing*.

9 The structure of this sentence has been adapted from Hutcheon, *Irony's Edge*, 5.

10 See, for example, Blanchot's *L'écriture du désastre* and Lyotard's *Heidegger et "les juifs."*

11 All English translations of Antelme's *L'espèce humaine* are from Haight and Mahler's *The Human Race*.

12 A kapo was a Nazi camp prisoner who was appointed by the SS to supervise other deportees. They received special privileges from the SS, such as more food and better clothing, that other internees did not. They were generally known for the brutality they showed toward other prisoners in order to stay in good favour with the SS.

13 The exact number of Spanish Republicans interned in Buchenwald has been difficult to determine. Historians estimate that anywhere between three hundred fifty and five hundred Spaniards were deported to the camp. For further reading, see Pike, *Spaniards in the Holocaust*, and Izquierdo, *Campos de concentración*.

14 Most of Semprun's works, including all of his Buchenwald testimonies, were originally written in French. The narrator of his 1994 witness text *L'écriture ou la vie* explains that Semprun writes primarily in French because he sees the experience of exile as his homeland: "I had personally chosen French, the language of exile, as another mother tongue, as another native language. I had chosen new origins for myself. I made a homeland out of exile" (my translation) [Pour ma part, j'avais choisi le français, langue de l'exil, comme une autre langue maternelle, originaire. Je m'étais choisi de nouvelles origines. J'avais fait de l'exil une patrie (353)]. However, the author's well-known tendency to fictionalize aspects of his own experiences makes it difficult to take such a statement at face value. In several places in *L'écriture ou la vie*, for example, the text's narrator refers to Spanish as a language of freedom and anguish for the survivor (see especially pp. 136–7 and 283), and provides theoretical commentary on the relationship between language and selfhood (see pp. 276–81). In an interview with Lila Azam Zanganeh given shortly before his death, Semprun further states that his French helps to rein in the craziness and shameless grandiloquence of his Spanish, and that, to him, Spanish is richer, more flexible, and less systematic than French (179). He also explains that "practical reasons" dictated his decision to write the few texts that he did in Spanish, as they were all about political subjects that are primarily of interest to a Spanish audience (178).

15 Theweleit's understanding of desire draws heavily from the work of Gilles Deleuze and Félix Guattari, particularly in their *Anti-Oedipus*.

16 Born Jans Chaim Mayer, Améry was born and raised in Vienna. In 1938 he fled the city first to France and then to Belgium to escape Nazi rule. Originally captured and tortured for his activities in the Belgian Resistance, he was deported to Auschwitz in 1943.

17 This is not to say that literature plays no role in representing atrocity. Rather, I am arguing against a certain belief in literature held by some members of the deportee community and by some readers of witness literature. The belief in the literary as a transcendent experience in which all human beings can share leads directly to its status as a defence mechanism that ignores the experiences of victims. In the works of Semprun in particular, the literary is constantly deployed, unironically, when his ability to share in another's experience is contested and, ultimately, exposed as impossible. Literature

is not useless when representing atrocity, but it has limits, it's status as something that allows people to share in others' experiences being one of them.

18 There is a significant body of scholarship that distinguishes the experiences of men and women in the Holocaust, the Nazi camps, and resistance movements in Europe, as well as studies that contest the relevance of discussing gender given the Nazis' racial categorizations and dehumanization of their victims. See, for example, Bauer's *Rethinking the Holocaust*, Bridenthal, Grossman, and Kaplan's *When Biology Became Destiny*, Heineman's *Gender and Destiny*, Hirsch's *Family Frames* and *The Generation of Postmemory*, Laska's *Women in the Resistance and in the Holocaust*, Ofer and Weitzman's *Women in the Holocaust*, Ringelheim's "Women and the Holocaust: A Reconsideration of Research," Rittner and Roth's *Different Voices*, and Tec's *Resilience and Courage*. For useful overviews of the development of this area of inquiry, see the introductions to Baer and Goldenberg's *Experience and Expression*, Goldenberg and Shapiro's *Different Horrors, Same Hell*, and Loew's *The Memory of Pain*. For a study of women's camp writing in the French context, see Hutton's *Testimony from the Nazi Camps*.

19 The first volume of Delbo's trilogy, titled *Aucun de nous ne reviendra*, was originally published as a stand-alone text in 1965. It was republished by Les Éditions de Minuit in 1970 as the first volume of the trilogy *Auschwitz et après*.

20 For further reading on Delbo's life and her complex relationship with the French Communist Party, see the biography co-authored by Violaine Gelly and Paul Gradvohl as well as Gradvohl's article "Charlotte Delbo et le communisme, Charlotte Delbo et les communistes."

21 For studies of these aspects of Delbo's work, see especially Caron, *My Father and I*; Carroll, "Les restes de la communauté – les femmes entre elles"; Chambers, *Untimely Interventions*; Rothberg, *Multidirectional Memory* and *Traumatic Realism*; Trezise, "The Question of Community in Charlotte Delbo's *Auschwitz and After*"; and Yaeger, "Proximity without Intimacy." For an overview of the development of Delbo scholarship, see Christiane Page's introduction to her edited volume *Charlotte Delbo, œuvre et engagements*.

22 Of course, as some scholars have argued, irony can also be used as a tool of exclusion by creating in-groups. For an overview of these studies, see Hutcheon's *Irony's Edge*.

23 See in particular the second chapter of *L'écriture ou la vie*.

24 Many conceptualizations of irony articulated since the romantic period have focused on philosophical concerns such as these. Richard Rorty, in particular, has argued for irony's value as a private philosophical attitude that can serve as the basis for ethics in postmodern societies, an idea he

bases on readings of theoretical reflections on irony advanced by Nietzsche, Heidegger, and Derrida, among others. For further reading, see Rorty's *Contingency, Irony, and Solidarity*. For useful overviews of irony's development as a concept, including its relationship to questions of subjectivity and ethics, see Claire Colebrook's *Irony* and Linda Hutcheon's *Irony's Edge*.

25 Literature must recognize its own limits as a means of representing atrocity if it is to cultivate this form of ethical commitment in its readers. Literature itself may not offer an experience that allows us to share completely in victims' experiences. However, it can bring out its own inadequacies as a representation of victims' experiences and allow readers to see those inadequacies so as to acknowledge them and remain engaged in spite of them.

26 My translation.

27 My translation.

28 In this respect, the rhetorical effect of Delbo's ironies contrasts starkly with the sting, cut, or "edge" that Linda Hutcheon identifies as a defining feature of the device. For further reading, see *Irony's Edge*.

29 See Felman and Laub's *Testimony*, LaCapra's *Writing History, Writing Trauma* and *History and Memory after Auschwitz*, and Caruth's *Unclaimed Experience*.

1 Literature, Theory, and Fraternity

1 All translations of Semprun's *L'écriture ou la vie* in this chapter are my own, and page numbers refer to the original French text.

2 In this chapter, I will use the name "Jorge" to refer to the main character of *L'écriture ou la vie* and the name "Semprun" for the text's narrator.

3 Semprun was a member of the Executive Committee of the Spanish Communist Party until 1964. Although the Spanish Communist Party announced that Semprun had decided to leave the movement to focus on his writing, he was actually banished for his criticisms of the Party's abuses of power, one of many subjects treated in his Spanish-language text *Autobiografía de Federico Sánchez*. His activities in the Party mainly consisted of organizing clandestine activities at Spanish universities. Federico Sanchez was the name by which he was known to most Party members. In addition to the *Autobiografía*, Semprun wrote another book in which his alias figures prominently, the French-language *Federico Sanchez vous salue bien*, which reflects on his tenure as Spain's Minister of Culture from 1988 to 1991 for Felipe Gonzalez's Socialist government. The second Federico Sanchez text has for its mission to uncover the secret workings of the Gonzalez government. In this text, Semprun focuses his attack on Gonzalez's vice president, Alfonso Guerra, and his abuses of power during Spain's transition to democracy.

4 The narrator of *L'écriture ou la vie* further explains that the author's traumatic past resurfaced after the war in spite of the joy that the act of writing brought him. An exemplary quote from the text reads: "The joy of writing, I was beginning to discover, never erased the misfortunes of memory. Quite the contrary: it sharpened them, made them worse, revived them. It made them unbearable. Only forgetting could save me" [Le bonheur de l'écriture, je commençais à le savoir, n'effaçait jamais ce malheur de la mémoire. Bien au contraire: il l'aiguisait, le creusait, le ravivait. Il le rendait insupportable. Seul l'oubli pourrait me sauver (212)].

5 See also Ana Maria Amar Sanchez. Amar Sanchez suggests in her work on Semprun's *Autobiografía de Federico Sánchez* that another form of artifice that Semprun uses in his work is, in the style of the *nouveau roman*, to have multiple narrators that provide different points of view on the events of the text. She proposes that one of these narrators is located inside of the text, and the other one looks in on the text from the outside, splitting the text both temporally and spatially (450).

6 A notable exception to this trend is Claude Lanzmann. For further reading and bibliographic references, see Azam Zanganeh.

7 For a more detailed analysis of Semprun's handling of narrative time in *Le grand voyage*, see Silk, "Writing the Holocaust" and "The Dialogical Traveler."

8 In her article "Historical Trauma and Literary Testimony," Suleiman uses the term "working through" in the sense that Dominick LaCapra attributes to the concept in his work on Freud. For further reading, see LaCapra's texts *History and Memory after Auschwitz*, and *Writing History, Writing Trauma*.

9 For a different understanding of how Semprun's narrators come to terms with the author's experience of trauma, see Ofelia Ferrán's *Working through Memory* and "Cuanto más escribo." Ferrán argues that Semprun's narrators use *memory*, and not fiction, to recreate the experience of Buchenwald in order to reposition themselves in a situation of mastery before events that rob them of any control ("Cuanto más escribo" 277). Though she does not reference LaCapra's rethinking of "working through," Ferrán's evaluation of the relation between Semprun's narrator and the resurfacing of traumatic memory draws on a similar reading of the concepts of "repetition compulsion" and "the return of the repressed" described in Freud's *Beyond the Pleasure Principle*.

10 The narrator of *L'écriture ou la vie* develops this idea further to consider the author's experience of the camps alongside Heidegger's understanding of "radical Evil," *das radikal Böse*. For this rethinking of Heidegger, see *L'écriture ou la vie*, 119–22.

11 For further reading on Rancière's understanding of "master explicators," in particular their differences from "ignorant masters," see the introduction to this book, pp. 25–7.

12 In this respect, the narrator's description of this scene of collective witnessing reflects an important historical fact concerning the dynamics of French-speaking communities of deportees that were organized in Buchenwald. In his study of the French Resistance in Buchenwald, Olivier Lalieu notes that the French communist organization known as the "Collectif français" was known throughout the camp for the discipline of its deportees and the "exigence morale" of its leaders (249). This also meant that they punished their members more than any other national group did. For further reading, see Lalieu, 226–67.

13 Maspero died just days before Buchenwald was liberated. Approximately 2900 of the French men deported to Buchenwald survived the camp.

14 All English translations of Maspero's *Les abeilles et la guêpe* are mine, and page numbers refer to the original French text.

15 The official date listed for Maurice Halbwachs's death in Buchenwald's archive is 15 March 1945.

16 The concentration camp at Buchenwald was divided into two main parts, the Big Camp and the Little Camp. The two parts were separated from each other by a barbed-wire fence with guarded checkpoints. From 1943 to 1945, nearly every deportee, including Semprun, was initially placed in Buchenwald's Little Camp, where the mortality rate was incomparably higher than that of the Big Camp. Access to bunks in the Big Camp was determined in part by the clandestine communist movement, and which members of the population of new arrivals they chose to protect.

17 Men in Buchenwald were given free time on Sunday afternoons in which they did not have to work for the SS. This was obviously little consolation in light of the brutal conditions of the camp. For an idealized vision of camp life during Sunday afternoons in Buchenwald, see Semprun's *Quel beau dimanche!*

18 The quote comes from Wittgenstein's *Tractatus Logico-Philosophicus*, in which, among other things, the philosopher argues that the limits of language are not themselves expressible in language. This, of course, parallels my own argument here that *L'écriture ou la vie* demonstrates that the limits of literature are not themselves expressible in literature.

19 The narrator of *L'écriture ou la vie* explains that "Julien" is the name of a real person from the French region of Burgundy with whom Jorge Semprun fought in the French Resistance. "Hans Freiberg" is the name of a wholly fictional person who first appeared in Semprun's 1967 novel *L'évanouissement*.

Commenting on this use of fiction in *L'écriture ou la vie*, the narrator reflects: "I had invented Hans Freiberg [...] in order to have a Jewish friend. I had had some in my life at that time, and I wanted to have some in my novel as well" (54; my translation).

20 At the time, Jean Paulhan (1884–1968) was the editor of the *Nouvelle Revue Française*. He was one of the spiritual leaders of the French Resistance, and founded the clandestine journal *Résistance* which was published during the war and forced him into hiding. A quote from Paulhan's famous essay from the period, "L'abeille," serves as the epigraph for Maspero's *Les abeilles et la guêpe*.

21 Better known as "La Pasionaria," Dolores Ibárruri (1895–1989) was a leading member of the Spanish Communist Party for the better part of the twentieth century. Her rise to public prominence occurred in the Spanish Civil War thanks to a speech she gave during the Battle of Madrid and the slogan – "No Pasáran!" – that the Republicans appropriated from it. The train ride to which the narrator of *L'écriture ou la vie* refers would have taken place while Ibárruri was Secretary General of the Spanish Communist Party.

2 Speaking for Others

1 My translation.

2 Consider, for comparison, the reflections Eugen Kogon offers in *The Theory and Practice of Hell*, his political analysis of the camps published in Germany in 1946, in which he insists on the differences between the experiences of distinct groups within the camps: "Germans as well as Jews were not very popular in the camps, though this obviously was not true of many individuals [...] The roles of these two groups, to do them justice, would require a separate book with many case histories, carefully balanced according to their significance. Without doubt it could be shown that the non-German concentration camp literature that has been published so far literally teems with one-sided statements, oversimplifications, and erroneous judgments. In my opinion there were no groups whose role in the concentration camps is so difficult to grasp as the Germans and the Jews. Let this statement at least hint at their significance" (311).

3 Many survivors and scholars have reflected on the differences between various camps and the differing experiences that Jews and political deportees from France had of the Nazi system. See, for example, Caron, "Deux récits, deux exigences"; Delbo, *Le convoi du 24 janvier*; Grinspan, *J'ai pas pleuré*; Hilberg, *The Destruction of the European Jews*; and Wieviorka, *Déportation et génocide* and *Auschwitz, 60 ans après*. For an overview of the

development of French national memory of the camps, see chapter 3 in this book, pp. 104–5.

4 For further reading on the French Republican model of citizenship, including references to foundational texts on the subject, see Jennings, "Citizenship, Republicanism, and Multiculturalism in Contemporary France."

5 Of course, the experiences of political deportees in concentration camps are essential to our understanding of the Nazi system. However, as Griselda Pollock and Max Silverman propose, it is also important that this "concentrationary" memory be distinguished from Holocaust memory. For their theoretical reflections on the concentrationary and its relation to Holocaust memory, see the introduction to their co-edited text *Concentrationary Memories*.

6 For an overview of Semprun's relationship with and activities in the Spanish Communist Party, see chapter 1, note 3.

7 My translation.

8 Ferrán further argues that Semprun's narrative techniques in *Autobiografía de Federico Sánchez* offer resistance to the official "retórica de desmemoria" of Spain's transition to democracy.

9 For further reading on Stalin's influence on the leadership of the Spanish Communist Party, see Pike, *In the Service of Stalin*.

10 For further reading on the Communist Party's clandestine activities in Buchenwald, see Lalieu, *La zone grise?* Communist internees seized control of Buchenwald's deportee-run administration in 1943 after a bitter power struggle with the German criminals interned in the camp. The *Arbeitsstatistik* was the primary site of their resistance activities. When Semprun was placed in the bureau in February 1944, he was the only Spaniard in a division composed of twenty-eight Czechs, twenty-four Germans, seven Poles, seven Russians, three Frenchmen, two Austrians, one Dutchman, and one Belgian.

11 All English translations of Semprun's *Quel beau dimanche*! are from Sheridan's *What a Beautiful Sunday*.

12 The spelling "Sanchez" occurs in the original texts. The name is written without an accent in both the original French and the English translation.

13 Scholars have made similar claims regarding the treatment of exile in Semprun's work. For further reading, see Valis, "Reader, Exile and the Text."

14 Though there were Spaniards sent to other concentration camps in the Nazi system from the refugee camps in southwestern France, 90 per cent of them were deported to Mauthausen.

15 In 1941, Himmler classified the Nazi concentration camps into three categories, with the camps belonging to the first two categories both

housing prisoners considered capable of rehabilitation to varying degrees. The third category, which included only Mauthausen, Gross-Rosen, and Auschwitz II-Birkenau, was considered the worst. Himmler's categorizations did not encompass the Nazi extermination camps, in which the primary objective was the liquidation of Jews. For further reading, see Hilberg, *The Destruction of the European Jews*, and Pike, *Spaniards in the Holocaust.*

16 This figure does not take account of the Spaniards who died on the train ride to Mauthausen, nor those who were gassed upon arrival. Historians have estimated that the total number of Spanish Republicans *sent* to the camp was somewhere between nine and ten thousand, and that approximately seven thousand of this total did not survive the camp. For further reading, see Pike, *Spaniards in the Holocaust* 11–13.

17 The bulk of Mauthausen's survivors settled in France after the war, and the first testimonies that appeared about this community's experience of the camp were published by the Federación Española de Deportados e Internados Políticos (FEDIP) in France in 1969. Many of these testimonies, in particular those of Mario Constante, have since been discredited by historians and other Mauthausen survivors as grossly exaggerated or factually inaccurate. Constante's testimonies in particular inflate survivor death tolls and invent ordeals that he never experienced in the camps. For further reading, see Pierre and Véronique Salou Olivares, *Los republicanos españoles en el Campo de concentración de Mauthausen*, and Pike's *Spaniards in the Holocaust*.

18 All English translations of *L'écriture ou la vie* in this chapter are from Coverdale's *Literature or Life*.

19 See Brison's *Aftermath*.

20 The letter Magny reads is her famous *Lettre sur le pouvoir d'écrire*, in which she reflects on the nature of literary writing through an analysis of Semprun's poetry.

3 Seeing Responsibility

1 While there has been much speculation about the reasons for the name *Muselmänner* being used to designate these deportees, the origins of this term remain unknown. For further reading, see Agamben's *Remnants of Auschwitz*, Mesnard and Kahan's *Giorgio Agamben à l'épreuve d'Auschwitz*, and Davis's essay "Can the Dead Speak to Us?"

2 Agamben pursues many intersecting arguments about testimony in *Remnants of Auschwitz* that all hinge upon his understanding of the deportee-*Muselmann* relation. However, as Mesnard and Kahan have persuasively

demonstrated, the ways Agamben connects the different elements of his argument, particularly his use of analogies, omits some important distinctions between the different conceptual frameworks that he activates throughout the text.

3 "The survivor is therefore familiar with the common necessity of degradation," Agamben writes, "he knows that humanity and responsibility are something that the deportee had to abandon when entering the camp" (59–60).

4 Agamben's focus on shame in *Remnants of Auschwitz* is largely connected to Primo Levi's reflections on the subject, particularly in his texts *The Reawakening* and *The Drowned and the Saved*. Levi asserts that shame is a dominant sentiment of survivors yet, Agamben argues, the survivor is unable to explain exactly why. Agamben offers his own theoretical elaboration of the phenomenon in the chapter "Shame, or On the Subject" in which he draws from, among others, Kant, Nietzsche, Heidegger, and Benveniste, and ultimately displaces the question of shame raised by Levi onto the idea of "desubjectification." He writes: "In shame, the subject thus has no other content than its own desubjectification; it becomes witness to its own disorder, its own oblivion as a subject. This double movement, which is both subjectification and desubjectification, is shame" (106). For further reading on the relation of shame and desubjectification, and criticisms of Agamben's definitions and deployment of both, see Mesnard and Kahan's *Giorgio Agamben à l'épreuve d'Auschwitz*, Chambers' *Untimely Interventions*, and Trezise's *Witnessing Witnessing*.

5 I limit myself here to rethinking this one, highly influential line of thought from *Remnants of Auschwitz* in greater depth through the work of Charlotte Delbo. Agamben, of course, offers an extensive rethinking of ethics throughout his work, including reconceptualizations of the ethical that base their arguments on the Nazi camp experience. Perhaps most notable is Agamben's contention in *Homo Sacer* that concentration camp inmates are representative of a notion called "bare life." Agamben's understanding is that deportees "were persons sentenced to death or detained in a camp, the entry into which meant the definitive exclusion from the political community. Precisely because they were lacking almost all the rights and expectations that we customarily attribute to human existence, and yet were still biologically alive, they came to be situated in a limit zone between life and death, inside and outside, in which they were no longer anything but bare life. Those who are sentenced to death and those who dwelt in the camps are thus in some way unconsciously assimilated […] to a life that may be killed without the commission of homicide. Like the

fence in the camp, the interval between death sentence and execution delimits an extratemporal and extraterritorial threshold in which the human body is separated from its normal political status and abandoned, in a state of exception, to the most extreme misfortunes" (159). For an analysis of how Agamben's reflections in *Remnants of Auschwitz* relate to his other works, including *Homo Sacer*, see Mesnard and Kahan's *Giorgio Agamben à l'épreuve d'Auschwitz*.

6 I describe these women as being "from France" rather than "French" because Delbo's convoy was composed of both French women and foreign nationals who were living in France at the time, most of whom were deported for their activities in the French Resistance. For further reading, see Delbo's *Le convoi du 24 janvier*.

7 As Delbo herself puts it: "for Birkenau, in 1943, fifty-seven out of two hundred thirty after six months is exceptional, unique in the history of the camp" (my translation) [pour Birkenau, en 1943, cinquante-sept sur deux cent trente après six mois, c'est exceptionnel, unique dans l'histoire du camp (17)]. In comparison, consider the fact that a convoy of one thousand women from Holland that arrived in Birkenau in October 1942 had only one surviving member by January 1943. Most of the deaths in Delbo's convoy occurred in the first two and a half months of their internment. For further reading, see her *Le convoi du 24 janvier*.

8 On 3 August 1943, just over six months after their arrival in the camp, Delbo's convoy was placed in quarantine in a building outside of Birkenau. The reasons for the quarantine remain unknown. Of the fifty-seven women still alive at the time of the quarantine, five died as a result of illnesses or injuries obtained while still interned in Birkenau. No other members of the convoy died in the camp after this date. The only deaths that occurred after the members of Delbo's convoy were transferred out of Auschwitz were caused by Allied forces. Three women from the convoy died as the result of an Allied air raid on the train station at Mauthausen just days before the camp's liberation. For further reading, see Delbo, *Le convoi du 24 janvier*.

9 As Margaret-Anne Hutton has noted, Delbo's work differs from most French women's camp writing in its depiction of solidarity among female deportees from France. It should not, therefore, be viewed as representative of French women's camp testimonies in general. For further reading, see Hutton's *Testimony from the Nazi Camps*.

10 *Aucun de nous ne reviendra* was originally published in 1965, then re-released as volume 1 of the trilogy *Auschwitz et après* in 1970. Along with significant portions of the second volume of the trilogy, it was written in 1945 and 1946,

immediately after Delbo returned to France from the camps. For further reading, see Lawrence Langer's introduction to the English translation of the trilogy.

11 The general population of Auschwitz's women's camp was primarily composed of Jews, gypsies, prostitutes, and female political prisoners from throughout Europe, especially Poland. Delbo and the members of her convoy were the only French political prisoners in the camp. For further reading, see her *Le convoi du 24 janvier*.

12 Delbo was transferred to Ravensbrück along with fifty-one of the surviving women from the Convoy of January 24th in 1944. She and ten other convoy members remained there until liberation. Before the end of the war, thirty-three of the convoy members were transferred out of Ravensbrück to Mauthausen, and six to factories in Germany that were using deportees for slave labour. One convoy member was too sick to be transferred to Ravensbrück and remained in Auschwitz until she was freed by the Soviet army. For further reading, see *Le convoi du 24 janvier*.

13 The term "eidectic reduction" comes from Husserl. For further reading, see his *Ideas*.

14 What these three short passages do, in other words, is gain visibility for deportees who had been deemed beyond help, which differs drastically from blaming relatively more healthy deportees for their actions in such situations. These passages shift our focus, as readers, onto the plight of the physically weakest deportees, lead us to understand them, and to see our responsibility to people in their state. They do not lead us to see ourselves as better than or superior to any of the people portrayed in them.

15 Delbo and the women deported with her were interned in block 26, which had windows facing block 25's courtyard, thus giving them the closest view of the hell that the women of Auschwitz experienced once they had been marked for imminent death.

16 My translation.

17 In this respect, Delbo's use of the word "nakedness" differs from and should not be confused with what Agamben calls "bare life," or to a limit zone in which the human body becomes separated from its normal political status and abandoned to the most extreme misfortunes (see note 2 in this chapter). The word "naked" is used throughout *Auschwitz et après* to describe a state in which the familiar appears in unfamiliar guise.

18 My translation.

19 My translation.

20 An alternate translation of these lines more loyal to the original French would be: "Today people know/For several years they have known/They have

known that this dot on the map/is Auschwitz/They know this/And they think they know the rest."

21 Bringing us closer to the position of victims is, of course, different from bringing us to a position identical to the one victims inhabit. We can draw nearer to their standpoint, but it is forever out of reach.

22 My translation.

23 My translation.

24 My translation.

25 Of course, Delbo would technically be called a *Muselweib* in this instance, and this name was used most notably in Ravensbrück to designate women who had become unresponsive to their environment. I use the terms *Muselmann* and *Muselmänner* here for the sake of consistency with Agamben's terminology.

26 Colin Davis points out that this is also a major flaw in Agamben's analysis in *Remnants of Auschwitz*, which ends with the testimonies of several *Muselmänner*, but fails to consider how their own accounts of their experience directly challenge Primo Levi's. For further reading, see Davis's "Can the Dead Speak to Us?"

27 The final line of this passage – "Et c'est le désespoir de l'impuissance à leur dire l'angoisse qui m'a étreinte, l'impression d'être morte et de le savoir" – is difficult to translate into English while respecting the fluidity and word choice of the original French. An alternate translation would be: "Telling them of the anguish that gripped me, the feeling of being dead and knowing it, made me despair at my powerlessness."

28 As Thomas Trezise has demonstrated, however, Agamben's analyses depend on highly problematic readings of Levi, including Levi's reflections on the gray zone, shame, and the *Muselmann*. For further reading, see the chapter titled "Theory and Testimony" in Trezise's *Witnessing Witnessing*.

29 For an overview of understandings of the *Muselmann* in various survivor testimonies, see the beginning of the chapter titled "The *Muselmann*" in Agamben's *Remnants of Auschwitz*.

30 For my analysis of Semprun's response to the "death" of Maurice Halbwachs, see chapter 1 pp. 45–53 in this book.

31 My translation. This is an example of a passage that is severely distorted by Lamont's English translation, which entirely omits the lines "Chaque matin, elle se met près de moi. Elle espère que je lui laisserai quelques gouttes au fond de ma gamelle. Pourquoi lui donnerais-je de mon eau? Aussi bien elle va mourir."

32 This is a crucial distinction that a consideration of Delbo's theorizations of non-human figures such as the *Muselmänner* lays bare. Agamben's witness

abandons his or her sense of responsibility to others in the camps because he or she sees the *Muselmänner*, retreats into himself or herself, and ignores the facts about what these non-human figures experienced. This example from *Aucun de nous ne reviendra* in which Delbo abandons her sense of responsibility to Aurore indicates that her blindness is caused by the fact that she has reached an extreme physical state of her own. All deportees, of course, suffered from the miserable conditions of the camps, and this suffering was beyond what most non-deportees have or will experience. But not everyone's suffering in the camps was the same, and some states were clearly different from and more severe than others. The behaviour of relatively healthy internees must be distinguished from the behavior of non-human figures, as each group was capable of seeing their responsibilities to others to different degrees. Delbo's writing makes such crucial distinctions and is thus an important site for thinking through such questions.

33 My translation.

34 My translation.

35 In the initial staging of *Électre* in Paris, Louis Jouvet, Delbo's mentor and for whom she worked as a secretary for four years immediately prior to her joining the French Resistance, played the Beggar. Jouvet also directed the play, as well as many others authored by Giraudoux. For further discussion of the influence of Jouvet and Giraudoux on Delbo, see Davis, "Charlotte Delbo's Ghosts," Chiappone-Lucchesi, "L'intrusion de Giraudoux dans l'écriture de Charlotte Delbo," and Riera-Collet's "Parlons de Charlotte à bâtons rompus."

36 An alternate translation of this poem that respects the shifting use of the politically inflected word "dawn" (*aurore*) with the more neutral "daybreak" (*aube*) would be: "*A man to die for another man/that's something to look for/* don't say that any more Beggar/don't say it any more/there are thousands/ who stepped forward for everyone else/for you too/Beggar/so that you can salute the dawn/daybreak was livid/in the mornings of those at Mont Valerien/and now/this is called dawn/Beggar/it's daybreak with their blood."

37 Delbo and her husband were arrested at the same time for running a clandestine printing press that produced anti-Nazi literature. For further reading, see Trezise's essay "The Question of Community in Charlotte Delbo's *Auschwitz and After*" and chapter 4 in this book.

38 In the fictionalized accounts of Delbo's relationship with Dudach that appear throughout her writings, the word "aurore" frequently appears when he discusses his own political convictions. See, for example, *Une scène jouée dans la mémoire* and the passage titled "Françoise" from *Mesure de nos jours*.

39 In *Witnessing Witnessing*, Thomas Trezise argues that Primo Levi's work actually leads to a different conclusion than the one Agamben extracts from it: "Responsibility, for the Holocaust survivor who bears witness, thus means not only responding *to* but responding *for* the drowned. It means speaking as a delegate, and delegating to us the task of listening" (156; emphasis in original).

40 Both Thomas Trezise and Philippe Mesnard and Claudine Kahan express similar criticisms of Agamben's methodology in their works. In *Witnessing Witnessing*, Trezise proposes that Agamben's "universalizing impulse" causes his theory to "risk losing sight of the Holocaust, its victims, and its witnesses in their historical specificity" (6). Mesnard and Kahan suggest that Agamben is concerned with "unifying and subjecting everything (the camps, society, history, and modernity) to a single, simplistic paradigm" (my translation) ["tout unifier et de tout assujettir (camp, société, histoire et modernité) à un seul paradigme simplificateur" (56)], which results in the theoretical subordinating reality to its "transcendent" visions (99).

41 This is a contradictory aspect of Agamben's rethinking of ethics in *Remnants of Auschwitz* that the text never resolves. Agamben argues, on the one hand, that we view Primo Levi as a model of ethical witnessing because of his attempts to bear witness to the *Muselmänner*. Yet Agamben simultaneously argues that responsibility had to be abandoned by all deportees upon entering the camps; thus the camps should be considered a zone of non-responsibility.

42 It is important to note that the Final Solution did not begin in Auschwitz II-Birkenau until 1942, and that before and after this date, millions of Europe's Jews were killed in other places by the Nazis and their collaborators. In *Auschwitz, 60 ans après*, French historian Annette Wieviorka explains that, in the second half of 1942, the killings at Birkenau "only represent from 10 to 15 per cent of more than one million four hundred thousand Jews assassinated in this same period at Chelmno (in German Kulmhof), in the Wartheau, a region annexed into Germany, at Belzec, Sobibor and Treblinka, [and] in the General Government [of Poland]" (my translation) [ne représentent que de 10 à 15% de plus de un million quatre cent mille Juifs assassinés dans cette même période à Chelmno (en allemand Kulmhof), dans le Wartheau, région annexée à l'Allemagne, à Belzec, Sobibor et Treblinka, (et) dans le Gouvernement général (de Pologne) (111)]. It wasn't until 1943 that Birkenau became the principal site of the destruction of Europe's Jews. For a complete list of death tolls from the Holocaust by camp, country, and year, see Hilberg, *The Destruction of the European Jews* 338–9.

43 See also Michael Kelly. In an analysis focused in particular on how suffering and death are articulated in cultural representations from the immediate postwar era, Kelly argues that the French engaged "in a cultural *bricolage*" to represent the Second World War, "using such discourses as would not jeopardize the developing national unity" (236; emphasis in original). This included an extensive use of religious symbolism for political ends, which contrasted with the largely secular imagery deployed by Pétain's regime.

44 Scholars have offered varying arguments for this shift from Buchenwald to Auschwitz as the primary site of concentration camp memory in France. Rousso, for example, sees three historical events of international importance – the Eichmann Trial (1961), the Six-Day Arab-Israeli War (1967), and the events of May '68 – as catalysts for Auschwitz's emergence in French consciousness. Annette Wieviorka, on the other hand, sees the Eichmann Trial alone as the turning point, which she further believes inaugurated the "era of the witness" in France. See Rousso's speech, "Collective memory and the Shoah," given at the Mémorial de la Shoah in 2005 and Wieviorka's *L'ère du témoin*.

45 Wieviorka observes that "[a]mong deportees from France, the only ones whose destiny attracted attention in the years following their return were those for whom deportation was the final stage of a glorious, heroic path" (my translation) [(p)armi les déportés de France, les seuls dont le destin attira l'attention dans les années qui suivirent leur retour sont ceux dont la déportation était l'ultime étape d'un glorieux chemin de héros (175)]. Auschwitz survivor Simone Veil further explains that, upon their return to France, people refused to listen to what Jewish survivors like her had to say, and that testifying to what they had been through became a humiliating experience each time. "We would scarcely begin to tell our stories," Veil explains, "before being interrupted as if we were children who were too excited or talkative by parents who were the ones burdened with real concerns" (my translation) [À peine commencions-nous à raconter que nous étions interrompus comme des enfants excités et trop bavards par des parents accablés, eux, de vrais soucis (quoted in Finkelkraut *La mémoire vaine* 39)].

46 Chaouat's argument builds on remarks that Alain Finkelkraut has made since the 1980s about French memory of the Jewish experience of the camps. Finkelkraut has proposed, among other things, that extremely simplified understandings of both the Nazis and their victims have long circulated in France. See his texts *Au nom de l'autre*, and *La mémoire vaine*.

47 The trial of Klaus Barbie in 1987 was a particularly striking example of this fact. Some political deportees argued at this time that the acts Barbie perpetrated against them should be considered crimes against humanity

rather than war crimes, a distinct change from how deportees presented their suffering to the French public immediately after the war. For further reading, see Alain Finkelkraut's *La mémoire vaine* and Joan Wolf's *Harnessing the Holocaust*.

48 Rothberg advances this argument through an analysis of Delbo's *Les belles lettres* – her first published work – which pertains to the Algerian War.

49 My translation.

50 My translation.

51 My translation.

52 My translation.

53 My translation.

54 My translation.

55 My translation.

56 My translation.

57 My translation.

4 Irony and Community

1 All translations of *Auschwitz et après* in this paragraph are my own.

2 An alternate translation of this poem that reflects the ambiguous nature of the line "une frange d'eux veut comprendre" would be: "Do not say that they do not hear us/they hear us/they want to understand/obstinately/meticulously/a small part of them wants to understand/a sensitive edge on the margin of their selves/it's their deep self/their truth/that remains distant/that flees when we think we've reached it/that retracts and contracts and escapes/is it not because they feel pain/where we no longer feel pain/that they retreat and withdraw…" The word "frange" literally translates as "fringe" in English, and can be used as a synonym for the word "minority" as well as to denote an edge or border of an object, particularly a decorative border made of thread or cord that hangs from clothing, furniture, or textiles more generally. The use of the term in this poem is more ambiguous than Lamont's translation of it as "the edge of their being" would suggest. "Une frange d'eux" also invokes the idea of a small group of people wanting to understand survivors' testimonies, not just a small part of themselves wanting to understand.

3 Delbo's critique differs drastically from those that have dominated studies of Second World War memory, most notably Henry Rousso's highly influential reflections on the subject. Rousso proposes that, after a brief period immediately after the war in which the French nation promoted a totalizing understanding of the camps in order to unify a divided nation,

a period of total amnesia was witnessed in French society in the 1950s and 1960s, when the ethical "duty to remember" that persists to this day initially emerged. For further reading, see *Le syndrome de Vichy* and Rousso's speech given at the Mémorial de la Shoah. For an overview of the development of Second World War memory in France, see chapter 3 in this book, pp. 104–5.

4 My translation.

5 My translation.

6 All of the return narratives in *Mesure de nos jours* fictionalize and transform the testimonies assembled by Delbo in *Le convoi du 24 janvier* to varying degrees, including the five narratives with imaginary protagonists. These five passages are not named for real women who were part of Delbo's convoy and each one alludes to details from several of the testimonies and biographies in *Le convoi du 24 janvier*. *Mesure de nos jours* also contains three narratives about survivors who were deported to Auschwitz on different convoys – "Ida," "Loulou," and "Jacques." "Ida" offers a modified version of the story of Ida Grinspan, author of *J'ai pas pleuré*. I have been unable to identify the remaining two survivors.

7 My translation.

8 My translation.

9 This translation and the following one from *Une connaissance inutile* are mine.

10 This scene also appears as part of the first act of Delbo's play *Ceux qui avaient choisi*, published by Les Provinciales in 2011.

11 All translations of Delbo's *Une scène jouée dans la mémoire* are mine.

12 My translation.

13 My translation.

14 My translation.

15 My translation.

16 My translation.

17 My translation.

18 This translation and the one in the following sentence are mine.

19 My translation.

20 Ross specifically suggests that the politically radical dimensions of May '68 and its disruption of the social roles and functions prescribed by the French state were both transformed afterwards by "ex-*gauchistes* who had claimed the role of custodians of May's memory" and reconfigured the event "in light of personal ethics" (12; emphasis in original). For further reading, see the introduction and first chapter of *May '68 and Its Afterlives*.

21 My translation.

22 All translations of Delbo's *Ceux qui avaient choisi* are mine.

23 My translation.

24 My translation.
25 My translation.
26 While *Mesure de nos jours* does not directly address this issue, factual information is of course also indispensable in the fight against Holocaust denial.
27 My translation.
28 My translation.

Conclusion

1 It has been suggested that Bernhard Walter and/or Ernst Hoffman, two SS officers in Auschwitz, took the majority of the photos that appear in *L'Album d'Auschwitz*. A companion album depicting Auschwitz's SS officers during the same period has also been discovered. For further reading, see *L'Album d'Auschwitz*, 10.
2 *L'Album d'Auschwitz* was first published in France by Le Seuil in 1983. An American volume of these photos was published in 1981. For further reading on its publication history, see *L'Album d'Auschwitz*, 8–29.
3 Unless otherwise noted, all translations in this chapter are my own, and page numbers refer to the original French texts.
4 I would like to thank Michael Kosko for this insight.
5 All English translations of Barthes' *La chambre claire* are from Richard Howard's *Camera Lucida*.
6 Brad Prager has argued, in contrast, that we seek to interact with and save the people we see in photographs of them on their way to death. For further reading, see "On the Liberation of Perpetrator Photographs in Holocaust Narratives."
7 Marianne Hirsch advances a different argument about our responses to the Holocaust in light of Barthes's second punctum. "The punctum of time is precisely that incongruity or incommensurability between the meaning of a given experience, object, or image *then*, and the one it holds *now*. It is the knowledge of the inevitability of loss, change, and death. And that inevitability constitutes the lens through which we, as humans, look at the past" (*Generation* 63; emphasis in original).
8 This rivalry between history and memory was especially bitter in France through the mid-1990s. For further reading, see Guillon and Laborie's *Mémoire et Histoire*, and Vernant's "La mémoire et les historiens."
9 Assmann's study provides an excellent overview of the history-memory debate in the field of Holocaust studies. For further reading on the subject, see also Friedlander, "The *Shoah* between Memory and History."

10 Hirsch develops her concept of "postmemory" in relation to the responses of the children of Holocaust survivors in her works *Family Frames* and *The Generation of Postmemory*. "Postmemory is not identical to memory: it is "post," she explains (*Generation* 31). "[B]ut, at the same time, I argue, it approximates memory in its affective force and its psychic effects. Eva Hoffman describes what was passed down to her as a fairy tale: 'The memories – not memories but emanations – of wartime experiences kept erupting in flashes of imagery; in abrupt but broken refrains.' These 'not memories,' communicated in 'flashes of imagery,' and these 'broken refrains,' transmitted through 'the language of the body,' are precisely the stuff of the *postmemory* of trauma, and of its return" (emphasis in original).

11 All translations of Didi-Huberman's *Écorces* are my own.

12 Marianne Hirsch presents a similar argument regarding the ways in which contemporary artists have incorporated perpetrator images into their memorial work. "[I]f perpetrator images can mediate the visual knowledge of those who were not there," she writes, "it is only because their contemporary reproductions mobilize some powerful idioms that obscure their devastating history and redirect the genocidal gaze that shaped them" (*Generation* 130).

Works Cited

Adorno, Theodor. "Cultural Criticism and Society." *Prisms*. Trans. Samuel and Shierry Weber. Cambridge, MA: MIT Press, 1981. 17–34.

Agamben, Giorgio. *Homo Sacer: Sovereign Power and Bare Life*. Trans. Daniel Heller-Roazen. Stanford, CA: Stanford UP, 1998.

Agamben, Giorgio. *Remnants of Auschwitz: The Witness and the Archive*. Trans. Daniel Heller-Roazen. New York: Zone, 1999.

Amar Sanchez, Ana Maria. "La Ficción del Testimonio." *Revista Iberoamericana* 151 (1990): 447–61.

Améry, Jean. *At the Mind's Limits: Contemplations by a Survivor on Auschwitz and Its Realities*. Trans. Sidney Rosenfeld and Stella P. Rosenfeld. Bloomington and Indianapolis: Indiana UP, 1980.

Antelme, Robert. *L'espèce humaine*. Paris: Gallimard, 1957.

Antelme, Robert. *The Human Race*. Trans. Jeffrey Haight and Annie Mahler. Evanston, IL: Marlboro P, Northwestern UP, 1992.

Assman, Aleida. "History, Memory, and the Genre of Testimony." *Poetics Today* 27.2 (2006): 261–73. http://dx.doi.org/10.1215/03335372-2005-003.

Azam Zanganeh, Lila. "Jorge Semprún: The Art of Fiction No. 192." *The Paris Review* 180 (2007): 163–88.

Baer, Elizabeth R., and Myrna Goldenberg, eds. *Experience and Expression: Women, the Nazis, and the Holocaust*. Detroit: Wayne State UP, 2003.

Barthes, Roland. *Camera Lucida: Reflections on Photography*. Trans. Richard Howard. New York: Hill and Wang, 1981.

Barthes, Roland. *La chambre claire: Note sur la photographie*. Paris: Seuil, 1980.

Bauer, Yehuda. *Rethinking the Holocaust*. New Haven and London: Yale UP, 2002.

Blanchot, Maurice. *L'écriture du désastre*. Paris: Gallimard, 1980.

Booth, Wayne. *A Rhetoric of Irony*. Chicago and London: U of Chicago P, 1974.

Bridenthal, Renate, Atina Grossmann, and Marion Kaplan, eds. *When Biology Became Destiny: Women in Weimar and Nazi Germany*. New York: Monthly Review P, 1984.

Brison, Susan. *Aftermath: Violence and the Remaking of a Self*. Princeton: Princeton UP, 2002.

Caron, David. "Deux récits, deux exigences: *Les jours de notre mort* de David Rousset et *La nuit* d'Elie Wiesel." *Nottingham French Studies* 36.2 (1997): 71–82. http://dx.doi.org/10.3366/nfs.1997-2.007.

Caron, David. *My Father and I: The Marais and the Queerness of Community*. Ithaca, NY: Cornell UP, 2009.

Carroll, David. "Les restes de la communauté – les femmes entre elles." *Les revenantes: Charlotte Delbo, la voix d'une communauté à jamais deportée*. Ed. David Caron and Sharon Marquart. Toulouse: Presses Universitaires du Mirail, 2011. 147–66.

Caruth, Cathy. *Unclaimed Experience: Trauma, Narrative, and History*. Baltimore, MD: Johns Hopkins UP, 1996.

Chambers, Ross. *Untimely Interventions: AIDS Writing, Testimonial, and the Rhetoric of Haunting*. Ann Arbor, MI: U of Michigan P, 2004.

Chaouat, Bruno. "Forty Years of Suffering." *Esprit Créateur* 45.3 (2005): 49–62. http://dx.doi.org/10.1353/esp.2010.0441.

Chiappone-Lucchesi, Magali. "L'intrusion de Giraudoux dans l'écriture de Charlotte Delbo." *Écritures théâtrales du traumatisme: Esthétiques de la résistance*. Ed. Christiane Page. Rennes, France: Presses Universitaires de Rennes, 2012. 85–96.

Chirac, Jacques. "Témoigner, transmettre, honorer, agir." Speech published in *Le Monde*. 28 January 2005.

Colebrook, Claire. *Irony: The New Critical Idiom*. London and New York: Routledge, 2004.

Davis, Colin. "Can the Dead Speak to Us? De Man, Levinas, and Agamben." *Culture, Theory & Critique* 45.1 (April 2004): 77–89. http://dx.doi.org/10.1080/14735780410001686469.

Davis, Colin. "Charlotte Delbo's Ghosts." *French Studies: Quarterly Review* 59.1 (January 2005): 9–15. http://dx.doi.org/10.1093/fs/kni063.

Delbo, Charlotte. *Aucun de nous ne reviendra*. Paris: Minuit, 1970. Vol. 1 of *Auschwitz et après*. 3 vols. Paris: Minuit, 1970–1.

Delbo, Charlotte. *Auschwitz and After*. Trans. Rosette Lamont. New Haven and London: Yale UP, 1995.

Delbo, Charlotte. *Les belles lettres*. Paris: Minuit, 1961.

Delbo, Charlotte. *Ceux qui avaient choisi*. Saint-Victor-de-Morestel: Les Provinciales, 2011.

Delbo, Charlotte. *Le convoi du 24 janvier*. Paris: Minuit, 1966.

Delbo, Charlotte. "'Je me sers de la littérature comme d'une arme': Entretien avec Charlotte Delbo." *Charlotte Delbo: La voix d'une communauté à jamais deportée*. Ed. David Caron and Sharon Marquart. Toulouse: Presses Universitaires du Mirail, 25–7.

Delbo, Charlotte. *Mesure de nos jours*. Paris: Minuit, 1971. Vol. 3 of *Auschwitz et après*. 3 vols. Paris: Minuit, 1970–1.

Delbo, Charlotte. *Une connaissance inutile*. Paris: Minuit, 1970. Vol. 2 of *Auschwitz et après*. 3 vols. Paris: Minuit, 1970–1.

Delbo, Charlotte. *Une scène jouée dans la mémoire, Qui rapportera ces paroles*. Aigues-Vives, France: HB Éditions, 2001.

Deleuze, Gilles, and Félix Guattari. *Anti-Oedipus: Capitalism and Schizophrenia*. Trans. Robert Hurley. New York: Penguin, 2009.

Didi-Huberman, Georges. *Écorces*. Paris: Minuit, 2011.

Didi-Huberman, Georges. *Images In Spite of All: Four Photographs from Auschwitz*. Trans. Shane B. Lillis. Chicago and London: U of Chicago P, 2008.

Didi-Huberman, Georges. *Images malgré tout*. Paris: Minuit, 2003.

Fassin, Didier. *Humanitarian Reason: A Moral History of the Present*. Berkeley and Los Angeles: U of California P, 2011. http://dx.doi.org/10.1525/california/9780520271166.001.0001.

Felman, Shoshana, and Dori Laub. *Testimony: Crises in Witnessing in Literature, Psychoanalysis, and History*. New York and London: Routledge, 1992.

Ferrán, Ofelia. "'Cuanto más escribo, más me queda por decir': Memory, Trauma, and Writing in the Work of Jorge Semprún." *MLN* 116.2 (2001): 266–94. http://dx.doi.org/10.1353/mln.2001.0018.

Ferrán, Ofelia. "Memory and Forgetting, Resistance and Noise in the Spanish Transition: Semprún and Vázquez Montalbán." *Disremembering the Dictatorship: The Politics of Memory in the Spanish Transition to Democracy*. Ed. Joan Ramon Resina. Amsterdam and Atlanta: Rodopi, 2000. 191–222.

Ferrán, Ofelia. *Working through Memory: Writing and Remembrance in Contemporary Spanish Narrative*. Lewisburg, PA: Bucknell UP, 2007.

Finkelkraut, Alain. *Au nom de l'Autre: Réflexions sur l'antisémitisme qui vient*. Paris: Gallimard, 2003.

Finkelkraut, Alain. *La mémoire vaine: Du crime contre l'humanité*. Paris: Gallimard, 1992.

Fondation pour la Mémoire de la Shoah. *L'Album d'Auschwitz*. Paris: Éditions Al Dante, 2005.

Freud, Sigmund. *Beyond the Pleasure Principle*. Trans. James Strachey. New York: Norton, 1975.

Friedlander, Saul. "The *Shoah* between Memory and History." *Breaking Crystal: Writing and Memory after Auschwitz*. Ed. Efraim Sicher. Urbana, IL: U of Illinois P, 1998.

Gelly, Violaine, and Paul Gradvohl. *Charlotte Delbo*. Paris: Fayard, 2013.

Goldenberg, Myrna, and Amy H. Shapiro, eds. *Different Horrors, Same Hell: Gender and the Holocaust*. Seattle, WA: U of Washington P, 2013.

Gradvohl, Paul. "Charlotte Delbo et le communisme, Charlotte Delbo et les communistes." *Charlotte Delbo, œuvre et engagements*. Ed. Christiane Page. Rennes, France: Presses Universitaires de Rennes, 2014. 39–52.

Grinspan, Ida. *J'ai pas pleuré*. Paris: Robert Laffont, 2002.

Guillon, Jean-Marie, and Pierre Laborie, eds. *Mémoire et Histoire: la Résistance*. Toulouse: Private, 1995.

Heinemann, Marlene. *Gender and Destiny: Women Writers and the Holocaust*. New York, Westport, CT, and London: Greenwood P, 1986.

Hilberg, Raul. *The Destruction of the European Jews*. New York: Holmes and Meier, 1985.

Hirsch, Marianne. *Family Frames: Photography, Narrative, and Postmemory*. Cambridge, MA: Harvard UP, 1997.

Hirsch, Marianne. *The Generation of Postmemory: Writing and Visual Culture after the Holocaust*. New York: Columbia UP, 2012.

Hirsch, Marianne, and Leo Spitzer. "Testimonial Objects." Marianne Hirsch, *The Generation of Postmemory: Writing and Visual Culture after the Holocaust*. New York: Columbia UP, 2012. 177–99.

Husserl, Edmund. *Ideas: General Introduction to Pure Phenomenology*. Trans. W.R. Boyce Gibson. New York: Humanities P, 1969.

Hutcheon, Linda. *Irony's Edge: The Theory and Politics of Irony*. London and New York: Routledge, 1994.

Hutton, Margaret-Anne. *Testimony from the Nazi Camps: French Women's Voices*. London and New York: Routledge, 2004.

Izquierdo, Manuel. *Campos de concentración*. Madrid: Ediciones Endymion, 1996.

Jennings, Jeremy. "Citizenship, Republicanism, and Multiculturalism in Contemporary France." *British Journal of Political Science* 30.4 (2000): 575–98. http://dx.doi.org/10.1017/S0007123400000259.

Kelly, Michael. "Death at the Liberation: The Cultural Articulation of Death and Suffering in France 1944–1947." *French Cultural Studies* 5.3 (October 1994): 227–40. http://dx.doi.org/10.1177/095715589400501503.

Kogon, Eugen. *The Theory and Practice of Hell: The German Concentration Camps and the System behind Them*. New York: Farrar, Strauss, and Giroux, 2006.

LaCapra, Dominick. *History and Memory after Auschwitz*. Ithaca, NY: Cornell UP, 1998.

LaCapra, Dominick. *Writing History, Writing Trauma*. Baltimore, MD: Johns Hopkins UP, 2001.
Lalieu, Olivier. *La zone grise? La Résistance française à Buchenwald*. Paris: Tallandier, 2005.
Lang, Berel. *The Future of the Holocaust: Between History and Memory*. Ithaca, NY: Cornell UP, 1999.
Lang, Berel. *Holocaust Representation: Art within the Limits of History and Ethics*. Baltimore, MD: Johns Hopkins UP, 2000.
Langer, Lawrence. *The Age of Atrocity*. Boston: Beacon P, 1978.
Laska, Vera. *Women in the Resistance and in the Holocaust: The Voices of Eyewitnesses*. New York, Westport, CT, and London: Greenwood P, 1983.
Laub, Dori. "Bearing Witness, or the Vicissitudes of Listening." Shoshana Felman and Dori Laub, *Testimony: Crises in Witnessing in Literature, Psychoanalysis, and History*. New York and London: Routledge, 1992. 57–74.
Levi, Neil, and Michael Rothberg, eds. *The Holocaust: Theoretical Readings*. New Brunswick, NJ: Rutgers UP, 2003.
Levi, Primo. *The Drowned and the Saved*. Trans. Raymond Rosenthal. New York: Summit Books, 1988.
Levi, Primo. *The Reawakening*. Trans. Stuart Woolf. New York: Simon & Schuster, 1965.
Liebman, Stuart. *Claude Lanzmann's Shoah: Key Essays*. Oxford and New York: Oxford UP, 2007.
Loew, Camila. *The Memory of Pain: Women's Testimonies of the Holocaust*. Amsterdam and New York: Rodopi, 2011.
Lyotard, Jean-François. *Heidegger et "les juifs."* Paris: Galilée, 1988.
Magny, Claude-Edmonde. *Lettre sur le pouvoir d'écrire*. Paris: Seghers, 1947.
Maspero, François. *Les abeilles et la guêpe*. Paris: Seuil, 2002.
Mesnard, Philippe, and Claudine Kahan. *Giorgio Agamben à l'épreuve d'Auschwitz*. Paris: Éditions Kimé, 2001.
Nancy, Jean-Luc. *The Inoperative Community*. Trans. Peter Connor, Lisa Garbus, Michael Holland, et al. Minneapolis and London: U of Minnesota P, 1991.
Novac, Ana. *Les beaux jours de ma jeunesse*. Paris: Gallimard, 1999.
Ofer, Dalia, and Lenore J. Weitzman, eds. *Women in the Holocaust*. New Haven and London: Yale UP, 1998.
Page, Christiane, ed. *Charlotte Delbo, œuvre et engagements*. Rennes, France: Presses universitaires de Rennes, 2014.
Pike, David Wingeate. *In the Service of Stalin: The Spanish Communists in Exile, 1939–1945*. New York: Oxford UP, 1993. http://dx.doi.org/10.1093/acprof:oso/9780198203155.001.0001.

Pike, David Wingeate. *Spaniards in the Holocaust: Mauthausen, the Horror on the Danube*. New York and London: Routledge, 2000.

Pollock, Griselda, and Max Silverman, eds. *Concentrationary Memories: Totalitarian Terror and Cultural Resistance*. London and New York: I.B. Tauris, 2014.

Prager, Brad. "On the Liberation of Perpetrator Photographs in Holocaust Narrative." *Visualizing the Holocaust: Documents, Aesthetics, Memory*. Ed. David Bathrick, Brad Prager, and Michael D. Richardson. New York: Camden House, 2008. 19–36.

Rancière, Jacques. *The Emanicipated Spectator*. Trans. Gregory Elliot. London and New York: Verso, 2009.

Rancière, Jacques. *The Ignorant Schoolmaster: Five Lessons in Intellectual Emancipation*. Trans. Kristin Ross. Stanford, CA: Stanford UP, 1991.

Riera-Collet, Claudine. "Parlons de Charlotte à bâtons rompus." *Écritures théâtrales du traumatisme: Esthétiques de la résistance*. Ed. Christiane Page. Rennes, France: Presses Universitaires de Rennes, 2012. 99–104.

Ringelheim, Joan. "Women and the Holocaust: A Reconsideration of Research." *Different Voices: Women and the Holocaust*. Ed. Carol Rittner and John K. Roth. New York: Paragon House, 1993. 373–405.

Rittner, Carol, and John K. Roth, eds. *Different Voices: Women and the Holocaust*. New York: Paragon House, 1993.

Rorty, Richard. *Contingency, Irony, and Solidarity*. Cambridge and New York: Cambridge UP, 1989.

Ross, Kristin. *Fast Cars, Clean Bodies: Decolonization and the Reordering of French Culture*. Cambridge, MA.: MIT Press, 1996.

Ross, Kristin. *May '68 and Its Afterlives*. Chicago and London: U of Chicago P, 2002.

Rothberg, Michael. "Between Auschwitz and Algeria: Multidirectional Memory and the Counterpublic Witness." *Critical Inquiry* 33.1 (2006): 158–84. http://dx.doi.org/10.1086/509750.

Rothberg, Michael. *Multidirectional Memory: Remembering the Holocaust in the Age of Decolonization*. Stanford, CA: Stanford UP, 2009.

Rothberg, Michael. *Traumatic Realism: The Demands of Holocaust Representation*. Minneapolis, MN: U of Minnesota P, 2000.

Rousset, David. *L'univers concentrationnaire*. Paris: Minuit, 1965.

Rousso, Henry. Conference on Collective Memory and the Shoah. Mémorial de la Shoah, Paris. 15 Feb. 2005.

Rousso, Henry. *Le syndrome de Vichy, de 1944 à nos jours*. Paris: Seuil, 1987.

Salou Olivares, Pierre, and Véronique Salou Olivares. *Los republicanos españoles en el Campo de concentración Nazi de Mauthausen: el deber colectivo de sobrevivir*. Paris: Éditions Tirésias, 2005.

Semprun, Jorge. *Autobiografia de Federico Sánchez*. Barcelona: Editorial Planeta, 1977.

Semprun, Jorge. *The Autobiography of Federico Sanchez and the Communist Underground in Spain*. Trans. Helen R. Lane. New York: Karz, 1979.

Semprun, Jorge. *L'écriture ou la vie*. Paris: Gallimard, 1994.

Semprun, Jorge. *L'évanouissement*. Paris: Gallimard, 1967.

Semprun, Jorge. *Federico Sanchez vous salue bien*. Paris: Bernard Grasset, 1993.

Semprun, Jorge. *Le grand voyage*. Paris: Gallimard, 1965.

Semprun, Jorge. *Literature or Life*. Trans. Linda Coverdale. New York: Viking, 1997.

Semprun, Jorge. *Quel beau dimanche!* Paris: Bernard Grasset, 1980.

Semprun, Jorge. *What a Beautiful Sunday!* Trans. Alan Sheridan. New York: Harcourt Brace Jovanovich, 1982.

Silk, Sally M. "The Dialogical Traveler: A Reading of Semprun's *Le grand voyage*." *Studies in Twentieth Century Literature* 14.2 (1990): 223–40.

Silk, Sally M. "Writing the Holocaust/Writing Travel: The Space of Representation in Jorge Semprún's *Le Grand Voyage*." *CLIO: A Journal of Literature, History, and the Philosophy of History* 22.1 (1992): 53–65.

Suleiman, Susan. *Crises of Memory and the Second World War*. Cambridge, MA: Harvard UP, 2006.

Suleiman, Susan. "Historical Trauma and Literary Testimony: Writing and Repetition in the Buchenwald Memoirs of Jorge Semprun." *Journal of Romance Studies* 4.2 (2004): 1–19. http://dx.doi.org/10.3167/147335304782369159.

Tec, Nechama. *Resilience and Courage: Women, Men, and the Holocaust*. New Haven and London: Yale UP, 2003.

Theweleit, Klaus. *Male Fantasies*. Vol. 1, *Women, Floods, Bodies, History*. Minneapolis, MN: U of Minnesota P, 1987.

Theweleit, Klaus. *Male Fantasies*. Vol. 2, *Psychoanalyzing the White Terror*. Minneapolis, MN: U of Minnesota P, 1989.

Trezise, Thomas. "The Question of Community in Charlotte Delbo's *Auschwitz and After*." *MLN* 117.4 (September 2002): 858–86. http://dx.doi.org/10.1353/mln.2002.0067.

Trezise, Thomas. *Witnessing Witnessing: On the Reception of Holocaust Survivor Testimony*. New York: Fordham UP, 2013. http://dx.doi.org/10.5422/fordham/9780823244485.001.0001.

Valis, Noël M. "Reader, Exile and the Text: Jorge Semprún's *Autobiografia de Federico Sánchez*." *Monographic Review/Revista Monografica* 2 (1986): 174–88.

Vernant, Jean-Pierre. "La mémoire et les historiens." *Mémoire et Histoire: la Résistance*. Ed. Jean-Marie Guillon and Pierre Laborie. Toulouse: Private, 1995.

Wiesel, Elie. *La nuit*. Paris: Minuit, 1958.

Wieviorka, Annette. *Auschwitz, 60 ans après*. Paris: Robert Laffont, 2005.

Wieviorka, Annette. *Déportation et génocide: entre la mémoire et l'oubli*. Paris: Plon, 1992.

Wieviorka, Annette. *L'ère du témoin*. Paris: Plon, 1998.

Wittgenstein, Ludwig. *Tractatus Logico-Philosophicus*. Trans. C.K. Ogden. Mineola, NY: Dover, 1999.

Wolf, Joan. *Harnessing the Holocaust: The Politics of Memory in France*. Stanford, CA: Stanford UP, 2003.

Yaeger, Patricia. "Testimony without Intimacy." *Poetics Today* 27.2 (2006): 399–423. http://dx.doi.org/10.1215/03335372-2005-010.

Index